Lecture Notes in Computer Science 12899

More information about this subseries at http://www.springer.com/series/7407

Markus Vincze · Timothy Patten ·
Henrik I Christensen · Lazaros Nalpantidis ·
Ming Liu (Eds.)

Computer Vision Systems

13th International Conference, ICVS 2021
Virtual Event, September 22–24, 2021
Proceedings

 Springer

Editors
Markus Vincze 🆔
TU Wien
Vienna, Austria

Timothy Patten 🆔
University of Technology Sydney
Sydney, Australia

Henrik I Christensen 🆔
University of California San Diego
La Jolla, CA, USA

Lazaros Nalpantidis 🆔
Technical University of Denmark
Kongens Lyngby, Denmark

Ming Liu 🆔
Hong Kong University of Science
and Technology
Hong Kong, China

ISSN 0302-9743   ISSN 1611-3349 (electronic)
Lecture Notes in Computer Science
ISBN 978-3-030-87155-0   ISBN 978-3-030-87156-7 (eBook)
https://doi.org/10.1007/978-3-030-87156-7

LNCS Sublibrary: SL1 – Theoretical Computer Science and General Issues

This Springer imprint is published by the registered company Springer Nature Switzerland AG
The registered company address is: Gewerbestrasse 11, 6330 Cham, Switzerland

Preface

In order to enable future intelligent machines to understand their environment in a similar manner as that of humans, they should be endowed with the ability to "see." Vision is one of the strongest components of perceiving the world, ultimately enabling the interaction with it. During the last decades, developments in various fields of research have significantly pushed computer vision systems to better interpret the world and thus support the operation of advanced machines. However, present artificial vision systems still lack the ability to operate in unconstrained, real-life environments and to cope with novel situations. Tackling and overcoming these challenges constitutes the main mission of the International Conference on Computer Vision Systems (ICVS).

The 13th edition of ICVS was held during September 22–24, 2021. In light of the unprecedented global COVID-19 pandemic, ICVS went fully virtual for the first time in its history. Past editions had taken the conference to different countries across multiple continents and brought together researchers from all around the world. Despite the virtual platform in 2021, ICVS remained vibrantly international with authors coming from 16 countries. It is our great hope that for the next edition, we will be able to meet in person in Vienna for ICVS 2023.

ICVS 2021 received 29 submissions, out of which 20 papers were accepted as oral presentations at the main conference. Each paper was reviewed by at least two members of the Program Committee or external reviewers. The authors of accepted submissions were then asked to submit their final versions, taking into consideration the comments and suggestions in the reviews. The best paper of the conference was selected by the general and program chairs, after suggestions from the Program Committee were made. Accepted papers cover a broad spectrum of issues falling under the wider scope of computer vision in real-world applications, including among others, vision systems for robotics, autonomous vehicles, agriculture and medicine. In this volume, the papers are organized into the sections: Attention Systems, Classification and Detection, Semantic Interpretation, Video and Motion Analysis, and Computer Vision Systems in Agriculture.

The technical program of ICVS 2021 was enhanced with three invited speakers. First, Prof. Peter Corke (Queensland University of Technology) described in his talk what is needed by computer vision systems and robotics to operate successfully in the real world. The second invited speaker, Prof. Renaud Detry (UCLouvain and KULeuven), shared his experience on autonomous robot manipulation for planetary and terrestrial applications. Finally, the third invited speaker, Dr. Donald Dansereau (University of Sydney), explored in his talk recent developments in the emerging field of robotic imaging, bringing together optics, algorithms, and robotic embodiment to allow robots to see and do.

The conference also hosted two workshops, which were organized in conjunction with the main conference. The Workshop on Object Recognition and Manipulation, organized by Markus Vincze, Mihai Andries, Andrea Cavallaro, Krystian Mikolajczyk, and Calli Berk, brought together projects sponsored by the CHIST-ERA scheme on "Object

Recognition and Manipulation by Robots: Data Sharing and Experiment Reproducibility." This workshop outlined the research advancements by the projects on the recognition and manipulation of objects in the context of robotics. The Workshop on Traffic Infrastructure Mapping and Automated Damage Assessment Systems was organized by Matthias Rüther. This workshop engaged the current research on mobile data capture, automated data processing and data management systems with the purpose of digitizing traffic infrastructure and assessing their condition.

We wish to thank the Robotics Institute of the University of Technology Sydney, Australia, and the Automation and Control Institute of TU Wien, Austria, for the institutional support. We express our sincere thanks to all the people who contributed to the organization and success of ICVS 2021; in particular, the 41 members of the Program Committee, external reviewers, invited speakers, workshop organizers, our secretary, as well as all the authors who submitted their work to and presented it at ICVS 2021. Finally, we thank Springer for publishing the proceedings in the *Lecture Notes in Computer Science* series.

August 2021   Markus Vincze
                                                                 Timothy Patten
                                                              Henrik I Christensen
                                                              Lazaros Nalpantidis
                                                                    Ming Liu

Organization

General Chairs

Markus Vincze	TU Wien, Austria
Timothy Patten	University of Technology Sydney, Australia

Program Chairs

Henrik I Christensen	University of California, San Diego, USA
Lazaros Nalpantidis	Technical University of Denmark, Denmark
Ming Liu	Hong Kong University of Science and Technology, Hong Kong

Conference Secretary

Maria Magdalena Molner	TU Wien, Austria

Program Committee

Sharath Chandra Akkaladevi	Profactor, Austria
Alen Alempijevic	University of Technology Sydney, Australia
Helder Araujo	University of Coimbra, Portugal
Antonis Argyros	University of Crete, Greece
Richard Bormann	Fraunhofer IPA, Germany
Darius Burschka	Technical University of Munich, Germany
Alessandro Carfi	University of Genoa, Italy
Dimitrios Chrysostomou	Aalborg University, Denmark
Diego Faria	Aston University, UK
Robert Fisher	University of Edinburgh, UK
Friedrich Fraundorfer	Graz University of Technology, Austria
Simone Frintrop	University of Hamburg, Germany
Dimitrios Giakoumis	Centre for Research and Technology Hellas, Greece
Raphael Guenot-Falque	University of Technology Sydney, Australia
Marc Hanheide	University of Lincoln, UK
Mahmoud Hassaballah	South Valley University, Egypt
Hannes Kisner	Chemnitz University of Technology, Germany
Walter G. Kropatsch	TU Wien, Austria
Cedric Le Gentil	University of Technology Sydney, Australia
Vincent Lepetit	Graz University of Technology, Austria
Elisa Maiettini	Italian Institute of Technology, Italy

Contents

Attention Systems

Thermal Image Super-Resolution Using Second-Order Channel Attention with Varying Receptive Fields

Nolan B. Gutierrez⦿ and William J. Beksi(✉)⦿

University of Texas at Arlington, Arlington, TX, USA
nolan.gutierrez@mavs.uta.edu, william.beksi@uta.edu

Abstract. Thermal images model the long-infrared range of the electromagnetic spectrum and provide meaningful information even when there is no visible illumination. Yet, unlike imagery that represents radiation from the visible continuum, infrared images are inherently low-resolution due to hardware constraints. The restoration of thermal images is critical for applications that involve safety, search and rescue, and military operations. In this paper, we introduce a system to efficiently reconstruct thermal images. Specifically, we explore how to effectively attend to contrasting receptive fields (RFs) where increasing the RFs of a network can be computationally expensive. For this purpose, we introduce a deep attention to varying receptive fields network (AVRFN). We supply a gated convolutional layer with higher-order information extracted from disparate RFs, whereby an RF is parameterized by a dilation rate. In this way, the dilation rate can be tuned to use fewer parameters thus increasing the efficacy of AVRFN. Our experimental results show an improvement over the state of the art when compared against competing thermal image super-resolution (SR) methods.

Keywords: Thermal imaging · Super-resolution · Compression via dilations

1 Introduction

The purpose of single image super-resolution (SISR) restoration is to determine the mapping between a possibly degraded low-resolution (LR) image and its high-resolution (HR) counterpart. Finding this arrangement is difficult due to the intractable nature of the problem. Techniques for discovering the mapping can be divided into two areas: *interpolated* and *learning-based*. Contemporary SISR has been dominated by deep learning which has demonstrated superiority over hand-crafted methods such as bicubic and bilinear interpolation.

The authors acknowledge the Texas Advanced Computing Center (TACC) at the University of Texas at Austin for providing software, computational, and storage resources that have contributed to the research results reported within this paper.

M. Vincze et al. (Eds.): ICVS 2021, LNCS 12899, pp. 3–13, 2021.
https://doi.org/10.1007/978-3-030-87156-7_1

Convolutional neural networks (CNNs) have been shown to be successful at attending to visual images on tasks such as SISR. This includes squeeze-and-excitation methods for global excitation of feature maps [11,16], and the use of weight excitations [17,20]. Furthermore, ablation studies have conclusively shown that excitation networks for feature maps bring performance gains [25]. On another note, a variety of methods exist for modifying the RF of a CNN either through concatenation [15], deformation [7], or dilation [23]. In this work, we study how dilated convolutions offer *compression through dilations*. Concretely, we show how they modify the effective receptive fields (ERFs) of a CNN and how they interact with an existing enhancement known as second-order channel attention (SOCA) [8].

The development of infrared thermographic cameras has spurred researchers to carry out innovative research in the thermal image domain. Representing traditional SR, Mandanici et al. [19] combined geometric registration with projection and interpolation to produce HR thermal images. Naturally, researchers have recently investigated color-guided thermal image SR [2,5]. For example, a pyramidal network provided by Gupta et al. [9] attains accurate results by extracting edge-maps from RGB images at various levels of the network. Chudasama et al. [6] present an efficient SR network for thermal images by eliciting high-frequency details with a limited number of feature extraction modules. Other works have introduced popular loss functions to the field of thermal image SR [1,13].

In this work we not only explore the use of efficient thermal SR, but we also provide complete benchmarks on three thermal imagery datasets. Furthermore, we compare the results of four architectural variants to assess performance gains or losses due to the compression of parameters in our SR network. In contrast to previous work on SISR, our proposed model applies SOCA to a concatenation of features produced from convolutions with changing RFs. An intermediate convolutional layer quantifies the importance of the values from each RF before passing this information to SOCA. The key contributions of our work are the following: (i) we show the effectiveness of SOCA for thermal image SR; (ii) we present a novel approach to sample from a foveated RF; (iii) we demonstrate an efficient network for multiple upscaling factors; (iv) we establish new benchmarks on public thermal image datasets. Our source code is available at [4].

The rest of this paper is organized as follows. In Sect. 2, we propose an architecture for transforming LR input images to super-resolved output images. We demonstrate our dilation-rate driven deep attention to varying receptive fields network through experimental results in Sect. 3. Finally, we conclude in Sect. 4.

2   Second-Order Channel Attention with Varying Receptive Fields

We establish a novel deep learning architecture for thermal image SR as follows. First (Sect. 2.1), we provide a detailed description of SOCA. Second (Sect. 2.2), we expound upon how dilated convolutions are computed. Third (Sect. 2.3), we

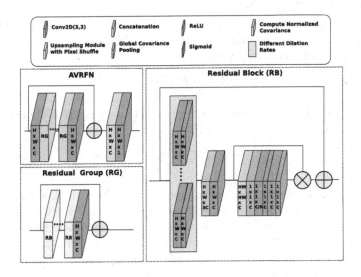

Fig. 1. An overview of our thermal imaging SR model.

describe how CNNs can be compressed with respect to an ERF via compression through dilations. Finally (Sect. 2.4), we apply SOCA to separate RFs (by dilation rates) within residual in residual to assist in the SR of LR images obtained with a bicubic degradation model.

2.1 Second-Order Channel Attention

We utilize an alternative SOCA network to enhance convolutional blocks by supplying a covariance matrix that allows for more discriminative representations. To produce these second-order statistics, the covariance normalization is obtained through Newton-Schulz iteration [10]. Additionally, this serves to speed up the computation. First, a feature map of dimension $H \times W \times C$ is reshaped into a feature map $\boldsymbol{X}$ of shape $HW \times C$. Second, the covariance matrix is calculated,

$$\boldsymbol{\Sigma} = \boldsymbol{X} \boldsymbol{I}_f \boldsymbol{X}^\top, \tag{1}$$

where $\boldsymbol{I}_f = \frac{1}{s}(\boldsymbol{I} - \frac{1}{s}\boldsymbol{1})$ and $s = HW$. $\boldsymbol{I}$ and $\boldsymbol{1}$ are the $m \times m$ identity matrix and the matrix of all ones, respectively. Then, the covariance matrix is prenormalized,

$$\hat{\boldsymbol{\Sigma}} = \frac{1}{\text{tr}(\boldsymbol{\Sigma})}\boldsymbol{\Sigma}, \tag{2}$$

where $\text{tr}(\cdot)$ denotes the matrix trace. Let $\boldsymbol{Y}_0 = \hat{\boldsymbol{\Sigma}}$ and $\boldsymbol{Z}_0 = \boldsymbol{I}$, then $\boldsymbol{Y}_n$ and $\boldsymbol{Z}_n$ are obtained by

$$\boldsymbol{Y}_n = \frac{1}{2}\boldsymbol{Y}_{n-1}(3\boldsymbol{I} - \boldsymbol{Z}_{n-1}\boldsymbol{Y}_{n-1}), \tag{3}$$

$$\boldsymbol{Z}_n = \frac{1}{2}(3\boldsymbol{I} - \boldsymbol{Z}_{n-1}\boldsymbol{Y}_{n-1})\boldsymbol{Z}_{n-1}, \tag{4}$$

with $\boldsymbol{Y}_n$ and $\boldsymbol{Z}_n$ quadratically converging to $\boldsymbol{Y}$ and $\boldsymbol{Y}^{-1}$, respectively. The final normalized matrix after five iterations of Newton-Schulz is found by compensating the pre-normalization step with

$$\hat{\boldsymbol{Y}} = \sqrt{tr(\boldsymbol{\Sigma})}\boldsymbol{Y}_N. \tag{5}$$

Afterwards, global covariance pooling is applied to obtain a scalar-valued statistic z_i for each channel i,

$$z_i = \frac{1}{C} \sum_j^C \hat{\boldsymbol{Y}}_{ij}. \tag{6}$$

This permits the channel attention to capture correlations higher than the first order. In the next step, the sigmoid activation function serves as a gating mechanism that entrusts the network to selectively choose what to add to the incoming input features. To create this gating mechanism, we use two convolutional layers, $\boldsymbol{W}_0$ and $\boldsymbol{W}_1$, with rectified linear unit (ReLU) and sigmoid activation functions. Concretely,

$$G(\boldsymbol{z}) = \boldsymbol{W}_1 * (\boldsymbol{W}_0 * \boldsymbol{z}), \tag{7}$$

where $*$ is the convolution operation and $G(\boldsymbol{z})$ is an attention map.

2.2   Dilated Convolutions

A dilated convolution multiplies a rate l by Δ during the convolution operation, i.e.,

$$(F *_l k)(\mathbf{p}) = \sum_{\Delta \in \Omega_r} F(\mathbf{p} - l \cdot \Delta)k(\Delta), \tag{8}$$

where $\Omega_r = [-r, r]^2 \cap \mathbb{Z}^2$, $k : \Omega_r \to \mathbb{R}$, $\boldsymbol{p} \in \mathbb{Z}^2$ is a location on $\boldsymbol{X}$, $F : \mathbb{Z}^2 \to \mathbb{R}$, and $*_l$ is an l-dilated convolution. In (8), k is known as the kernel function which slides over $\boldsymbol{X}$. This allows a convolutional network to sample pixel values from a larger RF over the input features.

In the case of SR, it is advantageous to sample from different sized RFs depending on a number of factors including depth, resolution, and the scaling factor. We use dilated convolutions to extract features within each residual block. Specifically, the feature sets of three convolutional layers with varying dilation rates are concatenated and passed to an intermediate layer which pools the information from contrasting RFs. This intermediate layer effectively pools information at each feature map's location from a foveated RF where more parameters are concentrated towards the center of the field.

2.3   Compression Through Dilations

We utilize dilated convolutions to artificially increase the ERFs of our CNN. An ERF is defined as the area containing any input pixel with a non-negligible impact on a particular output unit within a feature map [18]. In addition, we introduce the concept of compression through dilations as the case in which a

CNN uses fewer parameters to increase an ERF with dilated convolutions compared to without dilated convolutions. For example, assuming we are using bias, two single-layer CNNs defined by Conv2D(Input_Shape $= (32, 32, 3), 64, (5, 5)$) and Conv2D(Input_Shape $= (32, 32, 3), 64, (3, 3),$ Dilation_Rate $= 2$) have an ERF area of 25. However, our CNN has 160,064 and 57,664 parameters, respectively, giving a compression ratio of 2.776.

2.4 Model Overview

Our overall model is shown in Fig. 1. To upscale an input image, features are extracted from a series of residual groups and blocks within the RIR architecture similar to RCAN [25]. Pixel shuffle [22] is used to rearrange X of shape $(H, W, C \cdot r^2)$ to $(H \cdot r, W \cdot r, C)$ by periodically building a new feature map $PS(X)$ with pixel values from dissimilar channels according to the equation

$$PS(X)_{x,y,c} = X_{\lfloor x/r \rfloor, \lfloor y/r \rfloor, C \cdot r \cdot mod(y,r) + C \cdot mod(x,r) + c}. \tag{9}$$

Finally, a single-channel convolutional layer reduces the number of channels to the same number as in the LR image.

3 Experimental Results

Our experiments model the downscaling of HR thermal images using a bicubic degradation model with statistical noise.

3.1 Datasets

We use the Thermal Image Super-Resolution (TISR) 2020 Challenge dataset, the FLIR Thermal Dataset for Algorithm Training (TDAT) [24], and the KAIST multispectral pedestrian detection benchmark dataset [12]. The TISR dataset consists of three sets of 1,021 images from three distinct cameras. These cameras include a Domo, Axis, and FLIR with a resolution of (160×120), (320×240), and (640×480), respectively. Of these images, 60 were kept private, leaving 951 in the training set and 50 in the test set for each camera. For TDAT, we evaluate on only the first 100 images captured by a FLIR FC-6320 camera. Lastly, for the KAIST dataset, we collect every 200-th image from the day and night scenes and then evaluate on the set of 226 images. The images from the KAIST dataset were captured by a FLIR-A35 thermal camera with a resolution of 640×480.

The ground-truth dataset was created by first forming batches of 16 single-channel image patches where each patch is of size $scale \times 48$. The LR images were then obtained by bicubicly interpolating these patches to a size of 48×48. For both training and testing, the images were preprocessed by adding Gaussian noise with a mean of 0 and a variance of 10 for the bicubic with noise degradation model. Finally, all elements of each LR patch are normalized and clipped to [0,1].

3.2 Implementation

Our final architecture uses three residual groups with six residual blocks per group. Each convolutional layer has 64 filters resulting in a highly-efficient network. During training, the Adam optimizer [14], parameterized by a learning rate of $10^{-4}, \beta_1 = 0.9, \beta_2 = 0.999$, and $\epsilon = 10^{-7}$, is applied to minimize the MSE of each batch for 300 epochs. Training with four NVIDIA GeForce GTX 1080 Ti GPUs took less than three hours per model.

3.3 Evaluation

For the experiments, we tested four variants of our architecture to evaluate the performance gains of the network. The variants are as follows.

- Dilated residual in residual (DDRR): SOCA in the residual block of Fig. 1 is replaced by a convolutional layer with a 3×3 kernel size and no activation function.
- Residual in residual with SOCA (RRSOCA): Our different dilation rate module in the residual block of Fig. 1 is replaced with a series of two convolutional layers each with a kernel size of 3×3 and a ReLU activation function.
- Compressed RCAN (CRCAN) via dilated convolutions: This architecture is similar to RRSOCA, but the first and second convolutional layers have a dilation rate of 1 and 2, respectively.
- Attention to varying receptive fields network (AVRFN): This is our proposed model as shown in Fig. 1.

Figure 2 highlights example inputs, SR predictions, and the ground-truth images from the datasets. The added Gaussian noise produces heavily pixelated input images which presents very difficult conditions to evaluate our methods on. In all of our experiments, we use the peak signal-to-noise ratio (PSNR) and structural similarity index (SSIM) to evaluate each architectural variant. Table 1 shows the performance of our proposed AVRFN when evaluated on each of the datasets. Additionally, Table 2 provides an ablation study which compares the performance of the various types of compression with different channel attention networks. Note that we were unable to make a fair comparison with related work found in [6] since the performance of our baseline method did not match. However, each of our variants performed better than the baseline RCAN architecture.

An interesting finding is that adding compression through dilations in the residual block of RCAN leads to improved performance. After each residual connection, the ERF resets to the kernel size of the succeeding CNN due to the easy pass-through of low-level information found in residual networks [3]. Contemporary work has found a correlation between larger ERFs and performance gains [3]. We hypothesize that by introducing compression through dilations in each residual block, we increase the ERF at a faster rate thus allowing for performance gains. An unexpected result is that DDRR, the only variant without

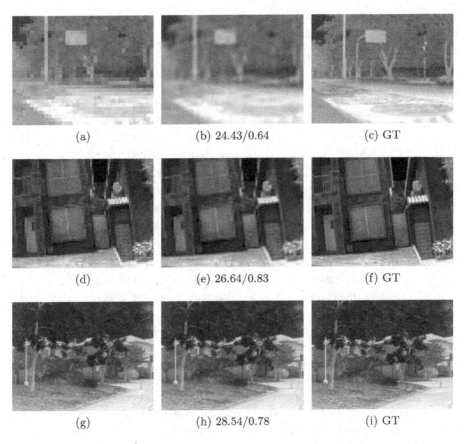

Fig. 2. Examples of (left column) downsampled images from (top row) low-resolution, (middle row) medium-resolution, and (bottom row) high-resolution thermal cameras, their ×4 upscaled counterparts (middle column), and the ground truth (GT) (right column). Additionally, (b), (e), and (h) show the PSNR and SSIM scores, respectively, when evaluated against the ground truth.

any form of channel-attention, performs significantly worse. This confirms previous ablation studies [25], but it also shows that most of the performance gains arise from channel attention and not compression through dilations. In addition, our varying dilation rate module (AVRFN) improves performance over the baseline which shows that attending to different RFs can improve performance. Nonetheless, our highest performance gains are obtained when we simply add compression through dilations to the RCAN baseline.

Table 1. The results of our AVRFN model on images captured by the TISR [21], TDAT [24] and KAIST [12] datasets.

Test set	Scale	Parameters	PSNR	SSIM
AXIS Domo P1290	2	2491009	30.097	0.846
AXIS Q2901		2491009	34.416	0.928
FLIR FC-6320		2491009	37.116	0.942
TDAT		2491009	31.184	0.733
KAIST		2491009	40.612	0.962
AXIS Domo P1290	3	2511809	26.831	0.747
AXIS Q2901		2511809	30.007	0.850
FLIR FC-6320		251180	33.668	0.898
TDAT		2511809	30.055	0.730
KAIST		2511809	39.065	0.958
AXIS Domo P1290	4	2507649	25.146	0.671
AXIS Q2901		2507649	27.724	0.784
FLIR FC-6320		2507649	31.574	0.857
TDAT		2507649	28.110	0.626
KAIST		2507649	37.793	0.951

Table 2. The results of our ×4 model variants on images captured by the TISR [21], TDAT [24] and KAIST [12] datasets.

Test set	Model	Scale	Parameters	PSNR	SSIM
AXIS Domo P1290	RRSOCA	4	1661377	25.487	0.691
	DDRR	4	2839873	25.458	0.691
	CRCAN	4	2839873	**25.491**	**0.692**
	RCAN	4	1661377	25.239	0.682
	AVRFN	4	1917313	25.368	0.685
AXIS Q2901	RRSOCA	4	1661377	28.167	0.802
	DDRR	4	2839873	28.159	0.801
	CRCAN	4	2839873	28.189	0.802
	RCAN	4	1661377	27.923	0.795
	AVRFN	4	1917313	27.990	0.797
FLIR FC-6320	RRSOCA	4	1661377	31.978	0.867
	DDRR	4	2839873	31.985	0.867
	CRCAN	4	2839873	32.002	0.867
	RCAN	4	1661377	31.756	0.861
	AVRFN	4	1917313	31.824	0.864

(*continued*)

Table 2. (*continued*)

Test set	Model	Scale	Parameters	PSNR	SSIM
TDAT	RRSOCA	4	1661377	28.388	0.641
	DDRR	4	2839873	28.427	0.645
	CRCAN	4	2839873	28.426	0.645
	RCAN	4	1661377	28.271	0.636
	AVRFN	4	1917313	28.298	0.637
KAIST	RRSOCA	4	1661377	37.977	0.949
	DDRR	4	2839873	37.456	0.918
	CRCAN	4	2839873	37.573	0.922
	RCAN	4	1661377	37.089	0.938
	AVRFN	4	1917313	37.827	0.943

4   Conclusion

In this work, we showed the advantage of attending to varying resolutions for the reconstruction of thermal images by efficiently parametrizing a convolutional layer with a dilation rate. Together with SOCA, our model achieves state-of-the-art results on the task of thermal image SR and yields up-to-date benchmarks for the research community. In the future, we intend to look at ways in which training may be further stabilized and how attention to uncertainty maps can improve the computational efficiency of thermal image SR.

References

1. Almasri, F., Debeir, O.: Multimodal sensor fusion in single thermal image super-resolution. In: Carneiro, G., You, S. (eds.) Computer Vision - ACCV 2018, pp. 418–433. Springer, Cham (2018). https://doi.org/10.1007/978-3-030-21074-8
2. Almasri, F., Debeir, O.: RGB guided thermal super-resolution enhancement. In: Proceedings of the IEEE International Conference on Cloud Computing Technologies and Applications, pp. 1–5 (2018)
3. Araujo, A., Norris, W., Sim, J.: Computing receptive fields of convolutional neural networks. Distill **4**(11), e21 (2019)
4. https://github.com/robotic-vision-lab/Attention-With-Varying-Receptive-Fields-Network
5. Chen, X., Zhai, G., Wang, J., Hu, C., Chen, Y.: Color guided thermal image super resolution. In: Proceedings of the IEEE International Conference on Visual Communications and Image Processing, pp. 1–4 (2016)
6. Chudasama, V., et al.: TherISuRnet - a computationally efficient thermal image super-resolution network. In: Proceedings of the IEEE/CVF Conference on Computer Vision and Pattern Recognition Workshops, pp. 86–87 (2020)

7. Dai, J., et al.: Deformable convolutional networks. In: Proceedings of the IEEE International Conference on Computer Vision, pp. 764–773 (2017)
8. Dai, T., Cai, J., Zhang, Y., Xia, S.T., Zhang, L.: Second-order attention network for single image super-resolution. In: Proceedings of the IEEE International Conference on Computer Vision, pp. 11065–11074 (2019)
9. Gupta, H., Mitra, K.: Pyramidal edge-maps based guided thermal super-resolution. arXiv preprint arXiv:2003.06216 (2020)
10. Higham, N.J.: Functions of Matrices: Theory and Computation. SIAM (2008)
11. Hu, J., Shen, L., Sun, G.: Squeeze-and-excitation networks. In: Proceedings of the IEEE Conference on Computer Vision and Pattern Recognition, pp. 7132–7141 (2018)
12. Hwang, S., Park, J., Kim, N., Choi, Y., So Kweon, I.: Multispectral pedestrian detection: benchmark dataset and baseline. In: Proceedings of the IEEE Conference on Computer Vision and Pattern Recognition, pp. 1037–1045 (2015)
13. Kansal, P., Nathan, S.: A multi-level supervision model: a novel approach for thermal image super resolution. In: Proceedings of the IEEE/CVF Conference on Computer Vision and Pattern Recognition Workshops, pp. 94–95 (2020)
14. Kingma, D.P., Ba, J.: Adam: a method for stochastic optimization. arXiv preprint arXiv:1412.6980 (2014)
15. Li, J., Fang, F., Mei, K., Zhang, G.: Multi-scale residual network for image super-resolution. In: Vedaldi, A., Bischof, H., Brox, T., Frahm, J.-M. (eds.) ECCV 2018. LNCS, vol. 12356, pp. 517–532. Springer, Cham (2018). https://doi.org/10.1007/978-3-030-58621-8
16. Li, T., Wu, B., Yang, Y., Fan, Y., Zhang, Y., Liu, W.: Compressing convolutional neural networks via factorized convolutional filters. In: Proceedings of the IEEE/CVF Conference on Computer Vision and Pattern Recognition, pp. 3977–3986 (2019)
17. Lin, X., Ma, L., Liu, W., Chang, S.-F.: Context-gated convolution. In: Vedaldi, A., Bischof, H., Brox, T., Frahm, J.-M. (eds.) ECCV 2020. LNCS, vol. 12363, pp. 701–718. Springer, Cham (2020). https://doi.org/10.1007/978-3-030-58523-5_41
18. Luo, W., Li, Y., Urtasun, R., Zemel, R.: Understanding the effective receptive field in deep convolutional neural networks. In: Proceedings of the International Conference on Neural Information Processing Systems, pp. 4905–4913 (2016)
19. Mandanici, E., Tavasci, L., Corsini, F., Gandolfi, S.: A multi-image super-resolution algorithm applied to thermal imagery. Appl. Geom. 11(3), 215–228 (2019). https://doi.org/10.1007/s12518-019-00253-y
20. Quader, N., Bhuiyan, M.M.I., Lu, J., Dai, P., Li, W.: Weight excitation: built-in attention mechanisms in convolutional neural networks. In: Vedaldi, A., Bischof, H., Brox, T., Frahm, J.-M. (eds.) ECCV 2020. LNCS, vol. 12375, pp. 87–103. Springer, Cham (2020). https://doi.org/10.1007/978-3-030-58577-8_6
21. Rivadeneira, R.E., et al.: Thermal image super-resolution challenge-PBVS 2020. In: Proceedings of the IEEE/CVF Conference on Computer Vision and Pattern Recognition Workshops, pp. 96–97 (2020)
22. Shi, W., et al.: Real-time single image and video super-resolution using an efficient sub-pixel convolutional neural network. In: Proceedings of the IEEE Conference on Computer Vision and Pattern Recognition, pp. 1874–1883 (2016)
23. Szegedy, C., et al.: Going deeper with convolutions. In: Proceedings of the IEEE Conference on Computer Vision and Pattern Recognition, pp. 1–9 (2015)

24. Teledyne FLIR LLC: Free FLIR Thermal Dataset for Algorithm Training (2021). https://www.flir.in/oem/adas/adas-dataset-form/
25. Zhang, Y., Li, K., Li, K., Wang, L., Zhong, B., Fu, Y.: Image super-resolution using very deep residual channel attention networks. In: Ferrari, V., Hebert, M., Sminchisescu, C., Weiss, Y. (eds.) ECCV 2018, vol. 11214, pp. 286–301. Springer, Cham (2018). https://doi.org/10.1007/978-3-030-01249-6

MARL: Multimodal Attentional Representation Learning for Disease Prediction

Ali Hamdi[1]([✉])(iD), Amr Aboeleneen[2]([✉]), and Khaled Shaban[2]([✉])

[1] RMIT University, Melbourne, Australia
ali.ali@rmit.edu.au
[2] Qatar University, Doha, Qatar
{aa1405465,khaled.shaban}@qu.edu.qa

Abstract. Existing learning models often utilise CT-scan images to predict lung diseases. These models are posed by high uncertainties that affect lung segmentation and visual feature learning. We introduce MARL, a novel *M*ultimodal *A*ttentional *R*epresentation *L*earning model architecture that learns useful features from multimodal data under uncertainty. We feed the proposed model with both the lung CT-scan images and their perspective historical patients' biological records collected over times. Such rich data offers to analyse both spatial and temporal aspects of the disease. MARL employs Fuzzy-based image spatial segmentation to overcome uncertainties in CT-scan images. We then utilise a pre-trained Convolutional Neural Network (CNN) to learn visual representation vectors from images. We augment patients' data with statistical features from the segmented images. We develop a Long Short-Term Memory (LSTM) network to represent the augmented data and learn sequential patterns of disease progressions. Finally, we inject both CNN and LSTM feature vectors to an attention layer to help focus on the best learning features. We evaluated MARL on regression of lung disease progression and status classification. MARL outperforms state-of-the-art CNN architectures, such as EfficientNet and DenseNet, and baseline prediction models. It achieves a 91% R^2 score, which is higher than the other models by a range of 8% to 27%. Also, MARL achieves 97% and 92% accuracy for binary and multi-class classification, respectively. MARL improves the accuracy of state-of-the-art CNN models with a range of 19% to 57%. The results show that combining spatial and sequential temporal features produces better discriminative feature.

Keywords: Multimodal representation learning · Visual uncertainty · Deep architecture · Lung disease prediction

1 Introduction

Deep representation learning models are proposed to learn discriminative features in various applications. Recently, lung disease prediction tasks, be it progression

© Springer Nature Switzerland AG 2021
M. Vincze et al. (Eds.): ICVS 2021, LNCS 12899, pp. 14–27, 2021.
https://doi.org/10.1007/978-3-030-87156-7_2

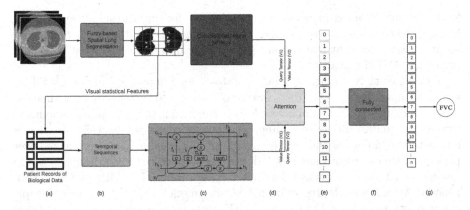

Fig. 1. Workflow of the proposed model architecture, MARL, for IPF lung disease prediction. (a) Inputing lung CT-scan images and patient data. (b-top) Applying Fuzzy-based spatial lung segmentation. (b-bottom) Preparing temporal sequences of the patient attributes and extracting statistical features from the segmented lung images. (c) Learning visual features using pre-trained CNN and temporal features using LSTM. (d and e) Injecting the visual and sequential feature vectors to an attention layer that learns the best set of weights. (f and g) Adding a fully-connected layer to learn the final feature vector from the multimodal data and learns the FVC score with a softmax layer.

regression or classification, have gained much attention due to the pandemic of COVID-19. Existing prediction models are challenged by uncertainty issues when determining the correct disease patterns [1,2]. These uncertainty issues effect lung disease prediction when performing lung segmentation and feature representation learning.

Lung segmentation is challenging due to the fuzziness of the visual compositions of the CT-scan images. These images contain radio-density Hounsfield scores that represent other human body parts. Conventional methods often depend on tissue thresholds over the CT-scan Hounsfield. Such methods also employ various morphological operations such as dilation to cover the lung nodules at far borders. However, these methods suffer from the uncertainty when separating the lung tissues. Therefore, we propose to apply Fuzzy-based spatial segmentation over the lung CT-scans to reduce noisy spots and spurious blobs in the images [3]. We then employ a pre-trained Convolutional Neural Network (CNN) to learn the visual features of the images.

Visual representation learning models depend, in most cases, on CNN to capture useful patterns in a given image [4]. However, CNNs suffer from challenges such as limited local structural information as they are designed to learn local descriptors using receptive fields [5]. This, in turn, leads to losing important global structures. We propose to address this issue by augmenting the CNN visual features with global temporal characteristics from patients biological and health records. We train our proposed hybrid model to learn these temporal features through a Long Short-Term Memory (LSTM) network. However, LSTM learns features from sequences at a fixed length limiting the significance of the learning feature space. We propose to overcome this limitation by employing an attention layer that learns what should be learnt from the visual CNN and sequential LSTM features.

As a case study, we utilise a public dataset for Idiopathic Pulmonary Fibrosis (IPF) lung disease [6]. IPF scars lung tissues and it worsens over time for unknown causes [1]. When infected, lungs cannot take in the required amount of oxygen due to difficulty of breathing. The dataset contains both CT-scan images and patients' biological and health records with different attributes collected over periods of times. Such multimodal data harnesses spatial visual features of the disease and temporal patient attributes. Our proposed MARL, a novel Multimodal Attentional Representation Learning model architecture, has multiple components as visualised in Fig. 1. MARL starts with preprocessing the input of the lung CT-scan images using a fuzzy-based spatial segmentation and preparing the temporal sequences from their corespondent patients' data records. Two different deep learning networks, including CNN and LSTM, are then employed to learn the visual and temporal features, respectively. The encoded pairs of feature vectors are injected into an attention layer. The final feature vectors are propagated through a fully-connected layer. These final feature vectors are evaluated against multiple downstream tasks such as regressing the disease progression and classifying the disease status.

In summary, the multimodal learnt feature vectors, produced by MARL, offer to solve the uncertainty issues in lung disease prediction through the following contributions:

- Producing accurate visual representation vectors by improving the CNN feature learning through a Fuzzy-based spatial segmentation.
- Developing effective temporal feature learning from the patient biological records and statistical information of the CT-scan images using an LSTM network.
- Introducing an attention mechanism that improves the feature representation by focusing on the critical input sequences and image parts.
- Carrying out an extensive experimental work to evaluate the proposed model on different lung disease prediction tasks such as lung declination regression and disease status classification.

The rest of the paper is organised as follows. Section 2 reviews related works and contrast that with our work in this paper. Section 3 explains the proposed MARL. Section 4 describes experimental setups, and discusses the results of performance evaluations. Section 5 concludes the paper.

2   Related Work

Recent research efforts have used CNNs visual representation learning to advance multiple applications [7]. CNN-based methods are widely utilised to produce visual feature vectors from CT-scan images for disease prediction. A CNN network was developed in [8] to classify the disease status into positive, possible-to-have, and negative. They collected a lung disease dataset of $1,157$ high-resolution images. Their experimental results showed the superiority of the deep learning models against the radiologists in both accuracy and speed. However, their results depended on a small dataset which limits the feature learning space. In this paper, we utilise a dataset of $33,026$ CT-scan lung images in addition to the patient tabular data. Besides, their dataset was annotated by one expert who might have erroneous decisions. On contrast, the dataset we use is created and published by Open Source Imaging Consortium that made substantial cooperative efforts between the academia and healthcare industry.

State-of-the-art of CNN-based models proposed various network architectures to improve image representation learning [4,9–13]. CNN-based models are designed to have large sets of layers to adapt to the increasing size and complexity of the training data [14]. However, they usually suffer from the problem of overfitting when having relatively small training data. Recently, the overfitting problem has been addressed by different techniques such as data augmentation. Moreover, CNNs neglect useful structures due to the limitations of their receptive fields and isotropic mechanism [5]. Therefore, we propose to combine the visual CT-scan data with their correspondent patients' data. Such multimodality adds useful features that increase the accuracy of lung disease prediction. The patient data is a set of patient attributes and disease progression measurements over time. Therefore, we employ LSTM to learn temporal features combined with the CNN visual representations in order to improve prediction. LSTM has been recently used to predict different disease developments such as Alzheimer [15], hand-foot-mouth [16], and COVID-19 [17]. LSTM learns better at equal intervals of regular spaced timestamps. Notwithstanding that CT-scan data are often collected at the patient needs making an irregular data collection sequences. The authors in [18] utilised adapted LSTM to learn irregular temporal data points for lung cancer detection. Moreover, LSTM learns features from sequences at a fixed length which effects the learning of the feature space. Therefore, we design our proposed MARL to combine CNN and LSTM to overcome their limitations.

The hybridisation between CNN and LSTM tends to have a potential increase in disease prediction accuracy. Recent work in [19] has reported that a hybrid model of LSTM and CNN outperformed the human experts in lung disease classification. However, their work did not consider the uncertainty in segmentation, and they used a small dataset of 102 patients. Therefore, there is still a need to address the above-discussed limitations and uncertainties in LSTM and CNN networks. We utilise Fuzzy-based spatial segmentation to improve the lung segmentation before the convolutional feature extraction. Using multimodal datasets contributes to accurate lung disease prediction [20]. The work in [21] predicted the recurrence of lung cancer based on a multimodal fusion of tomography images and genomics. However, using CNN and LSTM on multimodal data adds more complexity to the training process. We design an attentional neural layer at the bottleneck that connects the CNN and LSTM vectors with the fully-connected layer. This attention mechanism is designed to make the model focuses on essential features in the input sequences. The authors in [22] combined both medical codes and clinical text notes to implement multimodal attentional neural networks. Similarly, our proposed model, MARL, combines different data modalities such as CT-scan images, and patients' biological and health records. MARL, extract useful representations from CT-scan images, patient data, and visual statistical information.

3   Multimodal Attentional Representation Learning

We propose a novel representation learning model architecture for lung disease prediction. The proposed model is designed to address uncertainty issues that affect the downstream prediction tasks such as disease progression regression and disease status binary and multi-class classification. In this section, we explain the workflow phases of MARL.

3.1   Preprocessing

The given CT-scan images in the dataset have multiple issues regarding colour exposure and varying sizes. We start by correcting the black exposure to ensure high quality of the subsequent feature extraction step. We also crop and scale-up the dataset images to match a unified size.

Around the lung, the CT-scan images include other human body parts, such as bones and blood vessels. Therefore, the images must be segmented to extract the lung parts only. Pixels in the CT-scan images contain radio-density scores. The pixel value represents the mean attenuation of the tissue scale from $-1,024$ to $+3,071$ at Hounsfield scale. Hounsfield unit (HU) is a scaled linear transformation of the radio-density's attenuation coefficient measurements. HU values are calculated as in Eq. 1.

$$hu = pixel_{value} * slope + intercept \tag{1}$$

where slope and intercept are stored in the CT-scan file. The projected HUs are interpreted according to the ranges, such as, bone from $+700$ to $+3000$ and lung to be -500. However, segmenting the lung based on these numbers is cumbersome. The visual composition of the different body parts is uncertain at multiple locations. Therefore, we implement spatial segmentation based on Fuzzy C-Means (FCM) applied on the HUs.

3.2   Lung Segmentation with Spatial Fuzzy C-Means

The lung segmentation suffers from uncertainty due to the fuzzy area around the lung. This fuzziness happens because of the nature of the HU values that represent various human body parts around the lung. Using the Fuzzy spatial C-means has advantages over the classical Fuzzy C-Means. The latter is sensitive to noisy parts in the given images. Besides, the classic FCM expects data to have robust, and separated partitions to implement useful membership functions. Nonetheless, in our case, this assumption is not valid due to the high-dependency among the image segments. Spatial FCM computes the likelihood of a neighbourhood-pixel belongs to a specific segment, e.g., lung. The Fuzzy member function uses the spatial likeliness score to calculate the membership value. The work in [3] proposed to compute the membership values (m) based on score of spatial similarity and degree of hesitation, as in Eq. 2.

$$
m_{ij} = \frac{u_{ij}^p h_{ij}^q}{\sum\limits_{k=1}^{c} u_{kj}^p h_{kj}^q}
\tag{2}
$$

where m_{ij} denotes membership values of a neighbourhood pixel with coordinates of i and j, u denotes membership function calculated based on the degree of hesitation score, and p regulates the initial membership's weights, q controls spatial functions, and h is the spatial function. We at that stage apply standard morphological transformation methods. Specifically, we utilise erosion and dilation in order to remove the noise remain thereafter segmentation.

3.3 Patient Biological Data Enrichment

The dataset contains patient records of biological information. These tabular data are temporally tagged with different timestamps of their collections. The dataset has the following columns:

- Patient unique identifiers that link the biological data with the CT-scan images.
- Week numbers of which the CT-scan had been taken.
- FVC, the Forced Vital Capacity recorded for the patient lung in that week.
- The percent: a calculated field that estimates the FVC of a patient as a percentage of the average FVC for patients with similar attributes.
- Age of the patient.
- Sex denoting the gender of each patient.
- Smoking status of a patient as smoker, non-smoker, or ex-smoker.

The biological dataset is unbalanced. The patient ages, CT-scan times, and FVC percentages and scores show unbalanced distributions. Moreover, the dataset has records of males more than females, ex-smokers more than smokers and non-smokers. This fact adds more uncertainty due to the bias towards particular categories. Therefore, we enrich the biological tabular data with some visual statistical features. We compute the kurtosis, volume, mean, skewness, and moments for each CT-scan segmented lung. Adding such visual statistical information to the tabular biological data tends to be useful for achieving high accuracy. The generated visual statistics are computed based images of same person over time. Therefore, we implement an LSTM network to overcome the uncertainty issue due to the data unbalance by learning useful sequential patterns such temporal generated data.

3.4   Multimodal Representation Learning

We implement two deep neural networks. First, Convolutional Neural Network to extract the CT-scan images' visual features. Second, a double Long Short Term Memory Network to learn sequential temporal features from the biological and visual statistical data.

Convolutional Neural Networks. We employ Efficient-Net [4], which has recently outperformed other pre-trained networks in accuracy, size, and efficiency.

A CNN network is typically composed of one or more convolutional layers. Each layer i represents a function as in Eq. 3.

$$Y_i = \mathcal{F}_i(X_i) \tag{3}$$

where Y_i is output, $\mathcal{F}_i$ is a convolution operator, and X_i is the input features. X_i is a tensor of the shape of $< H_i, W_i, C_i >$ with H_i, W_i, and C_i denote the tensor spatial dimension and channel dimension. Thus, a convolutional network can be composed of multiple stages or groups of CNN layers as in Eq. 4 [10].

$$\mathcal{N} = \bigoplus_{i=1\ldots s} \mathcal{F}_i^{L_i} \left(X_{\langle H_i, W_i, C_i \rangle} \right) \tag{4}$$

where $\mathcal{N}$ represents the CNN neural network that has $\mathcal{F}_\rangle$ layer repeated L_i times in stages i. Most of the CNN architectures aim to find the best layer design and network scale of length L_i and width C_i. The employed Efficient-Net is designed to maximise the network performance according to the available resources.

$$
\begin{aligned}
&\max_{d,w,r} \text{ Accuracy } (\mathcal{N}(d,w,r)) \\
&\text{s.t. } \mathcal{N}(d,w,r) = \bigoplus_{i=1\ldots s} \hat{\mathcal{F}}_i^{d \cdot \hat{L}_i} \left(X_{\langle r \cdot \hat{H}_i, r \cdot \hat{W}_i, w \cdot \hat{C}_i \rangle} \right) \\
&\text{Memory}(\mathcal{N}) \leq \text{target\_memory} \\
&\text{FLOPS}(\mathcal{N}) \leq \text{ target\_flops}
\end{aligned} \tag{5}
$$

where w, d, r denote the width, depth, and resolution coefficients for scaling the network, $\hat{\mathcal{F}}_i, \hat{L}_i, \hat{H}_i, \hat{W}_i, \hat{C}_i$ are the predefined network parameters. The network depth scaling is a popular task in CNN. Most recent CNN networks assume that deeper networks capture rich and complex features. However, this intuition is difficult to train because of the vanishing gradient problem [23]. Recent advances have proposed to alleviate this issue via batch normalisation [24] and skip connection [10]. However, the network performance diminishes, and the accuracy does not increase even if the network depth is increased [4]. Wider networks are also assumed to be able to capture more fine-grained features and can also be trained easily [25]. However, having a wide but shallow network suffers difficulty learning high-level representations. Training a CNN on high-resolution images tends to produce better representations. In our case, the CT-scan images are in different resolutions. This varying image size also adds to the uncertainty problem in capturing useful visual representations. Therefore, we augment the visual feature vector with another feature vector that can be learnt from the biological and visual statistical data through an LSTM model.

Long Short Term Memory. The patient temporally recorded biological data are combined with visual statistical features from the CT-scan images at various timestamps. This data are then padded into identical sequences to be ready for LSTM learning. LSTM is a type of Recurrent Neural Networks having feedback connections by which it controls a sequence of data inputs instead of single inputs. An LSTM can be implemented with a forget gate as is Eq. 6

$$
\begin{aligned}
f_t &= \sigma_g \left(W_f x_t + U_f h_{t-1} + b_f \right) \\
i_t &= \sigma_g \left(W_i x_t + U_i h_{t-1} + b_i \right) \\
o_t &= \sigma_g \left(W_o x_t + U_o h_{t-1} + b_o \right) \\
\tilde{c}_t &= \sigma_c \left(W_c x_t + U_c h_{t-1} + b_c \right) \\
c_t &= f_t \circ c_{t-1} + i_t \circ \tilde{c}_t \\
h_t &= o_t \circ \sigma_h \left(c_t \right)
\end{aligned}
\tag{6}
$$

where $f_t \in \mathbb{R}^h$ denotes the activation vector of the LSTM forget gate, $x_t \in \mathbb{R}^d$ represents the input vector to the utilised LSTM network, $i_t \in \mathbb{R}^h$ is the activation vector of the LSTM input and update gate, $o_t \in \mathbb{R}^h$ is the activation vector of the LSTM output gate, $\tilde{c}_t \in \mathbb{R}^h$ represents the activation vector of the LSTM cell input, $c_t \in \mathbb{R}^h$ denotes the cell state vector, $h_t \in \mathbb{R}^h$ denotes the hidden state or output vector of the LSTM unit, $W \in \mathbb{R}^{h \times d}$ denotes the weights of the input, $U \in \mathbb{R}^{h \times h}$ denotes the weights of the recurrent connections, and $b \in \mathbb{R}^h$ denotes the parameters of the bias vector learnt throughout the training process. The superscripts h and d are the number of hidden units and input features, respectively. We implement two LSTM layers on biological and visual statistical data. The output feature vector will be injected into an attention layer alongside the previous CNN visual feature vector as denoted in Fig. 1.

Attention Layer and Feature Vector Concatenation. At this stage, we have extracted two feature vectors from the CNN and LSTM models. We then pass these feature vectors to an attention layer to learn the best features. We implement a dot-product attention layer based on Luong attention [26]. The attention layer expects query T_q and value T_v tensors. It starts with calculating the scores of the dot product operations as $scores = T_q * T_v$ computing the query-value dot product. Then, the $scores$ are used to compute the distribution based on softmax function as in Eq. 7.

$$
\text{Softmax} \left(x_i \right) = \frac{\exp \left(x_i \right)}{\sum_j \exp \left(x_j \right)}
\tag{7}
$$

The output distribution vector is utilised to create a linear combination of the value tensor T_v. The output attention vector is passed to a fully-connected layer to learn the final representation vector. The output feature vector is passed into an output softmax layer that learns a single regression values of the FVC score.

4   Experimental Work

We present a set of experiments to highlight MARL's efficacy. We implement its components as follows:

- Preprocessing the CT-scan images
    - Correcting the black exposure.
    - Unifying the image sizes.
    - Using the Fuzzy spatial C-Means to segment the lung.
- Preprocessing the patients' health records, as follow:
    - Adding visual statistical features of the correspondent images.
    - Making identical sequences to be ready for the LSTM sequential learning.
- Utilising multiple state-of-the-art CNN architectures to learn the visual features vectors form the lung images.
- Using a double LSTM architecture to learn sequential temporal features from the health and visual statistical records.
- Implementing two versions of the attention mechanism, as follows:
    - MARL V1: Using the CNN visual feature vectors as query tensors to find the best features for the LSTM to learn.
    - MARL V2: Using the LSTM feature vectors as query tensors to learn where to focus in the images.
- Adding a fully-connected layer to learn the final feature vectors.

The learnt feature vectors at the last step are now ready to be consumed by any downstream task. We introduce lung disease tasks as follows:

- Estimating disease progression by adding a regression layer on top of MARL.
- Classifying the lung disease status on binary and multi-class models.

In the next subsection, we discuss the utilised dataset and experimental results of both the regression and classification tasks.

4.1   IPF Lung Disease Dataset

The dataset includes $1,549$ patients' health records, $33,026$ CT-scan images, 880 of them are used for testing. Some CT-scan images have different resolutions, and some need colour correction. Moreover, the dataset provides unbalanced data categories where the number of males exceeds the number of females, and the number of ex-smokers exceeds the smokers and non-smokers.

4.2   Regression of IPF Lung Disease Progression

Table 1 reports the experimental results of lung disease regression using state-of-the-art CNNs on CT-scan images with three different setups, i.e., MARL V1, V2, and a fully-connected regression layers on top of the CNN architectures to extract the visual features as explained earlier. The results show that our model outperforms the other models. MARL manages to improve the accuracy of all CNN networks. The performance improvements range from 11% to 49% as shown in Table 1. We also evaluate the impact of each data modality and their combinations. Table 2 compares the performance of the regression models using each data source separately and combined. Using the biological data alone produces better results than the image and visual statistical data individually. The multimodal dominates the results over the other regression models. Besides, the table lists the performance results of MARL V1 and V2 on the multimodal data. MARL outperforms all with 91% and 89.6% R^2 scores for V1 and V2 setups, respectively. These results are higher than the other regression models by a range of 8% to 27% R^2 when compared to the results of the other models that are provided with multimodal data.

Table 1. Regression results of IPF lung disease progression using various CNN models and MARL V1 & V2.

Model	Fully-connected	**MARL V1**	MARL V2
VGG19 [9]	39%	52.10%	50%
Custom CNN	18%	67%	63%
InceptionV3 [27]	54%	68%	63%
ResNet [10]	43%	60%	65%
VGG16 [9]	40%	62%	66%
Xception [13]	37%	72%	74%
MobileNetV2 [12]	36%	79%	78%
DenseNet201 [11]	49%	79%	80%
InceptionResNetV2 [28]	56%	78%	84%
EfficientNetB0 [4]	46%	**91%**	90%
EfficientNetB5 [4]	48%	**91%**	0.89.6

Table 2. Regression results of IPF lung disease progression using various regression models and MARL V1 & V2 on different data modalities.

Model	Image	Bio	ViS	Bio+ViS	Multimodal
Linear	28%	50%	10%	50%	83%
LASSO	28%	58%	10%	59.87%	82%
Decision Tree	10%	23.80%	6%	24.02%	81%
Ridge	27%	57%	7%	57%	82.90%
ElasticNet	16%	35%	18%	67%	64%
Neural Network	15%	32%	12%	44%	67%
MARL V1	–	–	–	–	**91%**
MARL V2	–	–	–	–	89.60%

4.3   IPF Disease Status Classification

We evaluate the proposed MARL on binary and multi-class classification tasks. For the binary discritisation, we categorise data instances based on if the score of $FVC >= 2500$. For multi-class categorisation, the percent column is utilised to have three different classes, namely, sever (up to 60%), mild (60% to 80%), and good (above 80%). Table 3 lists the performance results of the binary and multi-class IPF lung disease status classification. Consistent with the regression results, MARL V1 and V2 improve the classification performance of state-of-the-art CNN models. The accuracy improvements range from 19% to 57% as shown in Table 1. Besides, we evaluate the utilisation of each data modality and their combinations as in the regression scenarios, see Table 4. Using the biological dataset has better results in the binary tasks than the multi-class where adding the visual statistical features contributes to higher performances. Models that use multiple data sources keep having the best results especially with our proposed MARL that has 97% and 92% accuracy for binary and multi-class classification, respectively.

Table 3. Results of binary and multi-class classification for IPF lung disease progression.

Model	Binary			Multi-class		
	Image	MARL V1	MARL V2	Image	MARL V1	MARL V2
Custom CNN	20%	76%	83%	12%	65%	63%
VGG19 [9]	56%	82%	83%	3%	66%	68%
VGG16 [9]	57%	82%	76%	3%	73%	69%
ResNet [10]	55%	87%	88%	1.20%	84%	85%
Mob.NetV2 [12]	44%	86%	81%	12%	88%	87%
Xception [13]	66%	91%	93%	32%	87%	88%
Inc.ResV2 [28]	69%	96%	93.50%	38%	91%	88.9%
InceptionV3 [27]	69%	95%	93%	37%	88%	89%
Dens.N.201 [11]	64%	90%	89.5%	40%	88%	89%
Eff.tNetB0 [4]	47%	84%	84%	35%	89%	91%
Eff.NetB5 [4]	40%	**97%**	95.30%	40%	**92%**	89.5%

Table 4. Results of binary and multi-class classification for lung disease progression.

Model	Binary classification					Multi-class classification				
	Image	Bio	ViS	Bio+ViS	Multi	Image	Bio	ViS	Bio+ViS	Multi
Extra Trees [29]	65%	93%	71%	91%	92%	37%	80%	49%	81%	85%
Light Gradient Boosting (GB) [30]	85%	93%	63%	93%	93%	65%	80%	40%	81%	85%
Extreme GB [31]	85%	93%	58%	88%	89%	65%	80%	44%	82%	85%
Random Forest	66%	92%	70%	87%	88%	38%	79%	44%	79%	84%
Random Forest [32]	86%	92%	66%	93%	93%	67%	79%	40%	78%	85%
CatBoost [33]	70%	91%	65%	88%	83%	38%	79%	40%	80%	84%
Gradient Boosting [31]	64%	90%	59%	89%	90%	35%	73%	36%	74%	81%
Decision Tree [30]	69%	88%	60%	88%	89%	38%	60%	39%	61%	45%
Ada Boost [34]	55%	87%	63%	85%	89%	29%	60%	43%	50%	64%
Logistic Regression [35]	68%	85%	68%	86%	88%	39%	56%	45%	60%	65%
Ridge Classifier	55%	85%	68%	86%	87%	29%	55%	44%	56%	57%
Naive Bayes	68%	80%	59%	76%	71%	36%	53%	43%	48%	55%
K Neighbors	67%	77%	74%	78%	84%	37%	47%	45%	48%	66%
SVM - Linear Kernel	51%	69%	49%	56%	67%	22%	7%	30%	25%	38%
Our V1	–	–	–	–	97%	–	–	–	–	92%
Our V2	–	–	–	–	95.30%	–	–	–	–	89.50%

5 Conclusion

We presented a novel multimodal attentional neural network architecture for representation learning. MARL, the proposed model, significantly improve accuracy to regress and classify IPF lung disease progression over state-of-the-art models. Multimodal data enable learning better feature representations than single sources. MARL includes several components designed to overcome uncertainties in the lung disease prediction when performing lung segmentation and feature representation learning. It is worthy to generalise the proposed architecture on other and different applications.

References

1. Kafaja, S., et al.: Reliability and minimal clinically important differences of FVC. Results from the scleroderma lung studies (SLS-I and SLS-II). Am. J. Resp. Crit. Care Med. **197**(5), 644–652 (2018)
2. Hamdi, A., Shaban, K., Erradi, A., Mohamed, A., Rumi, S.K., Salim, F.D.: Spatiotemporal data mining: a survey on challenges and open problems. Artif. Intell. Rev., 1–48 (2021)
3. Tripathy, B., Basu, A., Govel, S.: Image segmentation using spatial intuitionistic fuzzy c means clustering. In: 2014 IEEE International Conference on Computational Intelligence and Computing Research. IEEE, pp. 1–5 (2014)
4. Tan, M., Le, Q.: EfficientNet: rethinking model scaling for convolutional neural networks. In: International Conference on Machine Learning, pp. 6105–6114. PMLR (2019)

5. Luo, W., Li, Y., Urtasun, R., Zemel, R.: Understanding the effective receptive field in deep convolutional neural networks. In: Advances in Neural Information Processing Systems, pp. 4898–4906 (2016)
6. O. S. I. C. (OSIC) (2020). https://www.kaggle.com/c/osic-pulmonary-fibrosis-progression/
7. Hamdi, A., Salim, F., Kim, D.Y.: DroTrack: high-speed drone-based object tracking under uncertainty. In: Proceedings of the IEEE Conference on Fuzzy Systems (FUZZ-IEEE) (2020)
8. Walsh, S.L., Calandriello, L., Silva, M., Sverzellati, N.: Deep learning for classifying fibrotic lung disease on high-resolution computed tomography: a case-cohort study. Lancet Respir. Med. **6**(11), 837–845 (2018)
9. Simonyan, K., Zisserman, A.: Very deep convolutional networks for large-scale image recognition, arXiv preprint arXiv:1409.1556 (2014)
10. He, K., Zhang, X., Ren, S., Sun, J.: Deep residual learning for image recognition. In: Proceedings of the IEEE Conference on Computer Vision and Pattern Recognition, pp. 770–778 (2016)
11. Huang, G., Liu, Z., Van Der Maaten, L., Weinberger, K.Q.: Densely connected convolutional networks. In: Proceedings of the IEEE Conference On Computer Vision and Pattern Recognition, pp. 4700–4708 (2017)
12. Sandler, M., Howard, A., Zhu, M., Zhmoginov, A., Chen, L.-C.: Mobilenetv2: inverted residuals and linear bottlenecks. In: The IEEE Conference on Computer Vision and Pattern Recognition (CVPR), June 2018
13. Chollet, F.: Xception: deep learning with depthwise separable convolutions. In: Proceedings of the IEEE Conference on Computer Vision and Pattern Recognition, pp. 1251–1258 (2017)
14. Hamdi, A., Kim, D.Y., Salim, F.: flexgrid2vec: learning efficient visual representations vectors, arXiv e-prints, pp. arXiv-2007 (2021)
15. Hong, X., et al.: Predicting Alzheimer's disease using LSTM. IEEE Access **7**, 80 893–80 901 (2019)
16. Gu, J., et al.: A method for hand-foot-mouth disease prediction using geodetector and LSTM model in Guangxi, China. Sci. Rep. **9**(1), 1–10 (2019)
17. Chimmula, V.K.R., Zhang, L.: Time series forecasting of Covid-19 transmission in Canada using LSTM networks. Chaos Solitons Fractals **135**, 109864 (2020)
18. Gao, R., et al.: Distanced LSTM: time-distanced gates in long short-term memory models for lung cancer detection. In: Suk, H.-I., Liu, M., Yan, P., Lian, C. (eds.) MLMI 2019. LNCS, vol. 11861, pp. 310–318. Springer, Cham (2019). https://doi.org/10.1007/978-3-030-32692-0_36
19. Marentakis, P., et al.: Lung cancer histology classification from CT images based on radiomics and deep learning models. Med. Biol. Eng. Comput. **59**, 1–12 (2021)
20. Li, L., Zhao, X., Lu, W., Tan, S.: Deep learning for variational multimodality tumor segmentation in PET/CT. Neurocomputing **392**, 277–295 (2020)
21. Subramanian, V., Do, M.N., Syeda-Mahmood, T.: Multimodal fusion of imaging and genomics for lung cancer recurrence prediction. In: IEEE 17th International Symposium on Biomedical Imaging (ISBI). IEEE, pp. 804–808 (2020)
22. Qiao, Z., Wu, X., Ge, S., Fan, W.: MNN: multimodal attentional neural networks for diagnosis prediction. Extraction **1**, A1 (2019)
23. Zagoruyko, S., Komodakis, N.: Wide residual networks. In: British Machine Vision Conference 2016. British Machine Vision Association (2016)
24. Ioffe, S., Szegedy, C.: Batch normalization: accelerating deep network training by reducing internal covariate shift. In: International Conference on Machine Learning, pp. 448–456. PMLR (2015)

25. Tan, M., et al.: MnasNet: Platform-aware neural architecture search for mobile. In: Proceedings of the IEEE/CVF Conference on Computer Vision and Pattern Recognition, pp. 2820–2828 (2019)

26. Luong, M.-T., Pham, H., Manning, C.D.: Effective approaches to attention-based neural machine translation. In: Proceedings of the 2015 Conference on Empirical Methods in Natural Language Processing, pp. 1412–1421 (2015)

27. Szegedy, C., Vanhoucke, V., Ioffe, S., Shlens, J., Wojna, Z.: Rethinking the inception architecture for computer vision. In: Proceedings of the IEEE Conference on Computer Vision and Pattern Recognition, pp. 2818–2826 (2016)

28. Szegedy, C., Ioffe, S., Vanhoucke, V., Alemi, A.: Inception-v4, inception-ResNet and the impact of residual connections on learning. In: Proceedings of the AAAI Conference on Artificial Intelligence, vol. 31, no. 1 (2017)

29. Geurts, P., Ernst, D., Wehenkel, L.: Extremely randomized trees. Mach. Learn. $63(1)$, 3–42 (2006)

30. Hastie, T., Tibshirani, R., Friedman, J.: The Elements of Statistical Learning: Data Mining, Inference, and Prediction. Springer, New York (2009). https://doi.org/10. 1007/978-0-387-84858-7

31. Chen, T., Guestrin, C.: XGBoost: a scalable tree boosting system. In: Proceedings of the 22nd ACM SIGKDD International Conference on Knowledge Discovery and Data Mining, pp. 785–794 (2016)

32. Breiman, L.: Random forests. Mach. Learn. $45(1)$, 5–32 (2001)

33. Prokhorenkova, L., Gusev, G., Vorobev, A., Dorogush, A.V., Gulin, A.: CatBoost: unbiased boosting with categorical features, arXiv preprint arXiv:1706.09516 (2017)

34. Hastie, T., Rosset, S., Zhu, J., Zou, H.: Multi-class adaboost. Stat. Interface $2(3)$, 349–360 (2009)

35. Defazio, A., Bach, F.R., Lacoste-Julien, S.: SAGA: a fast incremental gradient method with support for non-strongly convex composite objectives. In: NIPS (2014)

Object Localization with Attribute Preference Based on Top-Down Attention

Soubarna Banik[1]([✉])[iD], Mikko Lauri[2][iD], Alois Knoll[1][iD], and Simone Frintrop[2][iD]

[1] Technical University of Munich, Munich, Germany
soubarna.banik@tum.de, knoll@in.tum.de
[2] University of Hamburg, Hamburg, Germany
{lauri,frintrop}@informatik.uni-hamburg.de

Abstract. We propose a weakly-supervised approach for object localization based on top-down attention which is able to consider both attributes and object classes as attentional cues. This enables to not only search for objects but additionally for objects with specific attributes such as colors or shapes. Our approach consists of two streams: an attribute stream and an object stream. By tracing backward through these two streams and localizing activated neurons in hidden layers, we generate two top-down attention maps, one for attributes and one for objects. Fusing these maps generates a joint attention map, which highlights regions with a specific attribute and object. We show experimentally that our method can localize objects in cluttered images by only specifying their attributes, and that instances of the same class can be discriminated based on their attributes.

Keywords: Object localization · Object attribute · Top-down attention

1 Introduction

Unconstrained environments, unknown objects, varying illumination, and limited computational resources challenge vision algorithms in real-world applications such as robotics. In human perception, attention mechanisms enable to cope with such challenges by prioritizing processing on the most relevant information [21]. For humans, the most relevant parts of a scene are determined by bottom-up and top-down factors [28]. Bottom-up factors guide our attention to salient parts of a scene that automatically draw attention, such as a flickering light or a strong color contrast. Top-down attention enables us to focus on behaviorally relevant regions: the bakery when we are hungry, or the station clock when hurrying to catch our train.

While many computational models of bottom-up attention (saliency) have been proposed [9,13,14], top-down attention is not as well investigated. Traditional top-down attention systems have mainly emphasized and localized target-specific features such as a certain color or orientation [8,19]. Recent top-down attention approaches based on convolutional neural networks (CNNs) localize

© Springer Nature Switzerland AG 2021
M. Vincze et al. (Eds.): ICVS 2021, LNCS 12899, pp. 28–40, 2021.
https://doi.org/10.1007/978-3-030-87156-7_3

(a) Input   (b) Object   (c) Object + Attribute

Fig. 1. (a) Input image, and top-down attention maps for (b) an object (dog), and for (c) a combination of both object and attribute (brown dog). (Color figure online)

objects by tracing back activations from class-specific neurons to hidden layer neurons [3,39]. This enables to quickly find the panda [3] or any other pre-trained object in a scene.

Existing methods search for either features [8,19] or objects [3,39], but it is known that both cues are important targets in human visual attention [17,37][1]: humans may look for a specific object class, but also guide their attention to attributes, for example to all red things or to striped objects. In applications such as service robotics or human-robot interaction, a combination of both is important: a robot should be able to not only focus on all cups on a table, but to select a cup with certain attributes ("Bring me the blue cup"). Additionally, a task a human gives to a robot does not necessarily include the object class, but sometimes only an attribute ("Pick up the red item over there").

In this paper, we propose a weakly supervised method for object localization using a top-down attention mechanism which is able to consider both attributes and object class information. The input to our system is an image and a desired target attribute and object, e.g., "brown" and "dog" in Fig. 1. The outputs of the system are an attribute- and an object-specific attention map. The attribute and object attention maps can be used separately, or they can be fused to obtain a combined attribute-object attention map that highlights the regions in the input image that correspond to both the desired attribute and object. Our approach is able to localize attributes in images, as well as discriminate between object instances. In attribute localization, we show our method performs better empirically than general visual question answering [35].

The rest of the paper is organized as follows. Section 2 discusses related work. Section 3 describes the architecture of our proposed approach and Sect. 4 presents the experimental results. Concluding remarks are given in Sect. 5.

2   Related Work

We briefly review relevant works in attribute classification and localization, top-down attention, weakly supervised object localization, and image captioning

---

[1] A third cue is spatial location, which we do not address here.

and visual question answering. We focus on how top-down attention is treated in these works, motivating our proposed approach.

Attribute Classification and Localization: Attributes can describe parts of an object (*has nose, has headlight*) [6], or the characteristic features of objects (*color, texture, pattern*) [2,12,24]. Existing attribute classification methods such as [5,18,22] use CNN extracted feature descriptors and support vector machines. In addition, approaches applying Bayesian theory [7,15] and deep learning [2,4,33,40] have been proposed. For attribute localization, Xiao et al. [34] focus on relative attributes between pairs of images to learn the spatial extent of the attributes. Wang et al. [30] propose a weakly supervised method for studying scene configuration and simultaneous attribute localization. However, these methods do not support adding a top-down signal or querying for an attribute.

Top-Down Attention: Different studies find that humans can direct their attention to not only objects, but also to spatial locations and features [17,37]. The guided search model of Wolfe [31] introduces top-down cues that boost target-relevant features. Inspired by these psychological theories, early computational models of top-down attention learn how much feature channels contribute to finding a target object. Some of these approaches excite target related features [39] while others also inhibit irrelevant features [8,29].

Deep-learning-based top-down object search [3,39] is realized by highlighting regions corresponding to the target class in the hidden layer activation maps. Cao et al. [3] introduced feedback layers in a classification network to infer the activation status of hidden layer neurons. During the backward pass, neurons in the feedback layers act as gates and open only connections associated with the target class. Zhang et al. [39] proposed Excitation Backprop (Ex-BP), which given a top-down signal for a target object, reveals the location of the target-specific activation in the input image. The algorithm applies to any deep classification network without the need for any modification, unlike [3].

Weakly Supervised Object Localization: Segmentation-based approaches for weakly supervised localization [10,30] classify each previously determined image segment, thereby giving the location information along with the object class. Oquab's fully convolutional model [20] is similar to the segmentation-based approaches, except instead of segments each sliding window is classified. However, the aforementioned approaches do not facilitate adding a top-down signal for a target object. Alternatively, recovering the location information from classification CNNs allows a mechanism for incorporating the top-down signal [25,41]. Approaches like Class Activation Mapping (CAM) [41] and Grad-CAM [25] are similar to Ex-BP [39] in functionality.

Image Captioning and Visual Question Answering: Some works in image captioning (IC) and visual question answering (VQA) learn to output attention maps corresponding to specific words in the generated caption or answer sentence [1,16,26,36]. The generated sentences may include object names,

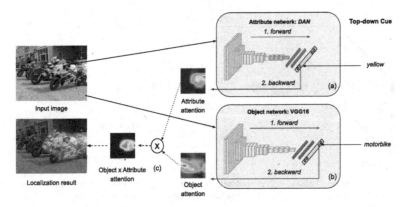

Fig. 2. Overview of the object localization process using attributes. Attention maps are generated from (a) the attribute network for the target attribute *(yellow)*, and from (b) the object network for the target object *(motorbike)*. (c) Object and attribute attention maps are combined to obtain the object-attribute attention map, showing the location of the target object having the target attribute (yellow motorbike). (Color figure online)

attributes, or relationships and the corresponding attention map shows the relevant region in the input image. However, these methods are not suited for generic object or attribute attention. Top-down signals in IC [16,36] are limited to the set of words from the generated caption. VQA methods such as [1,26] rely on question-answer annotations [11] and an object detection network that uses object and attribute annotations and their corresponding locations.

3   Architecture

Figure 2 shows an overview of our object localization process with attribute guidance. Our system contains two streams: an attribute classification stream ((a) in Fig. 2) trained to classify attributes such as color, shape, pattern, and texture; and an object classification stream (b) consisting of a standard object classification network, namely the VGG16 network [27]. The attribute network, named Deep Attribute Network (DAN) is described in Sect. 3.1. In both streams, a forward pass enables classification of attributes and objects, and a backward pass traces the activations in a top-down manner to output an attribute- and an object-specific attention map, as described in Sect. 3.2. The attribute and object attention maps can be used separately, or they can be combined to obtain an attribute-object attention map (c), which shows the locations in the input image that correspond to both the desired attribute and object.

3.1   Deep Attribute Network

Attributes are descriptive properties of objects [6]. Low-level attributes such as color, shape, or type of material can be shared by objects of different classes.

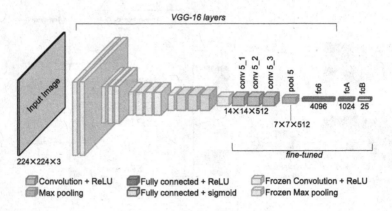

Fig. 3. The deep attribute network (DAN). The network is adapted from the VGG-16 model [27], by replacing the last two fully-connected layers with the new layers *fcA* and *fcB*. DAN is finetuned till layer *conv5_1*.

High-level object-part attributes, such as headlight, wheel, side mirror, are specific to certain objects and are not universally applicable. We consider only low-level attributes that can describe a wide range of objects. CNNs learn Gabor-like and color features in the first layers [38], which are useful for discriminating our target attribute groups - *color*, *shape*, *pattern* and *texture*. So, we modify VGG-16 [27], a standard object classification network, and finetune the last layers to adapt to the attribute classification similarly as in [2]. We obtain the Deep Attribute Network (DAN) for low-level attribute classification as shown in Fig. 3.

DAN is trained using transfer learning pre-trained on the ImageNet dataset [23]. All layers up to and including (*fc6*) are retrained. Two new fully-connected layers *fcA* with 1024 units and *fcB* with 25 units are added. The 25 units in the *fcB* layer correspond to the 25 target attribute classes in the ImageNet-Attribute dataset [24] in the attribute groups *color*, *shape*, *pattern* and *texture*. As object attribute classification is a multilabel classification task, the final layer *fcB* uses a sigmoid activation. All other layers use ReLU activation. We train DAN similarly as in [2], using weighted cross-entropy loss for attribute classification without any localization labels.

3.2   Top-Down Attention

Top-down attention localizes image regions likely to show the target object. In deep networks, target information is usually provided to the network at the output layer by indicating the class nodes which are target relevant, e.g. [3,41]. We use Grad-CAM [25], originally introduced to provide visual explanations for deep networks, to generate top-down attention maps. Given a top-down cue at an output node of the network, Grad-CAM generates an attention map highlighting the regions in the input image that activated the output node.

Grad-CAM calculates the top-down attention map for a target class c as a weighted sum of activation maps A_k in the last convolutional layer. The weights α_k^c are derived from the gradients of the output element corresponding to c with respect to elements of the activation map A_k. The weight indicates the importance of the activation map for the target class. The attention map L^c for class c is $L^c = \text{ReLU}(\sum_k \alpha_k^c A_k)$, where the ReLU ensures only positive contributions towards the target class c are considered.

We compute the attribute and object specific attention maps using Grad-CAM. To identify a target object with a specific attribute, the attribute-object attention map is computed by multiplying the individual maps as shown in Fig. 2(c). The greatest value in an attention map indicates the object location. As the attribute and object streams are independent, our method also works for unknown object classes, in which case only the attribute cue is used.

4   Experiments

We introduce the datasets we use in Sect. 4.1 and describe our evaluation methodology in Sect. 4.2. Section 4.3 demonstrates that object attributes can be successfully applied to localize objects in images. Section 4.4 then shows how much attributes help in object localization. We omit evaluation of object localization without attributes as this is covered in previous works [27].

4.1   Datasets

ImageNet-Attribute [24]: Contains annotations of 25 low-level object attributes in four categories: color, shape, pattern, and texture. The dataset consists of 9600 images from 384 synsets. Each image contains one object and is also annotated with the object class label and the corresponding bounding box. We divide the dataset into training, validation, and test sets with 5760, 1920, and 1920 images, respectively. DAN is trained on the training split of this dataset. The dataset is useful for training attributes, but not especially suitable for evaluating object or attribute localization since the images show mostly only a single object in large scale, often centered.

a-Pascal [6]: The images contain a varying number of objects from 20 classes annotated with bounding boxes, and 64 attributes describing shape, material, and high-level object components. The dataset is well suited for the attribute-object localization task. For our evaluation, we select the low-level attributes that are present in the training dataset: three shape attributes (*2D boxy, 3D boxy, round*) and five material attributes (*metal, wood, furry, shiny, vegetation*). The shape attributes *2D boxy* and *3D boxy* are not present in the training dataset. After manually reviewing the images, we found both attributes similar in appearance to the *rectangle* attribute of ImageNet-Attribute dataset. We merge these two attributes and evaluate them as the *rectangle* attribute.

Object-Attribute: We create a dataset for evaluating the attribute localization task. The new Object-Attribute dataset consists of 60 images from a cluttered kitchen environment. The number of objects per image is between 3 and 8. We annotate the images using the same color and shape attributes as in the ImageNet-Attribute dataset, and add bounding box annotations for objects.

4.2 Pointing Game Evaluation

Top-down attention maps highlight class-discriminative regions but do not provide pixel-precise boundaries of target classes. Due to this, we evaluate the performance of our approach with the *Pointing Game* experiment [39]. To calculate accuracy, the maximum saliency point (MSP) in a target-specific top-down attention map is selected. A hit is counted if the point is on any of the annotated instances of the cued target, otherwise a miss occurs. The pointing game accuracy is calculated as $hits/(hits + misses)$. This is equivalent to the top-1 accuracy metric used for evaluating object localization methods [27]. We also calculate the accuracy in a more relaxed setting from the top-3 most salient regions. The attention map is thresholded at 90% of the maximum saliency value of the map. The three regions with the greatest average saliency are selected. If any of the centroids of these regions lie in the ground truth bounding box area, a hit is counted. Otherwise, a miss is counted.

To calculate recall, we determine a hit or a miss similarly as for top-1 accuracy. We inhibit the area around the current MSP, and extract the next MSP, repeating k times. For top-k recall, we count the number of unique bounding boxes with hits among the first k MSPs, and calculate the ratio to the total number of applicable bounding boxes. We average across all images.

4.3 Experiment 1: Attribute Localization

Can attributes be used to localize objects without any information about the class of the target object? This is of interest for autonomous robots to find objects only based on their attributes such as with the given task "bring me the red object over there". We first compare variants of our attribute localization method using either Grad-CAM [25], Excitation-Backprop (Ex-BP) [39], or Class Activation Mapping (CAM) [41]. We also compare the attribute localization performance to a popular VQA method.

Pointing Game Accuracy and Recall: We generate attention maps at *pool5* of DAN, for Grad-CAM and Ex-BP. For CAM, we follow [41]: first, layers *(pool5-fcB)* in DAN are removed and a convolutional layer *conv6* with 512 filters of size 3×3, stride 1, padding 1 is added. We insert a global average pooling layer, a fully-connected layer *fcC* with 25 nodes and a sigmoid layer. The newly added layers *(conv6-fcC)* are trained for 6 epochs similarly as in [2]. We generate the attention maps for CAM at layer *conv6* of the modified network.

Table 1 reports the accuracy and recall of Ex-BP, CAM, and Grad-CAM on all datasets. Only attribute classes are used as top-down cues and the mean across all attribute classes is reported[2]. For all three methods, recall on the

---

[2] The types and number of attributes are different for the three datasets; see Sect. 4.1.

Table 1. Pointing game: mean attribute localization accuracy and recall for Imagenet-Attribute (IA), Object-Attribute (OA) and a-Pascal datasets.

	Accuracy						Recall					
	IA		OA		a-Pascal		IA		OA		a-Pascal	
	Top-1	Top-3	Top-1	Top-3	Top-1	Top-3	Top-1	Top-10	Top-1	Top-10	Top-1	Top-10
Ex-BP	0.88	0.90	0.65	0.72	0.52	0.57	0.88	0.88	0.58	0.61	0.44	0.45
CAM	0.85	0.88	0.69	0.75	0.47	0.52	0.87	0.87	0.62	0.64	0.42	0.43
Grad-CAM	0.79	0.83	0.70	0.71	0.56	0.60	0.80	0.80	0.61	0.64	0.48	0.50

Fig. 4. Sample attribute attention maps overlapped on the input image from (a) a-Pascal and (b) Object-Attribute datasets. (Color figure online)

Imagenet Attribute dataset is high, as is the top-1 accuracy. Among the test datasets, CAM and Grad-CAM achieve similar accuracy and recall on Object-Attribute dataset, whereas, in the more complex a-Pascal dataset, Grad-CAM performs the best on our model. Overall the result indicates that objects can be localized using only their attributes. Based on the test dataset performance, we conclude that Grad-CAM performs best for generating attention maps. Grad-CAM is exclusively used in all of the remaining experiments in the paper.

Figure 4 shows sample attention maps for the attributes *round, vegetation, red* and *green* from the a-Pascal and Object-Attribute datasets. The bounding box of the object with the target attribute is marked in red. The maximum saliency point, indicated by the red dot, shows the predicted location of the objects, even if they are partially occluded (the bucket in the rightmost image in Fig. 4(b)).

Comparison to Visual Question Answering: Since visual question answering methods can also be used for producing attention map for a specific query, we compare to one such method named "Ask, Attend and Answer" (AAA) [35]. We input an image and a query "Where is the x object?", where x is the attribute label. Table 2 reports the accuracy and recall on Object-Attribute dataset for all attributes, and separately for the attribute groups color and shape. This dataset is not used to finetune any of the models. Our simple method that focuses on attribute localization clearly outperforms the more general VQA method. AAA performs better on the shape attributes, particularly for the shapes 'long' and 'rectangle'. In contrast to AAA, our method is weakly supervised for object localization, using object and attribute annotation, but no location annotation.

Table 2. Comparison of attribute localization performance between our approach and Visual Question Answering method (AAA) on the Object-Attribute dataset.

Attribute type	Top-1 accuracy			Top-1 recall			Top-10 recall		
	All	Color	Shape	All	Color	Shape	All	Color	Shape
AAA [35]	0.55	0.53	0.59	0.48	0.48	0.47	0.50	0.48	0.55
Ours	**0.70**	0.75	0.55	**0.61**	0.69	0.38	**0.64**	0.72	0.41

Table 3. Pointing game: top-1 attribute-object localization accuracy. Number in parentheses shows improvement compared to object localization. Attribute attention improves accuracy for a majority of object classes, as highlighted in blue.

Obj/Attrib	loc acc →	0.84	0.65	0.58	0.48	0.41	0.41	0.35	Avg.
	loc acc ↓	Furry	Round	Metallic	Wooden	Shiny	Vegetation	Rectangular	improvement
Cat	0.96	0.94 (0)	–	–	–	–	–	–	0.00
Dog	0.90	0.90 (0.01)	–	–	–	–	–	–	0.01
Cow	0.90	0.95 (0.06)	–	–	–	–	–	–	0.06
Horse	0.86	0.93 (0.06)	–	–	–	–	–	–	0.06
Motorbike	0.83	–	–	0.74 (−0.06)	–	0.67 (−0.03)	–	–	−0.05
Aeroplane	0.82	–	1.00 (0)	0.89 (0.08)	0.60 (0)	0.83 (0.02)	–	0.68 (−0.04)	0.01
Train	0.82	–	0.78 (0.11)	0.87 (0.03)	–	0.76 (−0.06)	–	0.81 (−0.03)	0.01
Bus	0.81	–	–	0.78 (−0.04)	–	0.59 (−0.11)	–	0.58 (−0.15)	−0.10
Diningtable	0.78	–	0.75 (−0.06)	0.80 (0.10)	0.68 (−0.06)	0.81 (0)	–	0.77 (−0.06)	−0.02
Sofa	0.76	–	0.55 (−0.18)	–	0.69 (−0.08)	–	–	0.52 (−0.19)	−0.15
Tvmonitor	0.75	–	–	0.48 (−0.19)	–	0.52 (−0.23)	–	0.54 (−0.20)	−0.21
Bicycle	0.71	–	–	0.76 (0.04)	–	0.66 (0)	–	–	0.02
Boat	0.59	–	0.55 (0)	0.66 (0.17)	0.50 (0.06)	0.45 (0.09)	–	0.57 (0.03)	0.07
Car	0.57	–	–	0.60 (0.06)	–	0.47 (−0.04)	–	0.47 (−0.03)	0.00
Pottedplant	0.55	–	–	–	–	–	0.56 (0.01)	–	0.01
Chair	0.48	–	–	0.31 (0.06)	0.52 (0.03)	0.48 (0.09)	–	0.44 (0.04)	0.06
Bottle	0.41	–	–	0.44 (0.11)	–	0.35 (0.02)	–	–	0.07

4.4 Experiment 2: Joint Attribute-Object Localization

Does using attributes help to find objects? To answer this, we conduct the pointing game experiment for a combined object and attribute top-down signal, using Grad-CAM to create the attention maps. We evaluate on the a-Pascal dataset or its subsets. For object localization, we replace the softmax layer of VGG-16 [27] with a sigmoid layer with 20 output nodes corresponding to the object classes, and train with the cross-entropy loss.

Object vs Attribute-Object Localization: Table 3 reports the accuracy for the integrated attribute-object attention and the improvement over only using object attention in brackets. The average improvement is reported in the rightmost column. The object/attribute cases where the localization improved compared to only using object attention are highlighted in blue. The additional attribute cue improves the localization for 10 out of 17 classes. Accuracy decreases for 5 classes - *motorbike, bus, diningtable, sofa* and *tvmonitor*. This may be due to a dominance of the object classification stream which has been trained with a much larger dataset. For example, the greatest decreases are observed for the attributes *shiny* and *rectangle*. The average precision of

Table 4. Localization performance in images with visually similar objects. Attribute attention clearly improves performance.

Top-down cue	Top-1 accuracy	Top-1 recall	Top-10 recall
Object	0.56	0.33	0.35
Attribute-object	0.64	0.39	0.41

Table 5. Attribute-object localization performance for combinations of objects and attributes either in the training set or not.

Combination type	Top-1 accuracy	Top-1 recall	Top-10 recall
In training set	0.61	0.52	0.54
Not in training set	0.58	0.49	0.51

DAN on a-Pascal dataset for these two attributes are 0.32 and 0.55 respectively [2]. The poor attribute classification performance affects the corresponding attribute localization accuracy (0.41 and 0.35 respectively) and therefore, the combined object and attribute localization performance. Other failure cases are for the object/attribute combinations *sofa/round* and *tvmonitor/metallic*. This is explained by the contradictory annotations in the training (*rectangle*) and test dataset (*round*) for *sofa*, and by the absence of the object-attribute combination *tvmonitor-metallic* in the training dataset respectively. The overall performance in this experiment clearly shows that attributes are useful cues for localizing objects within the proposed top-down attention framework.

Searching Amongst Visually Similar Objects: We consider images with multiple instances of the target attribute with a different object class, e.g., images with both a red car and a red ball. These search cases are the most difficult: in psychological visual search tasks, humans are slower to find the target if there are distractors with similar appearance to the target [32]. We repeat the previous experiment on 287 such images in a-Pascal. Table 4 reports the accuracy and recall for object and attribute-object attention. Corresponding to the more difficult task, attribute-object localization performance is naturally lower in these cases than the average of the dataset (0.67). Nevertheless, localization accuracy and recall improve when an attribute top-down signal is used in addition to the class information. This shows a clear advantage of the attribute information for object localization.

Unobserved Object-Attribute Combinations: We find the combinations of objects and attributes that exist both in the training and test data, and also the combinations that appear only in the test data but not in the training data. We evaluate attribute-object localization performance on both of these subsets. Table 5 shows that the performance for object-attribute pairs that are not present in the training data decreases, as expected, but only by 3% compared to the cases present in the training data. This shows that our method generalizes well to unseen pairs of objects and attributes.

5   Conclusion

We present a simple yet effective approach for localizing attributes in images with top-down attention. We generate attribute and object attention maps to localize attributes, objects, or a combination of both. Our approach can search for objects, or for image regions of certain properties, and discriminate object class instances based on attributes, while generalizing to unseen combinations of objects and attributes. A limitation of our method is that the contribution of object and attribute localization streams is not controllable. This may lead to a localization failure when either one of the streams fails. Further experiments can be conducted to demonstrate applicability in a real-world robotics scenario. Finally, a comparison to object localization methods could further help to demonstrate the benefits and disadvantages of attribute-based localization.

References

1. Anderson, P., et al.: Bottom-up and top-down attention for image captioning and visual question answering. In: CVPR (2018)
2. Banik, S., Lauri, M., Frintrop, S.: Multi-label object attribute classification using a convolutional neural network. arXiv preprint arXiv:1811.04309 (2018)
3. Cao, C., et al.: Look and think twice: capturing top-down visual attention with feedback convolutional neural networks. In: ICCV (2015)
4. Chung, J., Lee, D., Seo, Y., Yoo, C.D.: Deep attribute networks. In: NIPS Workshop on Deep Learning and Unsupervised Feature Learning (2012)
5. Cimpoi, M., Maji, S., Vedaldi, A.: Deep filter banks for texture recognition and segmentation. In: CVPR (2015)
6. Farhadi, A., Endres, I., Hoiem, D., Forsyth, D.: Describing objects by their attributes. In: CVPR (2009)
7. Ferrari, V., Zisserman, A.: Learning visual attributes. In: NIPS (2008)
8. Frintrop, S., Backer, G., Rome, E.: Goal-directed search with a top-down modulated computational attention system. In: DAGM Symposium on Pattern Recognition (2005)
9. Frintrop, S., Werner, T., Martin Garcia, G.: Traditional saliency reloaded: a good old model in new shape. In: CVPR (2015)
10. Galleguillos, C., Babenko, B., Rabinovich, A., Belongie, S.: Weakly supervised object localization with stable segmentations. In: Forsyth, D., Torr, P., Zisserman, A. (eds.) ECCV 2008. LNCS, vol. 5302, pp. 193–207. Springer, Heidelberg (2008). https://doi.org/10.1007/978-3-540-88682-2_16
11. Goyal, Y., Khot, T., Summers-Stay, D., Batra, D., Parikh, D.: Making the V in VQA matter: elevating the role of image understanding in Visual Question Answering. In: CVPR (2017)
12. Hu, C., Bai, X., Qi, L., Chen, P., Xue, G., Mei, L.: Vehicle color recognition with spatial pyramid deep learning. IEEE Trans. Intell. Transp. Syst. **16**(5), 2925–2934 (2015)

13. Itti, L., Koch, C., Niebur, E.: A model of saliency-based visual attention for rapid scene analysis. IEEE Trans. PAMI **20**(11), 1254–1259 (1998)
14. Kümmerer, M., Wallis, T.S.A., Bethge, M.: Saliency benchmarking made easy: separating models, maps and metrics. In: Ferrari, V., Hebert, M., Sminchisescu, C., Weiss, Y. (eds.) ECCV 2018. LNCS, vol. 11220, pp. 798–814. Springer, Cham (2018). https://doi.org/10.1007/978-3-030-01270-0_47
15. Lampert, C.H., Nickisch, H., Harmeling, S.: Learning to detect unseen object classes by between-class attribute transfer. In: CVPR (2009)
16. Lee, K.-H., Chen, X., Hua, G., Hu, H., He, X.: Stacked cross attention for image-text matching. In: Ferrari, V., Hebert, M., Sminchisescu, C., Weiss, Y. (eds.) ECCV 2018. LNCS, vol. 11208, pp. 212–228. Springer, Cham (2018). https://doi.org/10.1007/978-3-030-01225-0_13
17. Liu, T., Slotnick, S.D., Serences, J.T., Yantis, S.: Cortical mechanisms of feature-based attentional control. Cereb. Cortex **13**(12), 1334–1343 (2003)
18. Liu, Z., Luo, P., Wang, X., Tang, X.: Deep learning face attributes in the wild. In: ICCV (2015)
19. Navalpakkam, V., Itti, L.: An integrated model of top-down and bottom-up attention for optimizing detection speed. In: CVPR (2006)
20. Oquab, M., Bottou, L., Laptev, I., Sivic, J.: Is object localization for free?-weakly-supervised learning with convolutional neural networks. In: CVPR (2015)
21. Pashler, H.: The Psychology of Attention. MIT Press, Cambridge (1997)
22. Razavian, A.S., Azizpour, H., Sullivan, J., Carlsson, S.: CNN features off-the-shelf: an astounding baseline for recognition. In: CVPR (2014)
23. Russakovsky, O., et al.: ImageNet large scale visual recognition challenge. Int. J. Comput. Vision **115**(3), 211–252 (2015)
24. Russakovsky, O., Fei-Fei, L.: Attribute learning in large-scale datasets. In: Daniilidis, K., Maragos, P., Paragios, N. (eds.) ECCV 2010. LNCS, Springer, Heidelberg (2010). https://doi.org/10.1007/978-3-642-15555-0
25. Selvaraju, R.R., Cogswell, M., Das, A., Vedantam, R., Parikh, D., Batra, D.: Grad-CAM: Visual explanations from deep networks via gradient-based localization. In: ICCV (2017)
26. Shih, K.J., Singh, S., Hoiem, D.: Where to look: focus regions for visual question answering. In: CVPR (2016)
27. Simonyan, K., Zisserman, A.: Very deep convolutional networks for large-scale image recognition. arXiv preprint arXiv:1409.1556 (2014)
28. Theeuwes, J.: Top-down and bottom-up control of visual selection. Acta Physiol. (Oxf) **135**, 77–99 (2010)
29. Tsotsos, J.K., Culhane, S.M., Wai, W.Y.K., Lai, Y., Davis, N., Nuflo, F.: Modeling visual attention via selective tuning. Artif. Intell. **78**(1–2), 507–545 (1995)
30. Wang, C., Ren, W., Huang, K., Tan, T.: Weakly supervised object localization with latent category learning. In: Fleet, D., Pajdla, T., Schiele, B., Tuytelaars, T. (eds.) ECCV 2014. LNCS, vol. 8694, pp. 431–445. Springer, Cham (2014). https://doi.org/10.1007/978-3-319-10599-4_28
31. Wolfe, J.M.: Guided search 2.0: a revised model of visual search. Psycho. Bull. Rev. **1**(2), 202–238 (1994)
32. Wolfe, J.M.: Visual search. In: Attention. Psychology Press/Erlbaum (UK) Taylor & Francis (2016)
33. Wu, F., et al.: Regularized deep belief network for image attribute detection. IEEE Trans. Circuits Syst. Video Technol. **27**(7), 1464–1477 (2017)

34. Xiao, F., Lee, Y.J.: Localizing and visualizing relative attributes. In: Visual Attributes. ACVPR, pp. 155–178. Springer, Cham (2017). https://doi.org/10.1007/978-3-319-50077-5_7

35. Xu, H., Saenko, K.: Ask, attend and answer: exploring question-guided spatial attention for visual question answering. In: Leibe, B., Matas, J., Sebe, N., Welling, M. (eds.) ECCV 2016. LNCS, vol. 9911, pp. 451–466. Springer, Cham (2016). https://doi.org/10.1007/978-3-319-46478-7_28

36. Xu, K., et al.: Show, attend and tell: Neural image caption generation with visual attention. In: ICML (2015)

37. Yantis, S., Serences, J.T.: Cortical mechanisms of space-based and object-based attentional control. Curr. Opin. Neurobiol. **13**(2), 187–193 (2003)

38. Yosinski, J., Clune, J., Bengio, Y., Lipson, H.: How transferable are features in Deep Neural Networks? In: NIPS (2014)

39. Zhang, J., Lin, Z., Brandt, J., Shen, X., Sclaroff, S.: Top-down neural attention by excitation backprop. In: Leibe, B., Matas, J., Sebe, N., Welling, M. (eds.) ECCV 2016. LNCS, vol. 9908, pp. 543–559. Springer, Cham (2016). https://doi.org/10.1007/978-3-319-46493-0_33

40. Zhang, N., Paluri, M., Ranzato, M., Darrell, T., Bourdev, L.: PANDA: pose aligned networks for deep attribute modeling. In: CVPR (2014)

41. Zhou, B., Khosla, A., Lapedriza, A., Oliva, A., Torralba, A.: Learning deep features for discriminative localization. In: CVPR (2016)

See the Silence: Improving Visual-Only Voice Activity Detection by Optical Flow and RGB Fusion

Danu Caus$^{(\boxtimes)}$ (ID), Guillaume Carbajal (ID), Timo Gerkmann (ID),
and Simone Frintrop (ID)

Department of Informatics, University of Hamburg, Hamburg, Germany
{danu.caus,guillaume.carbajal,timo.gerkmann,
simone.frintrop}@uni-hamburg.de

Abstract. In this work, we propose a novel approach for visual voice activity detection (VAD), which is an important component of audio-visual tasks such as speech enhancement. We focus on optimizing the visual component and propose a two-stream approach based on optical flow and RGB data. Both streams are analyzed by long short-term memory (LSTM) modules to extract dynamic features. We show that this setup clearly improves the one without optical flow. Additionally, we show that focusing on the lower face area is superior to processing the whole face, or only the mouth region as usually done. This aspect involves practical advantages, since it facilitates data labeling. Our approach especially improves the true negative rate, which means we detect frames without speech more reliably—we see the silence.

Keywords: Visual voice activity detection · Optical flow · Ensemble learning

1 Introduction

Voice activity detection (VAD) is the task of identifying the presence or absence of human speech segments in a stream of input data. Depending on the input modality used, we can distinguish between visual VAD, which uses only images to detect voice activity, and audio VAD, which separates the voice audio signal from the background noise signal. VAD is an important component in a variety of applications, such as speech enhancement [1,2] or source separation [3,4]. While most approaches in this field have focused on processing the audio data [5], there is a currently growing effort to combine audio VAD and visual VAD sub-systems. Both modalities complement each other and the joint processing obtains superior

This work was supported by the Alliance of Hamburg Universities for Computer Science (ahoi.digital) as part of the Adaptive Crossmodal Sensor Data Acquisition (ACSDA) research project and by the German Research Foundation (DFG) in the Transregional project Crossmodal Learning (TRR 169).

M. Vincze et al. (Eds.): ICVS 2021, LNCS 12899, pp. 41–51, 2021.
https://doi.org/10.1007/978-3-030-87156-7_4

performance. Visual voice activity detection in particular is more robust to noisy speech [6] and identifying whisper speech [7] than its audio-only counterpart. The merged audio-visual systems will generally be better if each of the individual components is optimized. However, most research focuses on the audio part, whereas the visual modality of VAD systems is often overlooked and standard solutions are applied, like extracting visual features with a ResNet before fusing them with the audio signals [8].

In this work, we focus on optimizing the visual VAD component. In particular, our aim is to improve the ability of the network to detect frames in which there is no speech, which will help reduce noise more effectively. We propose a novel visual VAD system, which combines RGB features and optical flow. Both modalities focus on different aspects of the data and are thus complementary. While the RGB stream extracts color features, the optical flow stream focuses on motion features, which is especially useful in detecting when someone is speaking. LSTM modules allow the system to exploit dynamic features and probabilistic-based fusion combines the two streams in an ensemble manner. Figure 1 shows an overview of our system.

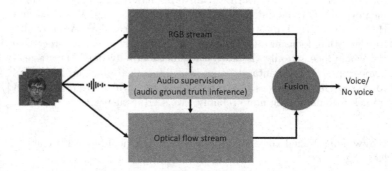

Fig. 1. Overview of our approach, consisting of an RGB and an optical flow stream. Both streams are fused to determine if voice activity is present in a frame or not, exploiting the complementary information of the streams. The audio channel from the video is used to generate ground truth labels that supervise the training of RGB and optical flow streams.

We focus our attention on facial features for voice activity detection, as opposed to body language and body motion, which are useful for large, in-the-wild scenes. Hence, we use a constrained dataset, were people's faces are clearly visible: the TCD-TIMIT dataset [9]. The contribution of this paper is twofold:

1. We show that adding optical flow to a deep learning approach via probabilistic fusion results in improving the true negative rate of the system (TNR) by as much as 7%. This is useful in audio-visual systems that rely on TNR in order to reduce transient noise and enhance speech.

2. We show that focusing on the lower face area of the speaker, including not only the mouth, but also nose and chin, offers better results than considering the mouth-only region, or entire face as done in previous work. Compared to extracting mouth-only regions of interest, our pre-processing is also more practical for real-world applications, avoiding precise mouth croppings and fine alignments, which require manual adjusting.

2   Related Work

The task of voice activity detection has a variety of solutions, which can broadly be classified as: audio-only, visual-only, and audio-visual combined approaches. We give an overview of relevant work in this section.

Audio-Only VAD. The task of voice activity detection has a rich history in the audio community. One important solution is based on sound energy thresholding to infer the VAD label such as [10]. Other approaches such as [11] have used statistical models which include the background noise statistics. These statistical models are robust to noise and also allow for computing the a posteriori probability of speech presence [12], i.e. to have a soft decision instead of a hard decision. More recently, researchers have leveraged deep learning for audio-only VAD and overcame traditional audio methods [13]. Additionally considering the time dimension via recurrent neural networks improved the results even more, as presented in [14].

Visual-Only VAD with Traditional Techniques. Early computer vision methods have studied VAD using manually extracted features and traditional machine learning techniques. The work of Joosten et al. [15] has shown that using mouth regions of interest is better than using full faces of speakers, although the authors did not apply their approach to sequence of frames, but rather on individual frames. We will show later that this also holds for videos, but even better results can be obtained using larger crops.

Tao et al. [7] have shown that it is important to have dynamic features rather than static ones. The manual features extracted from the RGB inputs such as mouth width and height, mouth area and perimeter were concatenated in feature vectors and the authors showed that computing first order differences between the vectors, so called dynamic representations, is beneficial for the task of visual VAD. They also used optical flow in this context as a natural dynamic feature.

Chakravarty and Tuytelaars [16] have used a support vector machine approach on full-body images as opposed to looking only at the face of speakers. The rational of the authors is that body language such as hand gesticulation and upper body motion are important especially in a multi-speaker environment such as a conference.

Visual-Only VAD Using Deep Learning. Surprisingly, visual only voice activity detection using neural networks has not been studied abundantly. The recent work of Guy et al. [17] is the most prominent work in this sense. They have investigated two types of datasets: a) unconstrained, in-the-wild datasets and

b) constrained, in-the-lab datasets; as well as two types of architectures: 1) facial landmarks extractor coupled with LSTM and 2) optical flow VGG16 ConvNet without any LSTM. They come to the conclusion that facial landmarks fed to an LSTM is the best all-round method for both types of datasets. Interestingly, the optical flow approach they investigated registered a particularly unexpected true negative rate for the constrained dataset that they used [18], roughly 15%, while the natural expectation would have been something in the range of 80%, which the other non-optical flow model they investigated did indeed reach.

Other works with deep learning approach have focused exclusively on in-the-wild scenes. For instance [19] use Hollywood movies which do not have a fixed structure. These types of datasets allow extraction of VAD labels from the subtitle timestamps of the movie, which makes the audio channel unnecessary for ground truth computation. They used 3D CNNs with bidirectional LSTMs on 1 s RGB video snippets and empirically showed that in the process of learning VAD classifications, the neural network also learns to pay attention to the face of the characters.

The recent work of Shahid et al. [20] has a similar use case as the work of [16], namely detecting active speakers during conferences, but uses a deep learning approach instead. Moreover, the work deliberately does not detect body parts of speakers, but rather focuses only on motion segmentation instead and learns to associate body motion with speech activity.

Audio-Visual VAD. Merging audio-only and visual-only VAD solutions has yielded synergistic results. In [21] the authors show improvement over single modality baselines by using a rule-based fusion approach which dictates what modality should be treated as the primary component depending on whether face or lip movements are detected or not. Tao et al. [22] show that if both modalities are used together, it is possible to improve the precision of boundary detection between speech and non-speech regions via the Bayesian information criterion/BIC algorithm. In a recent deep-learning framework [8], Ariav and Cohen combined raw audio data with cropped mouth regions as visual input via compact bilinear pooling [23] and obtained better results than with a single modality.

3   Our Approach

Our approach for visual voice activity detection consists of two streams: an RGB stream and an optical flow stream (see Fig. 2). Both streams are trained independently, and combined during the test phase in a probabilistic manner.

It is partially inspired by the ideas of [7], in which the authors use optical flow and manually engineered visual features on which they subsequently compute delta features. We build on this idea of delta features and integrate it into a deep learning framework. We keep the optical flow as a separate stream and use another stream that learns suitable RGB features depending on the dataset. By adding two LSTMs for the RGB and the optical flow stream, we allow the system to explore dynamic features, which is emulating the aforementioned delta

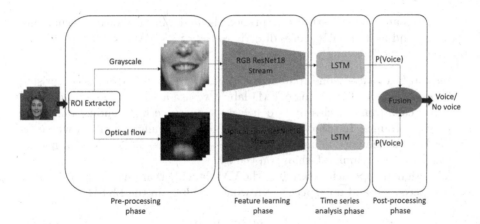

Fig. 2. Diagram of our system: from the input sequence, the lower part of the face is extracted and fed into an RGB branch (top) and an optical flow branch (bottom). In each stream a dedicated ResNet extracts static features, which are then fed into corresponding LSTM modules to exploit dynamic features. The results of both streams are fused via a probabilistic approach. The "ROI Extractor" includes: 1) nose, mouth and chin detection, 2) optical stabilization for a more robust optical flow calculation, and 3) cropping

features, but in a deep learning context. We note that adding an LSTM to optical flow, i.e. treating the optical flow as time series, is not encountered in other recent works. We also note that this setup offers the ability to infer indirectly the acceleration feature. This feature might be useful in future extensions to discriminate between language speech vs laughter or other lip gesticulations that do not involve speech.

Pre-processing: ROI Extractor. The first step of our VAD pipeline is a region of interest (ROI) extractor, which consists of detecting the lower face area, stabilizing the results and cropping the image patch. For detecting the lower face area, which contains not only the mouth as in other works, but additionally nose and chin, we first use a facial landmark detector [24]. We detect landmarks for the nose, mouth and chin area and concatenate them in a list. We then compute a center point per frame by averaging all detected landmarks. The center points are averaged over multiple frames (we use the last 30 frames) to achieve optical stabilization. The crop is then created with a size of 67×67 around the optically stabilized ROI center, computed via the running average. Optical stabilization is not critical for the RGB stream, but it does help the optical flow branch achieve better results. For more difficult, in-the-wild datasets, a Kalman filter would be recommended instead of a running average. The resulting lower face crop serves as input for the RGB and the optical flow stream.

RGB Stream. Our RGB branch is inspired by [8]: using ResNet18, we extract RGB features of the image patch containing the lower face regions. These features are then fed into an LSTM module. While the LSTM in [8] operates on both, audio and vision features, we pruned the audio branch for our visual-only approach and feed visual features directly to the LSTM. We modified [8] for our purposes in the following way:

- Instead of a many-to-one approach as in [8], where 15 video frames comprising 0.5 s are classified to a single VAD label, we use a many-to-many approach where each frame is classified to speech or non-speech depending on all the previous frames. In other words, we do not use a buffer approach where we need to accumulate a number of frames before classifying, but rather we classify in a streaming fashion, on the fly.
- The original approach determines the VAD label L as argmax of the two logits for speech (S) and non-speech (N), which result from the LSTM:

$$L = \text{argmax}(S, N) . \tag{1}$$

Since we need a probability P_{RGB} value for fusing the result of this stream with the optical flow stream, we specify:

$$P_{RGB} = \text{sigmoid}(J_{RGB}) , \tag{2}$$

where J_{RGB} is a joint speech/non-speech logit representation which we obtain from the LSTM. We can infer the hard RGB label L_{RGB} as:

$$L_{RGB} = \begin{cases} 0 & \text{if } P_{RGB} < 0.5, \\ 1 & \text{otherwise} . \end{cases} \tag{3}$$

While the probability P_{RGB} is required for the whole system during test time, the hard label L_{RGB} is used during training, in which each stream is trained separately. Our evaluation shows that these modifications improve the training and performance of the RGB stream (see Table 1).

Optical Flow Stream. The architecture of the optical flow stream is mirroring that of the RGB stream: we combine optical flow features, extracted using ResNet, with an LSTM module. We performed experiments without the LSTM module, i.e., replacing it with a multi-layer perceptron instead, but the results were worse than with the LSTM included. Hence, we keep the LSTM in the final system.

On the image patch of the lower face region, we compute a dense optical flow via the Gunnar Farneback algorithm [25]. This gives us the optical flow in Cartesian space. We then convert it to polar space and use the amplitude component to create activation maps. Mathematically: assuming we represent an image as $I(x, y, t)$, where x, y, t are the height, width and time dimensions, we can quantify the change of the image over time using Taylor series expansion and truncation of higher order terms as:

$$\frac{\partial I}{\partial x}\Delta x + \frac{\partial I}{\partial y}\Delta y + \frac{\partial I}{\partial t}\Delta t = 0. \tag{4}$$

Further dividing by Δt will give us the velocity, or optical flow components u and v:

$$\frac{\partial I}{\partial x}u + \frac{\partial I}{\partial y}v + \frac{\partial I}{\partial t} = 0. \tag{5}$$

Each pixel will therefore have an associated (u, v) optical flow in the Cartesian space, which we represent in polar coordinates as:

$$\vec{p} = Ae^{i\phi}, \tag{6}$$

where $\vec{p}$ is the pixel vector associated with (u, v) in Cartesian space, A and ϕ are the corresponding amplitude and angle of the optical flow in polar space. We then take the magnitude component A to create activation maps and feed these into a ResNet-18 for feature extraction. The resulting features are then fed into an LSTM module, which, after applying a sigmoid function, outputs the probability of speech P_{OF} obtained from the optical flow sequence:

$$P_{OF} = \text{sigmoid}(J_{OF}), \tag{7}$$

where J_{OF} is the logit computed by the optical flow LSTM module. To obtain the hard optical flow label L_{OF} we will threshold just like we did in the RGB case:

$$L_{OF} = \begin{cases} 0 & \text{if } P_{OF} < 0.5, \\ 1 & \text{otherwise}. \end{cases} \tag{8}$$

In analogy to the RGB stream, the hard label L_{OF} is used for training the optical flow stream separately.

Late Fusion. For the final fusion stage, we opt for a probabilistic strategy that is implemented only at test time. We compute the average of probabilities of the two streams and then threshold the average at 0.5 to determine the final VAD label:

$$F = \begin{cases} 0 & \text{if } \frac{P_{RGB}+P_{OF}}{2} < 0.5 \\ 1 & \text{otherwise}, \end{cases} \tag{9}$$

where F is the final label after fusion, P_{RGB} is the probability of speech as encoded by the RGB branch and P_{OF} is the probability of speech as encoded by the optical flow branch as defined above.

The intuition behind this approach is that when both streams agree that speech is present, the fused label will be resolved easily by unanimous vote. However, when the networks disagree, we enter a gray zone, and then system certainty is quantified in the form of averaging both probabilities and thresholding to resolve the conflict and come up with the final label. In our system we did not fuse via deep learning, because the current probabilistic fusion allows for a simple, yet effective explicit control over the probability threshold. This is a useful feature to have if we would like to manually adjust in favor of one metric over another without retraining.

4   Experimental Evaluation

In this section, we outline details about the dataset, the training, and the results we obtain.

4.1   Dataset and Training

For this work we made use of the TCD-TIMIT [9] dataset, which depicts 59 speakers in front of a green-screen and is already split into 42 train, 9 test and 8 validation speakers. Each speaker utters 99 different sentences. We resized the frames from the original 1920×1080 size to 224×224, because using originally-sized images causes landmark detection to run slow, whereas having images which are too small causes it to decrease accuracy.

The original videos were recorded with 30 frames per second (FPS), however we use a digital differential analyzer (DDA) interpolation algorithm [26] to achieve 62 FPS. This has the aim to synchronize the video frames with the audio frames that were used to generate the ground truth labels. Having a higher frequency of the audio frames allowed us to obtain more reliable labels, and hence it was natural to increase also the number of visual frames. Additionally, using a DDA can be thought of as data augmentation. We also augmented during training: we rotated frames by a random angle in the interval of $[-10°, 10°]$ and translated by a random amount in the interval of $[-0.1 \cdot H, \ 0.1 \cdot H]$ and $[-0.1 \cdot W, \ 0.1 \cdot W]$ respectively, where H is the image height and W is the image width.

Our approach is audio-visual from the perspective of label computation, i.e., we derive labels automatically from audio, unlike other works which derive labels from subtitle text [19] or create manual labels [8]. Since we have clean audio available, we implemented a sound energy-threshold detector. The alternative for noisy audio could be to use WebRTC [27]. We note that having 10% errors in the ground truth labels, provided they are random, i.e. not systemic, can be overcome by neural net approaches [17], which is another reason in favor of using deep learning for the VAD task.

4.2   Results

In this section, we show how our proposed approach improves the visual component for VAD systems. Our evaluation consists of three parts: first, we show that our modifications of the RGB stream from [8] are useful; second, we show the improvements we gain from adding optical flow to the pipeline; and third, we show that image crops of the lower face region improve the results and are additionally more convenient from a practical point of view than precise mouth crops.

Table 1 shows the results for the first two parts of the evaluation. The first two columns of the table compare the original RGB stream from the baseline with our modified RGB stream. We can see some clear improvements, especially with respect to the true negative rate. Note however that the system by Ariav & Cohen [8] is an audio-visual system, in which the focus is on the fusion part of the network. Thus, we do not claim to outperform [8] in general, but we show

Table 1. Comparison of baseline model [8] to our modified RGB, optical flow/OF and fused systems. All presented results are for the lower face, i.e. nose/mouth/chin regions extracted from the TCD-TIMIT dataset by our pre-processing routine.

Score type	Baseline RGB method [8]	Our modified RGB stream	Our OF stream	Our fusion
F1 ↑	87.6	89.4	90.9	**91.7**
TNR ↑	80.1	85.7	85.4	**87.2**
TPR ↑	92.7	93.3	**96.7**	96.5
Balanced accuracy ↑	86.4	89.5	91.1	**91.9**

that optimizing the visual stream alone results in clear performance gains, which will then most likely also be useful for complete audio-visual systems.

In column 4, we show the performance for the optical flow branch alone. We can see that it performs very similar to our RGB branch in terms of true negative rate. The true positive rate however is consistently better for the optical flow branch. When fusing both streams with our probabilistic approach (col. 5), we observe an overall improvement, especially with regard to the true negative rate. This indicates that the streams contain complementary information and profit from each other.

In Table 2, we show that focusing on the lower part of the face, i.e. nose, mouth and chin area does give better results than considering the full face. Moreover, it is better than using mouth-only images. Other works have considered just the mouth region, but including the nose and especially the chin area offers another speech specific cue, since they exhibit much movement for the optical flow branch during speech (note the visualization of the OF activation maps in Fig. 2, which shows clear activation in the chin area). This is also beneficial from a practical point of view for real-world applications, e.g. on a commodity household robot, because generating precisely cropped and well-aligned mouth regions in real time is harder than to approximate lower face crops.

Altogether, we show how the visual branch for voice activity detection can be improved by optimizing the RGB stream, adding optical flow, and focusing on image crops of the lower face region. The performance improves especially with respect to the detection of frames without voice activity. This will most likely also be useful for complete audio-visual systems.

Table 2. Fusion scores on full face, lower face, as well as precise mouth-only input crops. Using lower face images, i.e. nose, mouth and chin area, results in the best performance overall.

Score type	Full face	Mouth-only	Lower face
F1 ↑	90.1	90.4	**91.7**
TNR ↑	86.3	86.5	**87.2**
TPR ↑	94.2	94.6	**96.5**
Balanced accuracy ↑	90.3	90.6	**91.9**

5   Conclusion

In conclusion, we have presented an approach to improve the true negative rate for voice activity detection using unbalanced speech/non-speech datasets. Our method exploits the complementary advantages of RGB and optical flow and computes static as well as dynamic features from both streams. Additionally, we show that operating on crops of the lower face not only facilitates the processing, but also results in better performance, since especially the chin area contains useful information for VAD. In future work, we will integrate our visual-only VAD into an audio-visual framework.

References

1. Loizou, P.C.: Speech Enhancement: Theory and Practice. CRC Press, Boca Raton (2007)
2. Verteletskaya, E., Sakhnov, K.: Voice activity detection for speech enhancement applications. Acta Polytechnica **50**(4) (2010)
3. Vincent, E., Virtanen, T., Gannot, S. (eds.): Audio Source Separation and Speech Enhancement. Wiley, Hoboken (2018)
4. Liu, Q., Wang, W.: Blind source separation and visual voice activity detection for target speech extraction. In: 2011 3rd International Conference on Awareness Science and Technology (iCAST), pp. 457–460. IEEE (2011)
5. Ramirez, J., Górriz, J.M., Segura, J.C.: Voice activity detection. Fundamentals and speech recognition system robustness. Robust Speech Recogn. Understanding **6**(9), 1–22 (2007)
6. Bratoszewski, P., Szwoch, G., Czyżewski, A.: Comparison of acoustic and visual voice activity detection for noisy speech recognition. In: 2016 Signal Processing: Algorithms, Architectures, Arrangements, and Applications (SPA), pp. 287–291. IEEE (2016)
7. Tao, F., Hansen, J.H., Busso, C.: An unsupervised visual-only voice activity detection approach using temporal orofacial features. In: Sixteenth Annual Conference of the International Speech Communication Association (2015)
8. Ariav, I., Cohen, I.: An end-to-end multimodal voice activity detection using wavenet encoder and residual networks. IEEE J. Sel. Topics Signal Process. **13**(2), 265–274 (2019)
9. Harte, N., Gillen, E.: TCD-TIMIT: an audio-visual corpus of continuous speech. IEEE Trans. Multimedia **17**(5), 603–615 (2015)
10. Junqua, J.-C., Mak, B., Reaves, B.: A robust algorithm for word boundary detection in the presence of noise. IEEE Trans. Speech Audio Process. **2**(3), 406–412 (1994)
11. Sohn, J., Kim, N.S., Sung, W.: A statistical model-based voice activity detection. IEEE Signal Process. Lett. **6**(1), 1–3 (1999)
12. Gerkmann, T., Breithaupt, C., Martin, R.: Improved a posteriori speech presence probability estimation based on a likelihood ratio with fixed priors. IEEE Trans. Audio Speech Lang. Process. **16**(5), 910–919 (2008)
13. Zhang, X.-L., Wu, J.: Deep belief networks based voice activity detection. IEEE Trans. Audio Speech Lang. Process. **21**(4), 697–710 (2012)

14. Leglaive, S., Hennequin, R., Badeau, R.: Singing voice detection with deep recurrent neural networks. In: 2015 IEEE International Conference on Acoustics, Speech and Signal Processing (ICASSP), pp. 121–125 (2015)
15. Joosten, B., Postma, E., Krahmer, E.: Visual voice activity detection at different speeds. In: Auditory-Visual Speech Processing (AVSP) 2013 (2013)
16. Chakravarty, P., Tuytelaars, T.: Cross-modal supervision for learning active speaker detection in video. In: Leibe, B., Matas, J., Sebe, N., Welling, M. (eds.) ECCV 2016. LNCS, vol. 9909, pp. 285–301. Springer, Cham (2016). https://doi.org/10.1007/978-3-319-46454-1_18
17. Guy, S., Lathuilière, S., Mesejo, P., Horaud, R.: Learning visual voice activity detection with an automatically annotated dataset. In: 2020 25th International Conference on Pattern Recognition (ICPR), pp. 4851–4856. IEEE (2021)
18. Patterson, E.K., Gurbuz, S., Tufekci, Z., Gowdy, J.N.: CUAVE: a new audio-visual database for multimodal human-computer interface research. In: 2002 IEEE International Conference on Acoustics, Speech, and Signal Processing, vol. 2, pp. II-2017. IEEE (2002)
19. Sharma, R., Somandepalli, K., Narayanan, S.: Toward visual voice activity detection for unconstrained videos. In: 2019 IEEE International Conference on Image Processing (ICIP), pp. 2991–2995. IEEE (2019)
20. Shahid, M., Beyan, C., Murino, V.: S-VVAD: visual voice activity detection by motion segmentation. In: Proceedings of the IEEE/CVF Winter Conference on Applications of Computer Vision, pp. 2332–2341 (2021)
21. Petsatodis, T., Pnevmatikakis, A., Boukis, C.: Voice activity detection using audio-visual information. In: 2009 16th International Conference on Digital Signal Processing, pp. 1–5. IEEE (2009)
22. Tao, F., Hansen, J.H., Busso, C.: Improving boundary estimation in audiovisual speech activity detection using Bayesian information criterion. In: INTER-SPEECH, pp. 2130–2134 (2016)
23. Gao, Y., Beijbom, O., Zhang, N., Darrell, T.: Compact bilinear pooling. In: Proceedings of the IEEE Conference on Computer Vision and Pattern Recognition, pp. 317–326 (2016)
24. King, D.E.: DLIB-ML: a machine learning toolkit. J. Mach. Learn. Res. **10**, 1755–1758 (2009)
25. Farnebäck, G.: Two-frame motion estimation based on polynomial expansion. In: Bigun, J., Gustavsson, T. (eds.) SCIA 2003. LNCS, vol. 2749, pp. 363–370. Springer, Heidelberg (2003). https://doi.org/10.1007/3-540-45103-X_50
26. Bresenham, J.E.: Algorithm for computer control of a digital plotter. IBM Syst. J. **4**(1), 25–30 (1965)
27. Salishev, S., Barabanov, A., Kocharov, D., Skrelin, P., Moiseev, M.: Voice activity detector (VAD) based on long-term Mel frequency band features. In: Sojka, P., Horák, A., Kopeček, I., Pala, K. (eds.) TSD 2016. LNCS (LNAI), vol. 9924, pp. 352–358. Springer, Cham (2016). https://doi.org/10.1007/978-3-319-45510-5_40

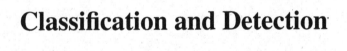

Classification and Detection

Score to Learn: A Comparative Analysis of Scoring Functions for Active Learning in Robotics

Riccardo Grigoletto[✉], Elisa Maiettini, and Lorenzo Natale

Humanoid Sensing and Perception, Istituto Italiano di Tecnologia, Genoa, Italy
`ricgri@kth.se`

Abstract. Accurately detecting objects in unconstrained settings is crucial for robotic agents, such as humanoids, that function in ever-changing environments. Current deep learning based methods achieve remarkable performance on this task on general purpose benchmarks and they are therefore appealing for robotics. However, their high accuracy comes at the price of computationally expensive off-line training and extensive human labeling. These aspects make their adoption in robotics challenging, since they prevent rapid model adaptation and re-training to novel tasks and conditions. Nonetheless, robots, and especially humanoids, being embodied in the surrounding environment, have access to streams of data from their sensors that, even though without supervision, might contain information of the objects of interest. The Weakly-supervised Learning (WSL) framework offers a set of tools to tackle these problems in general-purpose Computer Vision. In this work, we aim at investigating their adoption in the robotics domain which is still at a preliminary stage. We build on previous work, studying the impact of different, so called, scoring functions, which are at the core of WSL methods, on Pascal VOC, a general purpose dataset, and a prototypical robotic setting, i.e. the iCubWorld-Transformations dataset.

Keywords: Object detection · Active learning · Scoring function · Robotics

1 Introduction

Localizing and recognizing objects of interest is a crucial problem in modern robotic applications. Current approaches to address this task are based on Convolutional Neural Networks (CNN) [1], like, e.g., Mask R-CNN [2], EfficientDet [3] and YoloV4 [4]. These methods achieve remarkable performance on standard object detection benchmarks like Pascal VOC [5], Imagenet [6] and MS COCO [7]. However, they typically rely on Supervised Learning, therefore, they require carefully annotated training data to be optimized. For tasks like object detection or instance segmentation, the image annotation process is typically highly expensive as it requires an expert to manually provide both the names and locations (in terms of bounding box or contour, respectively) of all the objects of

© Springer Nature Switzerland AG 2021
M. Vincze et al. (Eds.): ICVS 2021, LNCS 12899, pp. 55–67, 2021.
https://doi.org/10.1007/978-3-030-87156-7_5

interest in the image. For this reason, these methods are not suited for agents that operate in unconstrained environments (like e.g., humanoids), which require the ability to quickly update the current model to novel conditions. It has been shown [8] that in constrained scenarios it is possible to acquire automatically annotated images, exploiting a human robot interaction and additional information from the other sensory modalities of a humanoid, like iCub [9]. However, recently it has been shown [8,10] that such an approach has limited generalization capabilities and that performance drop when the robot is asked to recognize objects in a different context.

Nonetheless, robots are autonomous agents that can actively explore the surrounding environment, having access to streams of images that, even if without supervision, might contain the objects of interest in different view poses and conditions. Therefore, they convey useful information for model adaptation or re-training, but they cannot be used within the Supervised Learning framework as they lack exact annotations. Moreover, they are typically redundant and strongly correlated in time. In these cases, Weakly-supervised Learning (WSL) [11,12] can be considered. This is a Machine Learning framework which targets those scenarios where it is required to learn from partially annotated data. For this work, the sub-classes of methods of WSL that are more relevant are Active Learning (AL) and Semi-supervised Learning (SSL). In particular, in AL [13,14], the informative unlabeled images are asked for annotations to an expert, with the aim of minimizing the labeling effort. The definition of the informativeness of an image is at the basis of each AL algorithm. SSL, instead, attempts to exploit the unlabeled images without querying for human annotation, by e.g., using high-confident predictions as pseudo ground-truth, in a self-supervised fashion. In both AL and SSL, it is fundamental to define evaluation functions which allow to express both the informativeness of the unlabeled images related to the task at hand and the confidence level of the predicted information. These functions are typically called *Scoring functions* [13,14].

Lately, WSL has been successfully applied to the object detection task [15–18], however their adoption in robotics is still at a preliminary stage. For instance, in [10], an on-line learning method for object detection [19] has been successfully integrated with a WSL pipeline [20], while in [21], different AL and SSL selection policies have been tested in robotics. The aim of this paper is, instead, to analyze the impact of different scoring functions, as they represent a core component of WSL methods, in a prototypical robotic scenario. Specifically, we compare different scoring functions, drawn from the Computer Vision literature, on two datasets for object detection: (i) the general purpose Pascal VOC [5] and (ii) the robotic dataset iCubWorld-Transformations [22]. Moreover, we provide insights on how the different functions affect the detection performance in terms of accuracy, training time and labeled data requirement on the two different tasks. We released the code to reproduce the experiments[1].

---

[1] https://github.com/RiccardoGrigoletto/SSM-Pytorch.

In the remaining of this paper, we report on the state-of-the-art on object detection and WSL (Sect. 2). Then, we describe the proposed method (Sect. 3) and we report on our experimental analysis (Sect. 4). Finally, we conclude commenting the obtained results (Sect. 5).

2   Related Work

In this section we present the state-of-the-art on object detection and WSL.

2.1   Deep Learning Based Object Detection

Approaches to the object detection task can be divided in two different categories: (i) grid-based and (ii) region-based detectors. In grid-based methods, for each image, classifiers are directly applied over a dense grid of cells, representing different object locations, scales, and aspect ratios. Recent examples of grid-based methods are: YOLO [4,23,24], SSD [25,26], RetinaNet [27], RefineDet [28] and CornerNet [29]. Instead, in region-based approaches, a previous step of region proposal generation is performed to predict a sparse set of candidate locations that might contain the objects of interest and that need to be further classified. As an example, Region-CNN (R-CNN) [30] can be mentioned, together with its optimizations: Fast R-CNN [31], Faster R-CNN [32], Region-FCN [33] and Mask R-CNN [2]. Typically, grid-based methods prove to be faster than region-based ones, but less precise [34].

All the aforementioned methods achieved high performance on general purpose Computer Vision benchmarks [5–7]. However, their application in robotics is not straightforward if fast adaptation capabilities are required. Indeed, these methods are generally composed of monolithic deep CNN-based architectures, trained end-to-end via stochastic gradient descent and back-propagation, thus requiring long training time and a large amount of carefully annotated images. Both these characteristics prevent fast and efficient adaptation to novel conditions. While the first issue has been recently addressed in [19,35–37], in this work we tackle the requirement of labeled data, by investigating WSL techniques, more specifically the scoring function component, to reduce the labeling human effort.

2.2   Weakly-Supervised Learning of Object Detection

The introduction of pipelines that allow to collect automatically annotated images (like, e.g. [8]) has alleviated the manually labeled data requirement of object detection methods. However, their usage may limit generalization capabilities of the learned model, since they typically require constrained scenarios for their functioning [8]. A solution to this problem is to consider WSL techniques, which allow to exploit unlabeled data to update and improve detection models [11,12]. AL and SSL (which have been introduced in Sect. 1) are two of the tools provided by the WSL framework. While their application to the object classification problem is well known (see, e.g. [14,38,39]), their adaptation to the object detection task is not straightforward, since each image can contain more than one object and the scoring function needs to take all of them into account. Moreover, the information of the location of the objects has to be considered as well. Recent work has been done in this direction [15–17,40,41]. Moreover, lately, SSL and AL have also been combined in a unique pipeline, called Self-supervised Sample Mining (SSM) [20] that is composed of (i) a CNN-based object detection method and (ii) a scoring function called Cross Image Validation (ICV) [20]. This latter is used to evaluate with a score the predictions on each unlabeled image. The produced score is used by the model to decide whether to ask it for annotation (AL) or accept the proposed prediction as a training label for that image (SSL). Finally, the newly obtained training set is used to fine-tune the detector. This process is repeated for different iterations over the unlabeled dataset.

While WSL techniques, and specifically SSM, have been recently integrated [10,21] with an on-line learning method for object detection for robotics [19], their adoption in robotics is still at a preliminary stage. In this work, we aim at investigating the impact of different scoring functions, a core component in all WSL pipelines, in a robotic scenario. Specifically, we integrate main state-of-the-art scoring functions with the SSM pipeline and we evaluate their robustness and efficiency on both general purpose and robotic datasets.

3   Methods

In this work, we consider the scenario of a robot provided with an object detection model pre-trained on a labeled, but scarce, dataset. The robot has access to a second set of unlabeled images and it can use them to refine the given detection model. We tackle this scenario with the WSL framework. Our aim is that of carrying out a systematic experimental evaluation, investigating the impact of the scoring function component in a WSL pipeline for object detection for robotics. In this section, we present the pipeline that has been used for our experimental analysis (Sect. 3.1) and the considered scoring functions (Sect. 3.2).

3.1   Overview of the Pipeline

The proposed pipeline builds on the SSM [20]. It is composed of three main building blocks (refer to Fig. 1 for a pictorial representation): (i) the *Object Detection module*, (ii) the *Dataset* and (iii) the *WSL module*.

Object Detection Module. For this part, in our experiments we chose the state-of-the-art approach Faster-RCNN [32]. This is a region-based method (see Sect. 2.1) and it is composed of: (i) a CNN based feature extractor, which computes convolutional descriptors for each image, (ii) a Region Proposal Network (RPN), which predicts a set of rectangular candidate regions in the image that might contain the objects of interest and (iii) a final Detector which classifies and refines all these proposals, providing a final set of predicted detections.

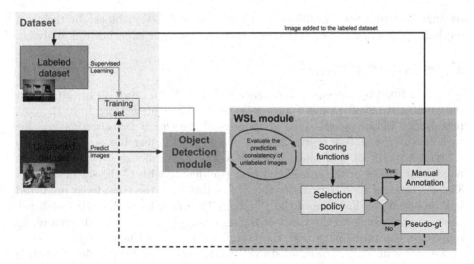

Fig. 1. Pictorial representation of the proposed pipeline. The blue arrows represent the *SL phase*, the orange ones represent the *WSL phase* (see Sect. 3.1 for details). (Color figure online)

In this work, for training Faster-RCNN we rely on the method proposed in [32]. Initially, we train it with the available labeled images, during the *Supervised Learning (SL) phase* (blue arrows in Fig. 1). Subsequently, the obtained detection model is iteratively refined using the unlabeled set of images, with the *WSL module*, during the *WSL phase* (orange arrows in Fig. 1).

Dataset. This component collects both the labeled and unlabeled sets of images at each iteration of the *WSL phase*. The former one is firstly used to pre-train the *Object Detection module* during the *SL phase*. Then, during the *WSL phase*, the unlabeled set is processed by the current *Object Detection module* and the predictions are evaluated by the *WSL module*. All the images with uncertain detections are asked for annotations (AL) and added to the labeled set, while all the confident ones are used as pseudo-groundtruth (SSL). Both of them are used as *Training set* for re-training the detection model during the current iteration of the *WSL phase*. At the end of each iteration, the *Training set* is re-initialized.

WSL Module. Finally, the *WSL module* consists of a (i) Scoring Function and a (ii) Selection Policy. During the *WSL phase*, the former one evaluates the predictions of the current *Object Detection module* on the unlabeled set of images, producing a consistency score [20] for each of them. The consistency score represents the confidence of the predictions and it is used by the Selection Policy to decide whether they are confident enough to be used as pseudo-labels (SSL) or if it is necessary to ask that image for manual annotation (AL). In this work, for the Selection Policy, we rely on the method proposed in [20]. Moreover, we refer to [21] for an empirical analysis of this latter component in a robotic setting. Our main contribution is in the scoring function block. In the next section, we describe the ones that we considered for our experimental analysis.

3.2   Scoring Functions

A scoring function calculates a consistency score $S(x)$, given an image x from the unlabeled set of images I and the corresponding predictions from the current model. In our pipeline, the predictions of the *Object Detection module*, for each image $x \in I$, are represented by a set of bounding boxes B_x. For each $b \in B_x$, a vector of confidence scores K is predicted, of size n, where n is the number of classes of the considered task (we denote with C the set of classes). The jth element in K represents the probability that the considered predicted box represents an instance of the jth class. Typically, for each b, the predicted class c_1 corresponds to the index of the maximum value k_b^* in K. Therefore, k_b^* represents the probability that the bounding box b depicts an object of class c_1, i.e., $k_b^* = \max_{\{c_1 \in C\}}(\hat{p}(c_1|b))$. In this work, we consider five different scoring functions from the state-of-the-art of Computer Vision and we evaluate them in a robotic setting. Specifically, two of them (namely, Maximum Confidence and Margin Sampling) have been drawn from the image classification literature [13] and adapted as follows for object detection while the others (namely, Cross Image Validation, Localization Tightness and Localization Stability) have been proposed for general purpose object detection with the purpose of integrating them in a robotic pipeline. We describe each of them in the following paragraphs.

Maximum Confidence (MC) [13]. This function computes the consistency score of an image x as the average of the k_b^* values for all the boxes in B_x:

$$S(x) = \frac{1}{|B_x|} \sum_{b \in B_x} k_b^* \tag{1}$$

Margin Sampling (MS) [13]. This function compares the difference between the first and second maximum values in K for each $b \in B_x$. It is computed as follows:

$$S(x) = \frac{1}{|B_x|} \sum_{b \in B_x} M_1(b) \tag{2}$$

where $M_1(b)$ represents the score for the single bounding box $b \in B_x$, such that:

$$M_1(b) = |\max_{\{c_1 \in C\}}(\hat{p}(c_1|b)) - \max_{\{c_2 \in C \setminus c_1\}}(\hat{p}(c_2|b))| \tag{3}$$

Cross Image Validation (ICV) [20]. It measures the confidence of the detections for an image by examining each predicted box as follows: (i) each detection is pasted into L different annotated images and (ii) the current detection model is used to predict them. The new predictions are compared with the ones of the original image and the score function is defined as:

$$S(x) = \frac{1}{|B_x|} \sum_{b \in B_x} M_2(b) \tag{4}$$

$M_2(b)$ represents the score for the single bounding box $b \in B_x$ such that:

$$M_2(b) = \frac{1}{\sum\limits_{l \in B_L} \hat{p}(c_1|l)} \sum\limits_{l \in B_L} \mathbf{1}(IoU(b,l) \geq \gamma)\hat{p}(c_1|l) \tag{5}$$

where B_L is the set of detections in the images in L corresponding to b. The $IoU(\cdot)$ is the Intersection over Union function, $\mathbf{1}(\cdot)$ is the indicator function and γ represents the acceptance threshold for an IoU ($\gamma = 0.5$, in our experiments).

Localization Tightness (LT) [40]. This function specifically applies to region-based object detection methods (see Sect. 2.1). It is computed as follows.

$$S(x) = \frac{1}{|B_x|} \sum\limits_{b \in B_x} M_3(b) \tag{6}$$

where $M_3(b)$ represents the score for the single bounding box $b \in B_x$ such that:

$$M_3(b) = |IoU(r,b) + k_b^* - 1| \tag{7}$$

where r is the region candidate from which b originated. The intuition behind this scoring function is that if r and b are too different it means that the Detector heavily modified the candidate regions predicted by the RPN during the refinement (see Sect. 3.1). This represents a "disagreement" of the two models on the position and size of the bounding boxes in an image, therefore they would benefit from re-training with the correct labels for that image.

Localization Stability (LS) [40]. This function measures the confidence of a detection for an image by repeating the prediction step on noisy versions of the same image and examining the consistency of the detections. Specifically, if N different Gaussian noise levels are chosen, the current detection model is applied N times on the N differently corrupted images ($N = 5$, in our experiments). For each initial predicted bounding box b, the most overlapping bounding box b_n is associated, which has been predicted by the detection model on the nth image of total N. The consistency score is computed as follows:

$$S(x) = \frac{\sum_{b \in B_x} k_b^* M_4(b)}{\sum_{b \in B_x} k_b^*} \tag{8}$$

where $M_4(b)$ represents the score for the single bounding box $b \in B_x$ such that:

$$M_4(b) = \frac{\sum_{n \in N} IoU(b, b_n)}{N} \tag{9}$$

4   Experiments

In this section, we present the experimental analysis carried out to evaluate and compare the scoring functions presented in Sect. 3.

4.1   Experimental Setup

For our analysis, we considered two different datasets: the Pascal VOC (VOC) [5] and the iCubWorld-Transformations (iCWT) [22]. Specifically, for VOC we used both train and validation sets of the two subsets, namely, *VOC2007* (∼5k images) and *VOC2012* (∼11k images), both depicting 20 object categories (which represent different animals, vehicles, furniture, etc.). The *VOC2007* is used for the *SL phase*, while *VOC2012* is used for the *WSL phase* (see Sect. 3.1). Therefore, in our experiments, *VOC2012* is treated as an unlabeled dataset. We used the test set of *VOC2007* to calculate accuracy (∼5k images). When using iCWT, instead, we selected 30 of the 200 available objects instances, gathering ∼2k, ∼6k and 4.5k images, respectively for the labeled, unlabeled training subsets and for the test set. This dataset has been acquired as described in [22], with a natural interaction with the iCub humanoid robot [9], simulating a teacher-learner scenario. The 200 depicted objects can be typically found in a domestic environment and, for each of them, several image sequences are available. For the acquisition procedure and the depicted objects, iCWT represents a suitable test bench to validate our system in the target robotic scenario. In the reported experiments, we chose ResNet50 [42] as CNN backbone for feature extraction for Faster R-CNN. In both cases, the training is done by fine-tuning a set of weights that has been pre-trained on MS COCO [7]. For the *SL phase*, we fine-tuned the network for 70k and 8k iterations for respectively VOC and iCWT while for the *WSL phase*, we iterate the selection policy for four times over the unlabeled part of the dataset, fine-tuning the weights, each time, for 20k and 4k iterations for respectively VOC and iCWT.

The evaluation is performed comparing 3 different metrics:

1 The mean Average Precision (mAP) as defined in [5].
2 The computational time[2] during the scoring function computation reported in terms of processed images per second (im/s). This aspect is critical in the considered robotics application.
3 The ratio between the number of images selected for manual annotation (AL) and the number of those that are automatically annotated with a self-supervision (SSL) (referred to as AL/SS ratio). This metric has practical relevance because it allows to understand how much the self-supervision is used by the different scoring functions.

We repeat each experiment for five trials for VOC and for three trials for iCWT and we present the results, reporting the mean and the standard deviation of the obtained results.

---

[2] The models have been trained on a single GPU Nvidia TESLA K40 and Intel(R) Xeon(R) CPU E5-2620 v4 @ 2.10 GHz.

4.2 Results Analysis on Pascal VOC

We report the obtained results in Fig. 2. In particular, we show the mAP and
AL/SS ratio trends for growing numbers of annotated images, respectively, in
Fig. 2A and Fig. 2B. As it can be noticed in Fig. 2A, the different scoring functions have similar mAP trends. This means that, for VOC, both approaches
drawn from the image classification literature (MC and MS) and the ones based
on the consistency of the predicted bounding boxes (ICV, LT and LS) present
similar accuracy performance for growing numbers of annotations. Notably, however, MC turned out to be the one that leads to less accurate results for small
annotation budgets and to a higher variability of the obtained mAP on the different experiment trials. Moreover, as it can be observed from Fig. 2B, ICV and
LS present AL/SS ratios which are, respectively, ~10 and ~7 times higher than
the other methods. On the contrary, MS, MC and LT present very low values.
This means that, for instance, ICV and LS achieve roughly the same accuracy
as LS and LT, with the same number of AL but less SSL.

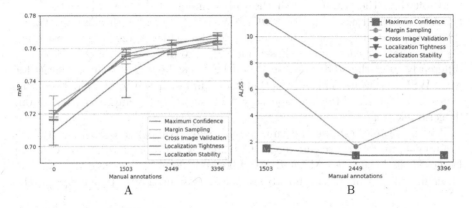

Fig. 2. Comparison of scoring functions on VOC in terms of mAP trend (A) and AL/SS
ratio (B) for growing numbers of manual annotations.

Table 1. Time performance comparison for the different scoring functions on both
datasets, VOC and iCWT.

Method	(im/s) on VOC	(im/s) on iCWT
MC	**2.19**	**2.07**
MS	**2.20**	**2.06**
ICV	0.56	1.06
LT	1.06	1.60
LS	0.55	1.04

4.3   Results Analysis on iCWT

In this section, we compare the scoring functions presented in Sect. 3.2 on the target robotic scenario, represented by the iCWT dataset. We report the obtained results in Fig. 3. Specifically, we show the mAP and AL/SS ratio trends for growing numbers of annotated images, respectively, in Fig. 3A and Fig. 3B. As it can be observed in Fig. 3A, mAP trends for iCWT for ICV and LS present the lowest slopes, while MC, LT and MS have the steepest ones especially for lower numbers of manual annotations. Notably, MC reaches the highest value of mAP ($\sim$0.71) with only 606 annotated images.

As a comparison, we trained Faster R-CNN with all the available annotated images (i.e. $\sim$16k) in iCWT for the chosen task. The obtained model represents the upper-bound of the results presented in Fig. 3 since it uses the full dataset for training, achieving an mAP of 0.866. Even if the results in Fig. 3 are reasonably lower than the upper-bound, it is worth noticing that, for instance, with MS it has been possible to obtain an mAP of ~ 0.71 with a significant lower amount of manually annotated images (606). This makes the proposed method a better trade-off than the training with the fully annotated dataset. Moreover, as it can be noted in Fig. 3B, as for VOC, ICV and LS present the highest AL/SS ratios. For instance, ICV (blue line in Fig. 3B) achieves 120 on the last step, meaning that for each image chosen for SSL, 120 are chosen for AL. However, differently from the VOC case, ICV and LS have the worst accuracy levels for early WSL iterations. This means that the samples chosen by the model as self-supervision for LT, MS and especially MC, significantly improved the overall detection accuracy.

Finally, Table 1 shows the time performance comparison. Specifically, the second column reports results for VOC, while the third one for iCWT. As it can be noted, in both cases MS and MC take considerably less time than all the other methods, while ICV and LS are the slowest methods. This is due to the

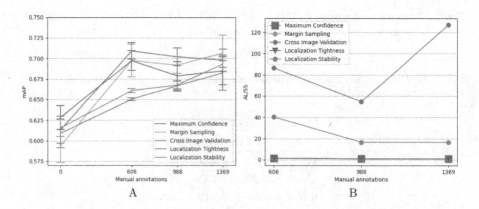

Fig. 3. Comparison of scoring functions on iCWT dataset in terms of mAP trend (A) and AL/SS ratio (B) for growing numbers of manual annotations. (Color figure online)

fact that both ICV and LS require to perform several inferences of Faster R-CNN for different images to evaluate the prediction consistency, while the others do it only once for the initial unlabeled image.

5   Discussion

In this work, we considered the scenario of a robot that is required to refine an object detection model with an incoming set of unlabeled images. We tackled this scenario with the WSL framework and we empirically evaluated the impact of the scoring function component in a WSL pipeline for object detection for robotics. Specifically, we compared five different scoring functions on both general purpose and robotics datasets, by means of the two benchmarks Pascal VOC and iCWT. Interestingly, we found out that while for Pascal VOC, the five methods have comparable accuracy performance, for the target robotic scenario they perform differently. Moreover, with the comparative analysis in terms of annotations and computation time required, we identified the most efficient methods. Notably, the three fastest scoring functions (namely, MC, MS and LT) present the best trends in terms of mAP and make a better use of self-supervision, representing valid options for a WSL based robotic application. We believe that the presented analysis provides useful insights on how to apply WSL techniques in a robotic setting, going towards the design of more efficient learning based robotic vision systems.

References

1. LeCun, Y., Bengio, Y., et al.: Convolutional networks for images, speech, and time series. In: The Handbook of Brain Theory and Neural Networks, vol. 3361.10, p. 1995 (1995)
2. He, K., et al.: Mask R-CNN. In: The IEEE International Conference on Computer Vision (ICCV), October 2017
3. Tan, M., Pang, R., Le, Q.V.: EfficientDet: scalable and efficient object detection (2020). arXiv:1911.09070 [cs.CV]
4. Bochkovskiy, A., Wang, C.-Y., Mark Liao, H.-Y.: YOLO4j: optimal speed and accuracy of object detection (2020). arXiv:2004.10934 [cs.CV]
5. Everingham, M., et al.: The pascal visual object classes (VOC) challenge. Int. J. Comput. Vis. 88(2), 303–338 (2010). ISSN 0920-5691, 1573-1405. https://doi.org/10.1007/s11263-009-0275-4. http://link.springer.eom/10.1007/s11263-009-0275-4
6. Krizhevsky, A., Sutskever, I., Hinton, G.E.: ImageNet classification with deep convolutional neural networks. In: Pereira, F., et al. (eds.) Advances in Neural Information Processing Systems, vol. 25, pp. pp. 1097–1105. Curran Associates Inc. (2012). http://papers.nips.cc/paper/4824-imagenet-classification-with-deep-convolutional-neural-networks.pdf
7. Lin, T.-Y., et al.: Microsoft COCO: common objects in context. arXiv:1405.0312 [cs], 20 February 2015. arXiv:1405.0312. URL: http://arxiv.org/abs/1405.0312. Accessed 21 May 2020

8. Maiettini, E., et al.: Interactive data collection for deep learning object detectors on humanoid robots. In: 2017 IEEE-RAS 17th International Conference on Humanoid Robotics (Humanoids), pp. 862–868, November 2017. https://doi.org/10.1109/HUMANOIDS.2017.8246973

9. Metta, G., et al.: The iCub humanoid robot: an open-systems platform for research in cognitive development. Neural Netw. Official J. Int. Neural Netw. Soc. **23**(8–9), 1125–34 (2010). https://doi.org/10.1016/j.neunet.2010.08.010. Jan

10. Maiettini, E., et al.: A weakly supervised strategy for learning object detection on a humanoid robot. In: 2019 IEEE-RAS 17th International Conference on Humanoid Robotics (Humanoids), p. 8 (2019)

11. Zhou, Z.-H.: A brief introduction to weakly supervised learning. Nat. Sci. Rev. **5**(1), 44–53 (2018). https://academic.oup.com/nsr/article/5/1/44/4093912. https://doi.org/10.1093/nsr/nwxl06. ISSN 2095–5138, 2053–714X. Accessed 28 May 2020

12. Zhang, D., et al.: Weakly supervised object localization and detection: a survey. IEEE Trans. Pattern Anal. Mach. Intell. 1 (2021). https://doi.org/10.1109/TPAMI.2021.3074313

13. Settles, B.: Active learning literature survey. Technical report, University of Wisconsin-Madison Department of Computer Sciences (2009)

14. Settles, B.: Active learning. In: Synthesis Lectures on Artificial Intelligence and Machine Learning (2012)

15. Aghdam, H.H., et al.: Active learning for deep detection neural networks. In: 2019 IEEE/CVF International Conference on Computer Vision (ICCV). Seoul, Korea (South), pp. 3671–3679, IEEE, October 2019, ISBN 978-1-72814-803-8. https://ieeexplore.ieee.org/document/9009535/. https://doi.org/10.1109/ICCV.2019.00377. Accessed 16 June 2020

16. Haussmann, E., et al.: Scalable active learning for object detection. In: IEEE Intelligent Vehicles Symposium (IV), IEEE 2020, pp. 1430–1435 (2020)

17. Li, Y., Huang, D., Qin, D., Wang, L., Gong, B.: Improving object detection with *selective* self-supervised self-training. In: Vedaldi, A., Bischof, H., Brox, T., Frahm, J.-M. (eds.) ECCV 2020. LNCS, vol. 12374, pp. 589–607. Springer, Cham (2020). https://doi.org/10.1007/978-3-030-58526-6_35

18. Dwibedi, D., Misra, I., Hebert, M.: Cut, paste and learn: surprisingly easy synthesis for instance detection. In: Proceedings of the IEEE International Conference on Computer Vision, pp. 1301–1310 (2017)

19. Maiettini, E., et al.: On-line object detection: a robotics challenge. Auton. Robot. 1573–7527 (2019). ISSN 0929-5593. http://link.springer.com/10.1007/S10514-019-09894-9. https://doi.org/10.1007/S10514-019-09894-9. Accessed 10 Feb 2020

20. Wang, K., et al.: Towards human-machine cooperation: self-supervised sample mining for object detection. arXiv:1803.09867 [cs], May 2018. http://eirxiv.org/abs/1803.09867. Accessed 30 Jan 2020

21. Maiettini, E., et al.: Data-efficient weakly-supervised learning for online object detection under domain shift in robotics (2020). arXiv:2012.14345

22. Pasquale, G., et al.: Are we done with object recognition? The iCub robot's perspective. Robot. Auton. Syst. 112, 260–281 (2019). ISSN: 09218890. arXiv:1709.09882. https://doi.org/10.1016/j.robot.2018.11.001. Accessed 13 Jan 2020

23. Redmon, J., et al.: You only look once: unified, real-time object detection. arXiv:1506.02640 [cs], 9 May 2016. arXiv:1506.02640. Accessed 26 May 2020

24. Redmon, J., Farhadi, A.: YOLOv3: an incremental improvement. CoRR abs/1804.02767 (2018). arXiv:1804.02767

25. Liu, W., et al.: SSD: single shot multibox detector, pp. 21–37. arXiv:1512.02325 [cs] 9905 (2016). arXiv:1512.02325. Accessed 26 May 2020. https://doi.org/10.1007/ 978-3-319-46448-0_2

26. Zhai, S., et al.: DF-SSD: an improved SSD object detection algorithm based on DenseNet and feature fusion. IEEE Access **8**, 24344–24357 (2020)

27. Lin, T.-Y., et al.: Focal loss for dense object detection, 7 February 2018. arXiv:1708.02002. Accessed 26 May 2020

28. Zhang, S., et al.: Single-shot refinement neural network for object detection. arXiv:1711.06897 [cs], 3 January 2018. arXiv:1711.06897. Accessed 26 May 2020

29. Law, H., Deng, J.: CornerNet: detecting objects as paired keypoints. In: arXiv:1808.01244 [cs], 18 March 2019. arXiv:1808.01244. http://cirxiv.org/abs/ 1808.01244. Accessed 26 May 2020

30. Girshick, R.B., et al.: Rich feature hierarchies for accurate object detection and semantic segmentation. CoRR abs/1311.2524 (2013). arXiv:1311.2524

31. Girshick, R.: Fast R-CNN. arXiv:1504.08083 [cs], 27 September 2015. arXiv:1504.08083. Accessed 20 May 2020

32. Ren, S., et al.: Faster R-CNN: towards real-time object detection with region proposal networks. arXiv:1506.01497 [cs], January 2016. arXiv:1506.01497. Accessed 29 Jan 2020

33. Dai, J., et al.: R-FCN: object detection via region-based fully convolutional networks. arXiv:1605.06409 [cs], 21 June 2016. arXiv:1605.06409. Accessed 26 May 2020

34. Huang, J., et al.: Speed/accuracy trade-offs for modern convolutional object detectors. arXiv:1611.10012 [cs], 24 April 2017. arXiv:1611.10012. Accessed 28 May 2020

35. Maiettini, E., et al.: Speeding-up object detection training for robotics with FALKON. In: 2018 IEEE/RSJ International Conference on Intelligent Robots and Systems (IROS), October 2018, pp. 5770–5776. https://doi.org/10.1109/IROS. 2018.8593990

36. Ceola, F., et al.: Fast region proposal learning for object detection for robotics (2020). arXiv:2011.12790 [cs.CV]

37. Ceola, F., et al.: Fast object segmentation learning with kernel-based methods for robotics (2020). arXiv:2011.12805 [cs.CV]

38. Kirsch, A., van Amersfoort, J., Gal, Y.: BatchBALD: efficient and diverse batch acquisition for deep Bayesian active learning. In: NeurIPS (2019)

39. Ash, J.T., et al.: Deep batch active learning by diverse, uncertain gradient lower bounds, January 2020. https://openreview.net/forum?id=0HjEAtQNNWD. Accessed 26 Oct 2020

40. Kao, C.-C., Lee, T.-Y., Sen, P., Liu, M.-Y.: Localization-aware active learning for object detection. In: Jawahar, C.V., Li, H., Mori, G., Schindler, K. (eds.) ACCV 2018. LNCS, vol. 11366, pp. 506–522. Springer, Cham (2019). https://doi.org/10. 1007/978-3-030-20876-9_32

41. Desai, S.V., et al.: An adaptive supervision framework for active learning in object detection. arXiv preprint arXiv:1908.02454 (2019)

42. He, K., et al.: Deep residual learning for image recognition. arXiv:1512.03385 [cs], December 2015. Accessed 09 July 2020

Enhancing the Performance of Image Classification Through Features Automatically Learned from Depth-Maps

George Ciubotariu[✉][iD], Vlad-Ioan Tomescu[✉][iD], and Gabriela Czibula[✉][iD]

Babeş-Bolyai University, Cluj-Napoca, Romania
george.ciubotariu@stud.ubbcluj.ro,
{vlad.tomescu,gabriela.czibula}@ubbcluj.ro

Abstract. This paper approaches a problem from Computer Vision, that of classifying indoor and outdoor images using *machine learning* and *deep learning* models. To do so, we are going to perform an unsupervised learning based analysis with the aim of determining the relevance of depth maps in the context of classification. For further tests to decide on the granularity of information extraction means, features are aggregated from sub-images of different sizes from DIODE data set to compare multiple scales of region attention. Four feature sets will be proposed and comparatively analysed in the context of indoor-outdoor image classification. To empirically confirm the advantage of using features automatically learned from depth maps, the features are fed into a supervised classification model. The performance of the classification using the proposed feature sets is then compared with the results of existing related work, highlighting the clear advantage of using features encoding depth information. Overall accuracy improvements consist of 18.8% for the machine learning approach and 1.1% for the deep learning one when depth information was added to the data.

Keywords: Computer vision · Depth estimation · Image classification · Deep learning

1 Introduction

Computer Vision (CV) aims to cover a wide range of visual tasks in order to automate the processes of decision making in domains such as *autonomous driving*, *robotic process automation*, *product quality control*, or creating virtual environments for Virtual Reality/Augmented Reality. Recently, all CV tasks are performed using *Deep Learning* (DL) models that consist of multiple types of layers for processing input images at different resolutions. The most popular architecture in image processing is the one of *Deep Convolutional Neural Networks* (DCNN) which has the *convolution* as core concept. The aim of such networks is to encode pictures' spatial information with the help of convolutions while decreasing the resolution of images in order to grasp more of the scene context.

© Springer Nature Switzerland AG 2021
M. Vincze et al. (Eds.): ICVS 2021, LNCS 12899, pp. 68–81, 2021.
https://doi.org/10.1007/978-3-030-87156-7_6

Such convolutions are intensely researched in order to maximise the amount of information extracted and minimise the computational cost of network training.

Depth estimation (DE) [2] or *depth extraction* aims towards gathering information about the structure of a scene using mathematical or learning means, hence every pixel of an image is supposed to be assigned a depth value. Stereo vision methods are highly dependent on illumination intensity and angle, therefore monocular depth estimation is more convenient for calibration or identification than stereo vision means [6]. *Monocular depth estimation* is a difficult task as even humans misinterpret *Depth of Field* when looking with one eye open.

The problem of determining the depth in a single image is an ill-posed one as stated in the literature [2], as we have to rely on features such as shapes, textures and occlusions in order to gain information about the scene geometry and different semantic meaningful regions that would help us compute the depth value of every pixel in an image. The great difficulty in this situation is that one 2D photo is not enough to reconstruct a 3D environment as there are infinite 3D layouts that can be projected into a 2D space to reproduce an image. As optical illusions have proven us, humans make assumptions about the shapes and sizes of the objects, ultimately leading them to the wrong conclusions. Still, that assumptions are also to be made by learning DL models when dealing with so little spatial information. Nonetheless, if depth information would be available, we could therefore use the advantages of combining RGB features with depth cues to enhance visual tasks, by offering the models extra guidance.

The goal of the research conducted in this paper is to study the usefulness of *depth* information applied to both *Machine Learning* (ML) and DL models in indoors and outdoors contexts that have totally different layouts and detail density. We decided to focus in our study on indoor–outdoor image classification, a classification task that could serve as a preliminary step in a more complex pipeline of image classification and scenery identification that becomes of increasing interest nowadays. The classification of images in indoor and outdoor classes is mostly used in content based image retrieval in order to perform queries on large volumes of data to find photos with similar characteristics [3]. Furthermore, another important application is in the field of image tagging, which could lead to better suggestions when using social media.

The contribution of the paper is twofold. Firstly, we are proposing four feature sets for characterizing the images with the aim of comparatively studying their relevance for the visual task of indoor-outdoor classification. One feature set is manually engineered, based on using RGB information and features extracted from depth-maps, while other three feature sets are automatically learned from images using a deep learning model. The relevance of the proposed feature sets will be investigated through an unsupervised learning classifier. Then, in order to confirm the hypothesis that the depth related features are useful in discriminating between indoor-outdoor images, a supervised learning classifier will be used to evaluate the performance of the image classification task on DIODE (Dense Indoor and Outdoor DEpth) data set [14]. To the best of our knowledge, a study similar to ours has not been performed in the literature yet.

To sum up, the current work is based on the following research questions:

RQ1 How relevant are depth maps in the context of indoor-outdoor image classification and to what extent does aggregating visual features from more granular sub-images increase the performance of classification?

RQ2 Which of the engineered and automatically learned features from depth-maps are able to better discriminate between indoor-outdoor images?

RQ3 How correlated are the results of the unsupervised based analysis and the performance of supervised models applied for indoor-outdoor image classification?

The study conducted in the paper serves as a proof of concept concerning depth-maps utility. The generalised benefits of including depth information in visual tasks is mostly that of using it into the training processes to speed up the convergence of the models and boosting their performance by offering them denser data to work with. Even though depth information may not be always available, the feature extraction enhancements offered by the exposure to depth cues would be valuable to deep models when working with raw RGB images.

The rest of the paper is structured as follows. Section 2 reviews the type of features and methods used in the literature for indoor-outdoor image classification. The methodology proposed for answering the previously stated research questions is introduced in Sect. 3, whilst Sect. 4 presents the results of our unsupervised and supervised learning-based analysis. Section 5 concludes the paper and indicates directions for further improvements and future work.

2   Literature Review on Indoor-Outdoor Image Classification

A review on indoor-outdoor scene classification, feature extraction methods, classifiers and data sets is done by Tong et al. [13]. It includes a collection of multiple remarkable methods, ranging from traditional ML to *neural networks* (NN), that achieved good performances in a time frame between 1998 and 2017. Most methods consisted of lightweight classifiers that analyse manually-extracted features. However, some later ones implement early versions of NNs capable of understanding scene context. The features analysed include color, texture, edge, as well as others, while the classification was done using machine learning methods, both classical approaches and deep learning, or by employing a method called bag of word (BoW), specific to computer vision. Multiple data sets were mentioned, but not DIODE, mainly due to the recent nature of the data set. The paper concludes that there is no ideal set of features for the indoor-outdoor classification task, but that deep learning classifiers have an edge over other models.

The method proposed by Raja et al. [9] used color, texture and entropy features that are fed into a KNN classifier, achieving a performance of 81.55% accuracy.

Furthermore, Cvetkovic et al. [3] employed a combination of multiple color and texture descriptors and a SVM classifier to obtain accuracies of 93.71% and 92.36% on two public data sets, while Tahir et al. [12] computes the GIST descriptor of the scene as a feature vector. A custom neural network classifier with one hidden layer then achieves 90.8% accuracy.

An approach to indoor-outdoor classification is done by Kumari et al. [5], in which a ResNet CNN Classifier is used both on RGB images, as well as depth maps. The model was on an indoor real data set, NYUV1, as well as the virtual outdoor one, KITTI. The comparison to related work was done on IITM-SCID2, a data set containing both indoors and outdoors images, achieving an average accuracy of up to 96%.

Velswamy et al. [15] introduced a model that classifies scene images into indoor and outdoor based on multiple factors including number of Euclidean shapes versus number of recursive shapes, number of straight lines, as well as brightness distribution. The best performing model presented in the paper achieves an average accuracy of 95.74%.

In some publications, the outdoor class is split into nature and city, effectively resulting in three classes, an example being [16]. Here, Yeo et al. used a semantic segmentation model in order to determine the objects in the images, which are then passed through a weight matrix for classification. They achieve a 92% accuracy on the COCO data set.

3 Methodology

This section describes the methodology we are proposing with the goal of answering the research questions stated in Sect. 1 and highlighting that depth-maps features improve the performance of indoor-outdoor image classification.

The classification problem we are focusing on is a binary classification one, that of learning to assign to an image a class $c \in \{I = indoor, O = outdoor\}$. To achieve the learning task, we are comparatively analysing the relevance of several image features in distinguishing the target class (I/O) for a specific image. The relevance of the proposed features is first assessed in an unsupervised learning scenario, by testing the ability of an unsupervised learning model to partition the input images in two clusters (corresponding to the two output classes). Then, in order to strengthen the unsupervised learning based analysis, the performance of a supervised learning classification model is evaluated considering various feature vectors characterizing the images.

We start by describing in Sect. 3.1 the data set used in our experiments, then we continue with introducing the previously summarised stages of our study: (1) feature extraction; (2) unsupervised learning-based analysis; (3) supervised learning-based analysis and performance evaluation.

3.1 Data Set

The image database used in our experiments is DIODE data set [14] consisting of 27858 RGB-D (R-Red, G-Green, B-Blue, D-Depth) *indoor* and *outdoor* images collected with a **FARO Focus S350** laser scanner. The data set is diverse, the photos have been taken both at daytime and night, over several seasons (summer, fall, winter). The full resolution of the images from the data set is 1024 × 768. Apart from RGB-D images, DIODE data set also provides us with normal maps that could further enhance the learning of depth and vice-versa. Normal maps are matrices with the same dimensions as the RGB images in which its components correspond to the X, Y, and Z coordinates, respectively, of the surface normal, which would help better determine regions with similar characteristics.

Figures 1 and 2 depict the frequencies of depth values represented as percentages of the total number of pixels. Depth values are measured in meters. There are almost twice as many outdoor images (18206) than indoors (9652) in order to capture the variety of different environments. Also, the data set is partitioned by default in train (25458) and validation (771) splits with a suggested test split of 1629 images.

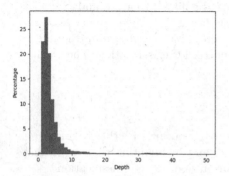 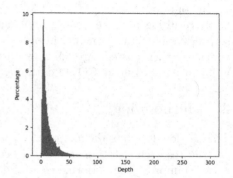

Fig. 1. Indoor depth frequency   **Fig. 2.** Outdoor depth frequency

In the experiments we chose to use a subset of every hundredth image from the train split, resulting in a 255 images sample from both indoors and outdoors settings. The resolution for the RGB/RGB-D experiments is the images' original one and for the DPT experiments a resolution of 384 × 384 was used.

3.2 Feature Extraction

The *feature extraction* stage refers to extracting a set of features relevant for representing the images in a vector space model. Formally, an image is encoded by a set $F = (F_1, F_2, \ldots F_m)$ of relevant features. Thus, an image Im will be represented as a high-dimensional numerical vector $Im = (i_1, i_2, \ldots, i_m)$, where i_j represents the value of feature F_j obtained for image I. An image will be, subsequently, visualized as a data point in $\mathbb{R}^m$.

We are proposing four feature sets for characterizing the images with the aim of comparatively studying their relevance for the visual task of indoor-outdoor classification. The first feature set is manually engineered, based on using RGB information and features extracted from depth-maps, while the next two feature sets are automatically learned by our DCNN model of choice from raw images and the last one follows the same procedure but for depth-augmented RGB encoded images.

Manually Engineered Features. In our approach we considered *RGB* of the images and the *Depth* of the depth-maps. Instead of resizing the images (which would have led to loss of information), we have chosen to aggregate the information of some regions of the image. We started from the intuition that smaller sub-images would generate more specific features.

The first vectorial representation proposed for the images is based on aggregating features (RGB information and features extracted from depth-maps) from sub-images of different sizes to compare multiple scales of region attention. Before the feature extraction step, the image is divided, recursively, in 4^n sub-images of equal sizes: the initial image is divided in 4, then each of the four sub-images is again divided in 4, and so on. An example of such a split is given in Fig. 3, for $n = 2$, resulting in 16 equally sized sub-images.

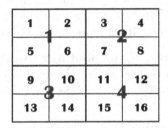

Fig. 3. Structure of 16 (4^2) image splits.

1. **RGBD features** (RGBD) are obtained by aggregating RGBD values from sub-images. Thus, for an image splitted in 4^n sub-images (as previously described), a vector of size $m = 4 \times 4^n$ is built by concatenating, in the order top-to-bottom and left-to-right (see Fig. 3), the average R, G, B, and D values for each sub-image.

Automatically Learned Features. As revealed by the literature review from Sect. 2, insufficient work on indoor-oudoor image classification has been carried out in what regards DCNNs, thus we looked into the potential of automatic feature extraction by proposing three feature sets that we studied with the help of a deep learning model, called *vision transformers* (DPT). The approach introduced by Ranftl et al. [10] leverages visual transformers in place of convolutions. The main advantage of this change is that compared to plain convolutions which have a limited spatial understanding due to their size and need downsampling to capture such information, DPT has included global receptive field information in each layer thanks to its custom fusion and residual blocks implemented in its DCNN architecture. Therefore, this leads to finer, sharper and more coherent predictions, establishing a new state-of-the-art in DE and *semantic segmentation* (SS) [10].

2. **DPT encoder DE features** (DPT-DE) are the features automatically learned by a pretrained DPT on MIX 6 DE data set [10].
3. **DPT encoder SS features** (DPT-SS) are the features automatically learned by a pretrained DPT on ADE20K SS data set [17].

For representations 2 and 3, the features are extracted after the encoder of the DPT model. We mention that an image will be represented as an m-dimensional numerical vector, where m is the dimensionality of the encoding layer of the DPT model.

The last set of features we propose is automatically learned from depth-augmented images using the DPT model. We consider the RGBA (RGB, A-Alpha which encodes pixel transparency) opaque images (that means the A value is 255 for each pixel) and we use $A_{ij} = 255 - clip(D_{ij})$ for every pixel in the image to create a progressively denser fog that simulates the depth of field. We clip the depth values D to a $[0, 255]$ meters interval so that they fit in a byte. Then, we blend the RGBA image with variable transparency with a white background and encode it to a RGB representation that the DPT model uses.

4. **DPT encoder SS depth-augmented features** (DPT-SS+D) are the features automatically learned by a pretrained DPT on ADE20K SS data set from the DIODE depth-augmented images [14,17].

3.3 Unsupervised Learning-Based Analysis

In our approach we are applying 3D t-SNE (*t-Distributed Stochastic Neighbor Embedding*) [7] for *non-linear* dimensionality reduction of the m-dimensional representation of the images from the data set, computed according to the representations 1.-4. t-SNE is used in exploratory data analysis for uncovering patterns in data useful for clustering. The model uses *Student t-distribution* [8] to better disperse the clusters.

The unsupervised learning-based analysis using t-SNE is conducted with the goal of providing useful insight about data organization and features' importance. Before the t-SNE visualization, for the RGBD data (representation 1) *data normalization* with the **inverse hyperbolic sine (asinh)** was applied in order to increase sensitivity to particularly small and large values. For automatic feature extraction (representations 2, 3, and 4), we did not use any preprocessing step, as DPT models are pretrained on raw RGB data.

In addition, for quantifying the quality of the t-SNE clustering, and measuring how well the indoor and outdoor images are separated in clusters, we are considering the *precision* (*Prec*) of the 3D t-SNE mapping which we define as the proportion of 3D data points from the t-SNE chart whose nearest neighbor (1-NN, considering the Euclidean distance) has the same label as the data point itself. More specifically, if we denote by $\mathcal{D}$ the 3D points representing the output of the t-SNE algorithm, the *precision* is defined as

$$Prec = \frac{\sum\limits_{x \in \mathcal{D}} \delta(f(x), f(nn(x)))}{|\mathcal{D}|}, \text{ where } \delta(x, y) = \begin{cases} 1 & if \ x = y \\ 0 & otherwise \end{cases} \ (nn(x) \text{ denotes}$$

the nearest neighbor of data point x and $f(x)$ denotes the label of instance x). *Prec* measure is ranging from 0 to 1, expressing how "close" are the images with the same label (indoor/outdoor class) on the 3D t-SNE space and how separated the two clusters are. Higher values for *Prec* indicate a better clustering of the data points.

3.4 Supervised Learning Based Analysis

To empirically analyze the relevance of the feature sets proposed in Sect. 3.2, the features are fed into a supervised classification model whose performance will point out the importance of the used features. As a supervised classification model we decided to use a simple, lightweight neural network model, the *Multilayer Perceptron* (MLP) [1]. The MLP classifier will be used for the indoor-outdoor image classification task. The goal of the supervised learning analysis is to strengthen the interpretation of the unsupervised learning one through the evaluation metrics used for assessing the performance of the MLP classifier. We expect the results of the unsupervised learning analysis (Sect. 3.3) to be correlated with the results of the MLP classifier, i.e. higher performance for MLP to be obtained for the feature set providing the best clustering using t-SNE.

Four evaluation metrics, usually used in the supervised learning literature, will be used for assessing the performance of the MLP classifier [4]: *accuracy* (Acc), *recall* or *sensitivity* (Sens), *specificity* (Spec) and *Area under the ROC curve* (AUC). All these measures range from 0 to 1, higher values for the metrics corresponding to better classifiers. The literature reveals that AUC is one of the best metrics used for measuring the performance of supervised classifiers, particularly for imbalanced data sets.

4 Results and Discussion

This section presents and analyzes the experimental results obtained by applying the methodology introduced in Sect. 3 on the DIODE data set described in Sect. 3.1. The experiments are conducted with the goal of answering research questions RQ1–RQ3, namely investigating the relevance of features extracted from depth maps in the context of indoor-outdoor image classification.

4.1 Experimental Setup

For both t-SNE and MLP we used the implementation from scikit-learn [11]. The version of the library we worked with is 0.22.2.post1. Regarding the DPT architecture used for automatic feature extraction, a resolution of 384×384 was used for the image and $m = 49152$ features were extracted after the encoder. For t-SNE the following parameters setting was used: a *perplexity* of 20, a learning rate of 3 (for obtaining a finer learning curve at the expense of slower convergence) and 1000 iterations.

For the supervised classifier, we used the MLP model with its default configuration from scikit-learn [11]. It uses 100 hidden layers, a batch size of 200, adam optimizer, ReLU activation function, a constant learning rate of 0.001 and we run the training for 200 epochs. For a thorough evaluation, we implemented the k-fold cross-validation testing methodology with $k = 10$. Therefore, we took the subset and split it in 10 batches, 9 of which we trained the models on and evaluated them on the remaining one. For each of the aforementioned performance metrics (Sect. 3.4) we reported the average value over the k folds, together with the 95% confidence interval (CI) of the mean, computed as $1.96 \cdot \sigma / \sqrt{k}$ (σ denotes the standard deviation of the values obtained during the k folds).

4.2   Results of the Unsupervised Learning Based Analysis

Figures 4, 5, 6 and 7 depict the 3D t-SNE visualization for the images represented with the four feature sets proposed in Sect. 3.2. For extracting the RGBD features (representation 1), four splits of the original image were used (i.e. $n = 1$). The t-SNE visualization using RGBD features (Fig. 4) depicts a good enough boundary region between the indoor and outdoor classes.

As we can see in Fig. 6, the DPT model trained for SS outputs a set of features with high relevance for indoor-outdoor classification as there are many object classes that are uniquely found only in indoor or outdoor settings. Concerning DE, the DPT model's features extracted from the encoder are less connected to the indoor-outdoor classification as there are fuzzier boundaries between the values of depth specific for each scene. Overall, Fig. 7 presents the best separation, having more distant and compact clusters with a better boundary region, benefiting of both semantic cues and depth augmentation.

Table 1 depicts the values for the *Prec* measure introduced in Sect. 3.3 computed for the t-SNE visualizations from Figs. 4, 5, 6 and 7. The best and the second best *Prec* values are highlighted. The values are perfectly correlated with the visual interpretation of the t-SNE mappings: the most accurate t-SNE visualization, providing a precision of 0.957, is obtained using features learned by the encoder of DPT trained on SS depth-augmented features, followed by the features learned by the DPT models trained for SS. As Table 1 and Figs. 4, 5, 6 and 7 present, our proposed method of augmenting RGB images with Depth information surpasses the baseline DPT-SS approach. Moreover, the RGBD aggregated features perform better than the DE pretrained DPT model. A baseline for the RGBD approach was not included as RGB aggregated features proved themselves to yield results too close to random guessing as our extensive experiments suggested.

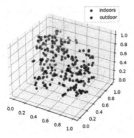

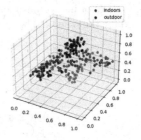

Fig. 4. t-SNE for RGBD representation with 4 splits.

Fig. 5. t-SNE of DPT DE learned features.

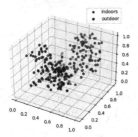

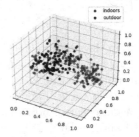

Fig. 6. t-SNE of DPT SS learned features.

Fig. 7. t-SNE for DPT encoder SS depth-augmented features.

Table 1. *Prec* values for the t-SNE transformations depicted in Figs. 4, 5, 6 and 7.

Measure	RGBD features (4 splits)	DPT DE learned features	DPT SS learned features	DPT SS depth augmented features
Prec	0.769	0.729	**0.945**	**0.957**

To conclude, the unsupervised learning based analysis previously conducted reveals that the best features are those learned by the encoder of DPT trained on SS depth-augmented features.

4.3 Results of the Supervised Learning Based Analysis

According to the methodology introduced in Sect. 3.4, the MLP classifier is applied on the DIODE data set with the aim of reinforcing the results of the t-SNE analysis conducted in Sect. 4.2. Table 2 presents the performance of the classifier for the feature sets introduced in Sect. 3.2 in terms of the evaluation metrics described in Sect. 3.4. In addition to the four feature sets introduced in Sect. 3.2, we also considered the RGB representation of an image, which is similar to the RGBD one but ignoring the Depth feature. Thus, for an image splitted in 4^n sub-images (as described in Sect. 3.2), a vector of size 3×4^n is built by concatenating, the average R, G, and B values for each sub-image. The best values are highlighted in Table 2, for each performance measure.

Table 2. Results of indoor-outdoor supervised classification on DIODE data set. 95% CIs are used for the results. The DPT encoder features are used in all the experiments.

Features	# Splits (n)	Acc	AUC	Spec	Sens
RGB	0	0.692 ± 0.077	0.525 ± 0.056	0.980 ± 0.028	0.070 ± 0.121
	1	0.688 ± 0.064	0.517 ± 0.022	**0.989 ± 0.014**	0.046 ± 0.049
	2	0.669 ± 0.049	0.545 ± 0.048	0.912 ± 0.068	0.163 ± 0.136
RGBD	0	**0.880 ± 0.039**	0.858 ± 0.041	0.898 ± 0.058	0.817 ± 0.081
	1	0.876 ± 0.043	**0.862 ± 0.044**	0.894 ± 0.046	0.829 ± 0.063
	2	0.838 ± 0.044	0.826 ± 0.053	0.848 ± 0.060	0.804 ± 0.099
DPT-DE	0	0.823 ± 0.131	0.831 ± 0.076	0.812 ± 0.185	0.850 ± 0.069
DPT-SS	0	**0.950 ± 0.027**	**0.942 ± 0.029**	0.969 ± 0.034	**0.915 ± 0.053**
DPT-SS+D	0	**0.961 ± 0.015**	**0.956 ± 0.021**	**0.970 ± 0.019**	**0.941 ± 0.041**

As seen in the experiments we performed, the results of the supervised classification using the MLP model are highly correlated with the unsupervised learning findings presented in Sect. 4.2. We observe a perfect correlation between the values for AUC (Table 2) and the values for *Prec* (Table 1), as the feature sets in the decreasing order of both AUC and *Prec* are: (1) DPT-SS+D; (2) DPT-SS; (3) RGBD and (4) DPT-DE.

Table 2 reveals that the best performance of the MLP classifier, in terms of AUC, as highlighted by the t-SNE analysis, is obtained using features automatically extracted from depth-augmented images by the DPT model trained on SS (DPT-SS+D feature set). By using this representation, an AUC of 0.956 and an accuracy of 0.961 have been reached. One may also observe that the second best performance in terms of AUC and accuracy is obtained using the features learned by DPT trained for SS.

As expected, in case of RGB features, the performance is poor, it did not surpass 70% in accuracy and the AUC metric is a little better than random guessing. Nevertheless, by adding the Depth feature (RGBD), the performance is significantly increased (88% accuracy) while being consistent and reliable as the AUC metric suggests. However, what is somehow surprising is that the third best AUC and accuracy (highlighted in red) are achieved by using RGBD features, surpassing the performance obtained using features learned by DPT trained on DE. The performance for RGBD representation is only 8%–9% lower than the best performance obtained using the features learned by DPT trained on SS. Thus, a good enough performance is achievable using RGBD features, but with a significantly reduced computational cost.

It has to be noted that neural networks learn very different features when comparing DE to SS. That happens because SS is a classification problem and it does not need learning the camera pose or its localisation in the scene context. The features learned by SS models consist of different patterns for predicting and localising the regions relevant objects are situated in. However, it does not necessarily need to know about depth information, as the most important features lay within the semantic regions. The results reveal that the solely learned depth cues do not help the indoor-outdoor classification as much as the semantic information about the present regions in the images.

Even though a direct comparison to the literature is somewhat difficult, due to the recent nature of the DIODE data set, our top accuracy (96%) surpasses others reported on the indoor-outdoor classification task (up to 93.71%), obtained from similar principles of selecting features and feeding them into a classifier, albeit on different data sets.

Moreover, the accuracy of MLP with RGBD features (88%) outperforms classical machine learning classifiers already applied in the literature (accuracy ranging from 81.55% to 87.70%, as shown in Sect. 2). Additionally, it is less computationally expensive overall compared to other work, as it aggregates features in a single step using basic mathematical operators from the images then inputs them into a lightweight MLP model. Using the RGBD features, we tried maximising the trade-off between cost and performance.

To summarise, there is a clear improvement obtained using depth-maps features. In addition, a main benefit of the features extracted from depth-maps (i.e. the RGBD representation) is that a good performance is obtained using a lightweight model (MLP) but using less features and parameters compared to other models, such as DPT. Additionally, the learning model requires low memory and computational cost compared to other deep learning methods, being a significant increase in performance when enhancing RGB information with depth cues. Moreover, the results have shown the benefits transfer learning brings in the context of our task of choice, as both pretrained DPT models perform well, especially the SS one when using depth augmented features. DPT proved itself to be a good platform for future research thanks to its ability to learn more contextual information.

5   Conclusions and Future Work

We have conducted in this paper a study towards determining the relevance of depth maps in the context of indoor-outdoor image classification. Four feature sets for characterizing the images were introduced and their relevance for the visual task of indoor-outdoor classification was analyzed. Among the proposed feature sets, one was manually engineered and defined based on RGB information and features extracted from depth-maps, while the other feature sets were automatically learned from raw images using a deep learning model. The advantage of depth-maps in the context of indoor-outdoor image classification has been empirically proven through experiments performed on DIODE data set, using both ML and DL models.

The research questions addressed in Sect. 1 were answered. The four feature sets proposed in this paper serve as a good proof of concept in what regards the addition of depth-maps information to the RGB images. Our handcrafted RGBD set of features brought a significant improvement compared to the RGB one for indoor-outdoor image classification. As we have experimentally proven, a more granular feature extraction method is better but up to a point, as we faced incomplete data that made the learning process harder.

Concerning the unsupervised based learning methods, we can confidently say that the t-SNE proved itself as a trustworthy means of anticipating the supervised results as we have seen in the comparative study on the proposed feature sets. Each method presented has its strengths, whether it's the computational efficiency or the overall performance and consistency. Nevertheless, the accuracy reached using so few features on the handcrafted RGBD feature set is remarkable, competing even with DL models. Eventually, the automatically learned features performed better because there were in a larger number, therefore the greater possibility of more patterns to be found and they had the flexibility of following their own learned rules instead of handcrafted ones. Moreover, we have proven the *transfer learning* usefulness of SS learned features in the context of our problem of choice.

Future work may refer to better a understanding of the learning patterns of SS and DE deep learning models in the context of transfer learning so that we could identify other domains of interest and adapt the studied problem of indoor-outdoor classification to a more general one. We are further aiming to extend our study to multiple data sets, using a wider variety of scenes, for a better validation of the current findings.

Acknowledgment. This work was supported by a grant of the Ministry of Research, Innovation and Digitization, CNCS/CCCDI—UEFISCDI, project number PN-III-P4-ID-PCE-2020-0800, within PNCDI III. The first author acknowledges the financial support received from Babeş-Bolyai University through the special scholarship for scientific activity for the academic year 2020–2021. The authors would like to thank the anonymous reviewers for their useful suggestions and comments that helped to improve the paper and the presentation.

References

1. Abirami, S., Chitra, P.: Energy-efficient edge based real-time healthcare support system. Adv. Comput. **117**(1), 339–368 (2020)
2. Bhoi, A.: Monocular depth estimation: a survey. CoRR abs/1901.09402 (2019). http://arxiv.org/abs/1901.09402
3. Cvetkovic, S., Nikolic, S., Ilic, S.: Effective combining of color and texture descriptors for indoor-outdoor image classification. Facta Universitatis Ser. Electron. Energ. **27**, 399–410 (2014). https://doi.org/10.2298/FUEE1403399C
4. Gu, Q., Zhu, L., Cai, Z.: Evaluation measures of the classification performance of imbalanced data sets. In: Cai, Z., Li, Z., Kang, Z., Liu, Y. (eds.) ISICA 2009. CCIS, vol. 51, pp. 461–471. Springer, Heidelberg (2009). https://doi.org/10.1007/978-3-642-04962-0_53
5. Kumari, S., Jha, R.R., Bhavsar, A., Nigam, A.: Indoor–outdoor scene classification with residual convolutional neural network. In: Chaudhuri, B.B., Nakagawa, M., Khanna, P., Kumar, S. (eds.) Proceedings of 3rd International Conference on Computer Vision and Image Processing. AISC, vol. 1024, pp. 325–337. Springer, Singapore (2020). https://doi.org/10.1007/978-981-32-9291-8_26
6. Lee, J.H., Han, M., Ko, D.W., Suh, I.H.: From big to small: multi-scale local planar guidance for monocular depth estimation. CoRR abs/1907.10326 (2019). http://arxiv.org/abs/1907.10326

7. van der Maaten, L., Hinton, G.: Visualizing data using t-SNE. J. Mach. Learn. Res. **9**, 2579–2605 (2008)
8. Martin, B.: Chapter 6 - sampling distributions associated with the normal distribution. In: Martin, B. (ed.) Statistics for Physical Science, pp. 105–122. Academic Press, Boston (2012)
9. Raja, R., Roomi, S.M.M., Dharmalakshmi, D., Rohini, S.: Classification of indoor/outdoor scene. In: 2013 IEEE International Conference on Computational Intelligence and Computing Research, pp. 1–4 (2013)
10. Ranftl, R., Bochkovskiy, A., Koltun, V.: Vision transformers for dense prediction. ArXiv preprint, pp. 1–15 (2021)
11. Scikit-learn: Machine learning in Python (2021). http://scikit-learn.org/stable/
12. Tahir, W., Majeed, A., Rehman, T.: Indoor/outdoor image classification using gist image features and neural network classifiers. In: 12th International Conference on High-capacity Optical Networks and Emerging Technologies, pp. 1–5 (2015)
13. Tong, Z., Shi, D., Yan, B., Wei, J.: A review of indoor-outdoor scene classification. In: Proceedings of the 2017 2nd International Conference on Control, Automation and Artificial Intelligence (CAAI 2017), pp. 469–474. Atlantis Press, June 2017
14. Vasiljevic, I., et al.: DIODE: a dense indoor and outdoor depth dataset. CoRR abs/1908.00463, 1–8 (2019)
15. Velswamy, R., Devadass, S., Velswamy, K., Venugopal, J.: Indoor and outdoor image classification: a mixture of brightness, straight line, euclidean shapes and recursive shapes based approach. Int. J. Intell. Unmanned Syst. (2019, ahead-of-print). https://doi.org/10.1108/IJIUS-04-2019-0024
16. Yeo, W.H., Heo, Y.J., Choi, Y.J., Kim, B.G.: Place classification algorithm based on semantic segmented objects. Appl. Sci. **10**(24) (2020). Article ID = 9069
17. Zhou, B., Zhao, H., Puig, X., Fidler, S., Barriuso, A., Torralba, A.: Scene parsing through ADE20K dataset. In: 2017 IEEE Conference on Computer Vision and Pattern Recognition, CVPR, pp. 5122–5130. IEEE Computer Society (2017)

Object Detection on TPU Accelerated Embedded Devices

Bertalan Kovács[1]([✉])[iD], Anders D. Henriksen[2], Jonathan Dyssel Stets[2][iD],
and Lazaros Nalpantidis[1][iD]

[1] Technical University of Denmark, Lyngby, Denmark
lanalpa@elektro.dtu.dk
[2] ProInvent A/S, Hørsholm, Denmark
{ahe,jds}@proinvent.dk

Abstract. Modern edge devices are capable of onboard processing of computational heavy tasks, such as artificial intelligence-driven computer vision. An increasing number of deep learning-based object detection networks are frequently proposed with lightweight structures to be deployed on mobile platforms without the need for cloud computing. Comparing these networks is challenging due to the variety in hardware and frameworks and because of different model complexity. This paper investigates models that can be deployed on cross-functional single-board computers without utilizing the power of GPUs. This paves the way towards performing accurate, cheap, and fast object detection, even suited for industrial applications within Industry 4.0. Four state-of-the-art neural networks are trained via transfer learning, then deployed and tested on the Raspberry Pi 4B and the Coral Edge TPU accelerator from Google as a co-processor. The comparison of the models focuses on the inference time, the versatility of the deployment, training, and finally the accuracy of the retrained networks on a selection of datasets with different feature characteristics.

Our code can be found in the following repository: https://github.com/kberci/Deep-Learning-based-Object-Detection.

Keywords: Object detection · Coral Edge TPU · Transfer learning

1 Introduction

Industry 4.0 is a digital transformation of industrial processes to create "smart factories". It utilizes sensor data, machine learning, and the Internet of Things (IoT). It often employs the power and scalability of cloud computing platforms. However, sending a large amount of data to the cloud can become problematic in terms of speed, bandwidth, security, and cost of transmission or storage. This can be overcome by edge computing which can host and control local tasks autonomously on an embedded device.

Computer vision is an important field within the industry that often relies on smart cameras to perform part inspection and gauging or robot guidance [12].

© Springer Nature Switzerland AG 2021
M. Vincze et al. (Eds.): ICVS 2021, LNCS 12899, pp. 82–92, 2021.
https://doi.org/10.1007/978-3-030-87156-7_7

These smart cameras are embedded devices with a built-in camera sensor and a small computer capable of running the manufacturer's image library. However, the devices currently available on the market have limited deep learning capabilities; they lack the ability for customization by using closed source software or limited APIs. Moreover, they are expensive.

Many hardware companies have put great efforts to provide alternative edge devices to smart cameras to instigate engineers assembling cheaper and state-of-the-art (SOTA) vision solutions. These edge devices always bring a tradeoff between being versatile, having reliable industrial variants, small size, cheap price, and low power consumption. Google's Coral Edge TPU is one of the devices that has managed to bring a favorable combination of the mentioned attributes to inference neural networks. It can be used as a co-processor attached to Single Board Computers such as a Raspberry Pi 4B (RPi4). This hardware combination is especially promising as several industrial AI gateways have already appeared which gives a great upscaling opportunity.

One of the biggest challenges is to utilize the hardware with the newest neural network architectures. For this reason, four recent object detection networks are chosen to be deployed on the RPi4 equipped with Google's Coral Edge TPU co-processor: MobileNetV2 + SSDLite [14], MobileDet [21], Tiny-YOLOv4 [1], and YOLOv5[1]. All models are pretrained on the Common Objects in Context (COCO) dataset [7]. Object detection in industrial applications often requires different feature characteristics which challenge the pretrained networks. Therefore, two different datasets are selected to use for retraining the four detection networks via transfer learning. One has similar, while the second has different feature characteristics, compared to the original COCO dataset.

The main contribution of this paper is to evaluate and analyze the performance of the four state-of-the-art networks for object detection on the selected hardware (RPi4 with Coral Edge TPU). More precisely, we investigate how efficient their implementations are and how effective they are in learning new datasets. The remaining of this paper is organized as follows: Sect. 2 presents the related works to the benchmarking and performance of similar edge devices as well as introduces the SOTA detection networks. Sect. 3 will describe the methodology and Sect. 4 contains the experimental results for both the deployment and latency as well as the transfer learning and accuracy. This is followed by the conclusion in Sect. 5.

2   Related Works

2.1   Mobile Object Detectors

Several survey and review papers examine the most important models and milestones of object detection from the last years [8,9,19]. The first large milestone of deep learning-based object detection is the winning of AlexNet at the ImageNet

---

[1] Git repository: https://github.com/ultralytics/yolov5.

Large Scale Visual Recognition Challenge (ILSVRC) in 2012 [6]. It was the starting point for the evolution of two-stage detectors. Their operation consists of a proposal generation followed by the prediction, which is the classification of the proposed areas of potential objects. The later and more novel one-stage detectors classify each region of interest and label them as either objects or backgrounds with a unified detection pipeline. In the last years, researchers gave extra focus to mobile networks which aim to develop smaller networks with short inference time and high accuracy. Figure 1 illustrates the most important one-stage networks of the last three years, which were considered to be compared against each other in this paper.

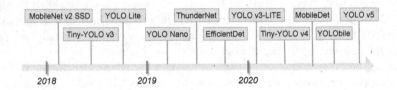

Fig. 1. Recent history of mobile object detection networks

After reviewing them, the following four have been selected:

MobileNetV2 + SSDLite was released in 2018 as an improved version of the previous MobileNet classification network together with a new detection framework called SSDLite [14]. The key feature of the network is the inverted residual structure. The residual connection is placed between the bottleneck layer as an expansion layer, to introduce nonlinearity by a depthwise convolution.

Tiny-YOLOv4 is implemented in the Darknet framework. It was created as a fast-variant of YOLOv4 [1] which was published in April 2020. YOLOv4 is famous for its bag of freebies (BoF) and the bag of specials (BoS). BoF is increasing the accuracy by keeping the same inference time while BoS is improving the accuracy, however, causing a minor inference cost.

MobileDet is also dated from April 2020 [21], implemented in TensorFlow. It improves the performance of non-GPU devices (i.e., CPU, DSP, and Edge TPU). The models are built by putting regular convolutions in the search space and then effectively placing them into the network as an outcome of neural architecture search. They get a family of models that outperform most of the existing solutions that can be deployed on the above-mentioned three hardware platforms.

YOLOv5 was released in June 2020, by Glenn Jocher. It is an unofficial naming, as it has no research papers published. Despite there being no academic publication, Jocher is acknowledged as the creator of mosaic augmentation in the YOLOv4 paper. It is a PyTorch implementation, based on the YOLOv3 model [13] with the improved augmentation and auto-learning bounding box anchors. The motivation for using it is to compare its performance with other published models.

2.2   Embedded Deep Learning

A number of recent works have been considered that either uses the Coral TPU as hardware or constitute the SOTA regarding object detection networks deployed on other embedded devices. These works are summarized in Table 1.

Table 1. SOTA regarding papers on embedded object detection

Paper	Published	Hardware	Neural network	Main motivation
[3]	2020 Jun	Coral TPU + RPi4	-	Application
[17]	2020 Sept	IPC, Xavier AGX, Xilinx Zynq	YOLOv3, CenterNet, MobilenetV2 + SSDLite	Hardware, network benchmark
[11]	2020 Oct	Coral Dev Board	MobileNetV2 + SSDLite	Application
[16]	2020 Nov	Drive PX2	YOLOv2-v5, EfficientDet 0-7	Network benchmark
[10]	2020 Nov	Jetson TX2	EfficientDet Lite, YOLOv3	Application
[5]	2020 Dec	Xavier AGX, NCS2, Coral TPU	GoogleNet, AlexNet	Hardware benchmark
[4]	2021 Mar	Coral TPU	Classification network	Application
Own	-	Coral TPU + RPi4	MobileNetV2 + SSDLite, MobileDet, YOLOv4-v5	Hardware validation, network benchmark

The works of [3–5, 11] use the Coral TPU to deploy neural networks as part of a particular application such as face mask detection. They use either older detection networks or classification, therefore none of them investigates the Coral TPU with SOTA models. On the other hand, [10, 16, 17] present broader benchmarks through various networks. However, they do not deploy them on the Coral device. It can be seen that there is no work that benchmarks the selected four object detection networks on the Coral TPU. There is also no work on investigating the network accuracy of the four detection networks on multiple datasets besides latency.

3   Methodology

Training and inference of the four object detection networks use different frameworks and hardware. Regarding training, the COCO dataset was used to obtain the pretrained models which are further trained on two new datasets via transfer learning. TensorFlow, PyTorch, and Darknet are used as frameworks to train the four models on Google Cloud's Tesla P100 and V100 GPUs on the two selected datasets. The trained models run on the inference hardware (RPi4), which can be extended with an accelerator for faster speed (Edge TPU). The inference engine (TensorFlow Lite) is used as the interface that enables running the network on the given hardware architecture. Figure 2 shows these blocks that are needed for the benchmark.

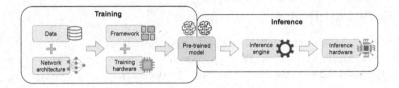

Fig. 2. System elements for training and inference

3.1   Framework and Quantization

TPU only runs TensorFlow Lite (TFLite) runtime, therefore all models have to be converted to the corresponding representation. The purpose of the conversion is to accelerate the running time as well as to reduce the model size. TFLite models can natively run on the RPi4.

The weights in the TFLite model have to be converted into an 8-bit integer fixed format to obtain the Edge TPU model. This process is called quantization which is one of the ways optimizing neural networks to reduce inference time and model size without significant accuracy loss.

There are two major ways of performing quantization on a neural network:

1. Quantization Aware Training: It emulates inference-time quantization by inserting fake-quantization nodes during the full-precision training procedure. This way, the model learns robust parameters against the loss of precision invoked with quantization.
2. Post Training Quantization: Quantizing already-trained float models to accelerate inference and reduce model size.

Further compiling is needed to obtain the Edge TPU compatible file from the 8-bit quantized representation. The process is done by mapping operations to the Edge TPU. Google's TPU has a limited number of operations that can be mapped. If the compiler finds an unsupported one, it stops the process and leaves two groups of nodes. One contains all mapped operations as one custom node in the graph which is executed on the TPU during inference. The other contains the others as separated nodes that will be executed on the CPU.

There are three possible outcomes of the pipeline:

1. All operations are converted to integer representation and all of them are supported types by the Edge TPU, therefore they are all mapped.
2. All operations are converted to integer format, however, some of them are not supported on the Edge TPU. The compiler will output a graph with two groups of nodes that can still run (slower) on the Edge TPU.
3. Some operations cannot be converted to integer representation, therefore the compiler does not consider the model quantized and the model cannot be used with the TPU.

The last option is to use quantization-aware pretrained models if there is any available. This achieves the highest accuracy and represents the most simple process.

3.2 Datasets

The goal with new datasets is to investigate how well the selected networks can achieve generalization and which ones are resistant to overfitting.

To achieve this, we use the COCO dataset as the standard dataset and the most popular evaluation frame for detection networks. We also select two additional datasets with different feature characteristics from the database of Northeastern University (NEU): The **Hard Hat Workers Dataset** [20] and the **Surface Defect Database** [2].

COCO [7] is an object detection dataset published in 2014. It contains objects in a wide range of scales, therefore it forces detection algorithms to be able to detect small size objects on an image. It contains around 328000 images in 80 categories.

The attributes of the additional datasets are summarized in Table 2.

Table 2. Summary of the two selected datasets: Hard Hat Workers and NEU Surface Defect Database

	Hard hat workers	NEU surface defect database
Source:	Northeastern University [20]	Northeastern University [2]
Publication date:	January 2019	November 2013.
Number of images:	7041	1800
Number of classes:	3	6
Class balance:	Imbalanced	Balanced
Class names:	Helmet, head, person	Rolled-in scale, patches, crazing, pitted surface, inclusion, scratches
Image size:	Varying	200×200
Coloring:	RGB, 3-channel	Grayscale, 1-channel

The Hard Hat Workers dataset is chosen because of the similar characteristics of a head and helmet to the COCO dataset on which the pretrained models were trained. The models are expected to be able to transfer the already known features.

The NEU Surface Defect Database is chosen because the objects consist of defective areas instead of clear shapes (except scratches). This gives rise to the question of whether the COCO object features can be transferred to the textural domain. It also challenges the models because of the fixed image size of 200×200 pixels. This is smaller than all of the network inputs. Upsampling is ensuring the proper input size, which reduces the resolution of the images and leaves the full capacity of the networks unused. The last challenge is that the dataset has grayscale images. Networks are developed to process 3-channel image inputs, therefore the grayscale 1-channel pictures reduce the available information for the learning process.

3.3   Transfer Learning

Transfer learning aims to study the transferability and co-adaptation phenomena among the four selected models. The accuracy of all models is known on the COCO dataset, therefore the goal is to measure their effectiveness on other datasets.

Full model retraining is used where the whole model is retrained, updating all layers. The pretrained model provides the initial knowledge of the network. It gives higher accuracy than the last layer-only method at the cost of additional training time. Furthermore, it requires more data samples to avoid overfitting.

The used accuracy metric in this paper is the so-called COCO metric that can be written as by mean Average Precision (mAP), COCO mAP, or mAP@.5:.05:.95. It uses ten Intersection over Union (IoU) values from $\Omega = 0.5$ to $\Omega = 0.95$, incremented by 0.05. For each Ω value, the mAP is calculated over all categories, finally, the average is calculated among all Ω.

4   Evaluation

4.1   Inference Time

All four models are compiled into quantized 8-bit TPU versions but with a different number of operations that cannot be mapped. Table 3 shows the ratio between the two defined partitions with the corresponding inference speed. It also shows the inference time of the TFLite models on the RPi4 as well as the inference time of the compiled representations with partly mapped operations running on the co-processor.

Table 3. Number of mapped operations for CPU and TPU after compiling, along with the corresponding inference times

	MobileNetV2 + SSDLite	MobileDet	Tiny-YOLOv4	YOLOv5s
TPU operations:	108/111	204/205	2/193	1/197
CPU operations:	3/111	1/205	191/193	196/197
Running time RPi4 (ms):	432.3	231.6	526.2	587.5
Running time RPi4 with TPU (ms):	16.4	17.7	465.3	779.6

All four models are converted to TFLite and run on the RPi4. MobileDet prevails in inference time with ~ 4.6 FPS which can already be useful in many industrial scenarios (e.g. fault inspection).

All four models are attempted to be compiled for the Edge TPU. The number of mapped operations explains the difference in speedup for the four models. There is an immense acceleration for the mobile models where almost all operations are successfully mapped. The running time of the MobileNetV2 + SSDLite and MobileDet models decrease to 5.5% and 7.6% respectively. The two models from the YOLO family are successfully deployed, however, with almost no mapped operations, resulting in minor changes in the execution time.

4.2   Accuracy

The four models are retrained on both the Hard Hat and the Surface Defect datasets. Figure 3 shows the comparison between the custom and the original COCO training accuracies.

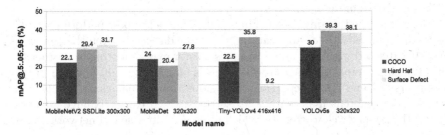

Fig. 3. Accuracy comparison among four object detection networks, between three datasets

YOLOv5s dominates regarding effectiveness. It shows a flexible behavior in learning different feature domains. It wins both the textural and COCO-similar feature learning.

It can be observed that the mobile networks are the only models that achieve their best results on the Surface Defect dataset. This can also be an argument for the simplicity of the low-resolution, grayscale images. Deeper networks with more parameters overfit while the more shallow mobile-optimized two networks adapt their weight easier compared to the more challenging features in the Hard Hat dataset. Their example demonstrates that shallow networks are suitable choices for datasets containing low-resolution simple images.

Example predictions can be observed in Fig. 4 from the YOLOv5s network, which performs the best on both custom datasets.

(a) Hard Hat dataset   (b) Surface Defect dataset

Fig. 4. Example of ground truth images (left) and bounding box predictions (right) on the two custom datasets from the YOLOv5s network

4.3   Versatility and Training Speed

Based on the findings of this paper, the two mobile networks are the only models that can be accelerated by the Edge TPU. Furthermore, they both come from the model family which is directly optimized to run inference on CPU and TPU devices. This can change in the future with the improvement of the Coral Edge TPU to execute more operations.

Regarding the training speed, Tiny-YOLOv4 has the best performance. This can be a useful feature for applications where the dataset is often changed or frequently extended with new image samples. Faster experimenting is another benefit of having a rapid training process. This is an advantage in research projects at universities and R&D departments of industrial companies. It enables iterative tests of different hyperparameter settings which can be a huge advantage due to the try-error characteristic which often describes neural network training processes.

4.4   Overall Performance

A comprehensive comparison is made between the four models by measuring the strengths and weaknesses of each object detection network. It is summarized in Fig. 5. The different perspectives are selected and evaluated by targeting deployment on embedded devices.

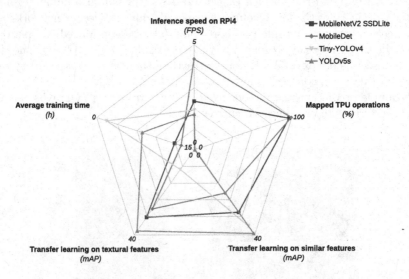

Fig. 5. General comparison among the four object detection models from various perspectives (the farther from the center of the diagram is better)

5 Conclusion

The most recent and most SOTA mobile object detection networks are examined: MobileNetV2 + SSDLite, MobileDet, Tiny-YOLOv4, and YOLOv5s; together with promising embedded hardware: RPi4 with an Edge TPU accelerator co-processor running TFLite.

All models are converted to a TFLite format and deployed on the RPi4 where MobileDet achieved the fastest running time ($\sim$4.6 FPS). Integer 8-bit representations are converted and the Edge TPU compatible formats are compiled for all detector models. Most of the neural network computations are successfully mapped to the Edge TPU for the case of the two mobile networks, while the YOLO models have a high number of unmappable operations. MobileNetV2 + SSDLite and MobileDet networks achieve the fastest inference time with $\sim$ 65FPS. The achieved speed demonstrates the power and topicality of the selected system components to run object detection on embedded devices with low latency.

All networks accomplish transfer learning on two datasets: the Hard Hat Workers and the Surface Defect databases. The most accurate model performance is achieved by the YOLOv5s model. The larger deep networks (the two YOLO models) are found to learn better the more complex but also more similar features to the original dataset of the pretrained models, while the shallow mobile networks learn simpler textural features easier.

The field of mobile object detection is rapidly progressing and new networks are constantly being presented, such as Scaled-YOLOv4 [18] and EfficientDet-Lite0 [15]. Thus, future updates of our work should be monitoring and including such new promising networks.

Acknowledgements. The authors would like to thank ProInvent A/S for its support.

References

1. Bochkovskiy, A., Wang, C.Y., Liao, H.Y.M.: YOLOv4: optimal speed and accuracy of object detection. arXiv preprint arXiv:2004.10934 (2020)
2. Dong, H., Song, K., He, Y., Xu, J., Yan, Y., Meng, Q.: PGA-Net: pyramid feature fusion and global context attention network for automated surface defect detection. IEEE Trans. Ind. Inform. **16**(12), 7448–7458 (2019)
3. Ghosh, A., Al Mahmud, S.A., Uday, T.I.R., Farid, D.M.: Assistive technology for visually impaired using tensor flow object detection in raspberry Pi and coral USB accelerator. In: 2020 IEEE Region 10 Symposium (TENSYMP), pp. 186–189. IEEE (2020)
4. Hosseininoorbin, S., Layeghy, S., Sarhan, M., Jurdak, R., Portmann, M.: Exploring edge TPU for network intrusion detection in IoT. arXiv preprint arXiv:2103.16295 (2021)
5. Kljucaric, L., Johnson, A., George, A.D.: Architectural analysis of deep learning on edge accelerators. In: 2020 IEEE High Performance Extreme Computing Conference (HPEC), pp. 1–7. IEEE (2020)

6. Krizhevsky, A., Sutskever, I., Hinton, G.E.: Imagenet classification with deep convolutional neural networks. Commun. ACM **60**(6), 84–90 (2017)
7. Lin, T., Maire, M., et al.: Microsoft COCO: common objects in context. CoRR abs/1405.0312 (2014), http://arxiv.org/abs/1405.0312
8. Liu, L., et al.: Deep learning for generic object detection: a survey. Int. J. Comput. Vis. **128**(2), 261–318 (2020)
9. Murthy, C.B., Hashmi, M.F., Bokde, N.D., Geem, Z.W.: Investigations of object detection in images/videos using various deep learning techniques and embedded platforms–A comprehensive review. Appl. Sci. **10**(9), 3280 (2020)
10. Nguyen, H.H., Tran, D.N.N., Jeon, J.W.: Towards real-time vehicle detection on edge devices with Nvidia Jetson TX2. In: 2020 IEEE International Conference on Consumer Electronics-Asia (ICCE-Asia), pp. 1–4. IEEE (2020)
11. Park, K., et al.: Real-time mask detection on google edge TPU. arXiv preprint arXiv:2010.04427 (2020)
12. Pedersen, M.R., et al.: Robot skills for manufacturing: from concept to industrial deployment. Robot. Comput-Integ. Manuf. **37**(282–291) (2015)
13. Redmon, J., Farhadi, A.: YOLOv3: an incremental improvement. arXiv preprint arXiv:1804.02767 (2018)
14. Sandler, M., Howard, A., Zhu, M., Zhmoginov, A., Chen, L.C.: MobileNetV2: Inverted residuals and linear bottlenecks. In: Proceedings of the IEEE Conference on Computer Vision and Pattern Recognition, pp. 4510–4520, January 2018
15. Tan, M., Pang, R., Le, Q.V.: EfficientDet: scalable and efficient object detection (2020)
16. Tran, D.N.N., Nguyen, H.H., Pham, L.H., Jeon, J.W.: Object detection with deep learning on drive PX2. In: 2020 IEEE International Conference on Consumer Electronics-Asia (ICCE-Asia), pp. 1–4. IEEE (2020)
17. Verucchi, M., et al.: A Systematic assessment of embedded neural networks for object detection. In: 2020 25th IEEE International Conference on Emerging Technologies and Factory Automation (ETFA). vol. 1, pp. 937–944. IEEE (2020)
18. Wang, C.Y., Bochkovskiy, A., Liao, H.Y.M.: Scaled-YOLOv4: Scaling Cross Stage Partial Network (2021)
19. Wu, X., Sahoo, D., Hoi, S.C.: Recent advances in deep learning for object detection. Neurocomputing **396**, 39–64 (2020)
20. Xie, L.: Hardhat (2019). https://doi.org/10.7910/DVN/7CBGOS, https://doi.org/10.7910/DVN/7CBGOS
21. Xiong, Y., et al.: MobileDets: searching for object detection architectures for mobile accelerators. arXiv preprint arXiv:2004.14525, July 2020

Tackling Inter-class Similarity and Intra-class Variance for Microscopic Image-Based Classification

Aishwarya Venkataramanan[1,2,3]([⊠]) [iD], Martin Laviale[1,3] [iD], Cécile Figus[1],
Philippe Usseglio-Polatera[1] [iD], and Cédric Pradalier[2,3] [iD]

[1] Laboratoire Interdisciplinaire des Environnements Continentaux,
Université de Lorraine, Metz, France
venkatar1@univ-lorraine.fr
[2] GeorgiaTech Lorraine-International Research Lab Georgia Tech - CNRS IRL 2958,
Metz, France
[3] LTER-Zone Atelier Moselle, Lorraine, France

Abstract. Automatic classification of aquatic microorganisms is based on the morphological features extracted from individual images. The current works on their classification do not consider the inter-class similarity and intra-class variance that causes misclassification. We are particularly interested in the case where variance within a class occurs due to discrete visual changes in microscopic images. In this paper, we propose to account for it by partitioning the classes with high variance based on the visual features. Our algorithm automatically decides the optimal number of sub-classes to be created and consider each of them as a separate class for training. This way, the network learns finer-grained visual features. Our experiments on two databases of freshwater benthic diatoms and marine plankton show that our method can outperform the state-of-the-art approaches for classification of these aquatic microorganisms.

Keywords: Micro-organisms classification · Automatic clustering · Intra-class variance · Inter-class similarity

1 Introduction

Micro-organisms are key components of aquatic ecosystems and analysing their distribution is a central question in aquatic ecology. This often requires manual identification of organisms by a human expert using a microscope. Organisms are grouped into taxa based on morphological features which can present a huge diversity. The classification task often turns out to be time-consuming, tedious and sometimes requires a high-level of expertise. Thus, methods are being developed to automate the process [5,17]. Over the years, the automatic classification has evolved from traditional hand-crafted methods [2,16] to deep-learning-based ones [8,10]. While the methods using deep learning have shown improved performance, we show that they are not sufficient to learn fine-grained visual features for reliable classification [11].

M. Vincze et al. (Eds.): ICVS 2021, LNCS 12899, pp. 93–103, 2021.
https://doi.org/10.1007/978-3-030-87156-7_8

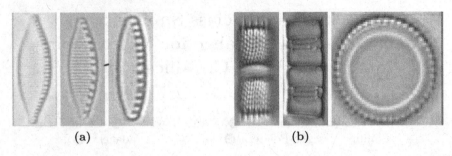

(a)   (b)

Fig. 1. Examples of diatom images usually misclassified due to high inter-class similarity (a) or intra-class variance (b). (a) Three different diatom species of the genera *Nitzschia*: *N. soratensis*, *N. subacicularis* and *N. costei*, from left to right. (b) A single diatom species *Aulacoseira pusilla* seen from the side or from the top, from left to right.

For this study, we consider the classification task of two typical aquatic microorganisms: freshwater benthic diatoms and marine plankton. Diatoms are unicellular micro-algae characterized by a highly ornamented silicified exoskeleton. Plankton includes a group of organisms drifting or floating in the water column, encompassing a large range of microbes, algae and larvae. Automated classification of these microscopic images is challenging notably due to two aspects: inter-class similarity and intra-class variance. Inter-class similarity occurs when objects belonging to different classes have visually similar appearance due to minute variations in the morphological features. Intra-class variance is when some objects belonging to the same class have drastically different appearances. This is prevalent in microscopic images due to the restrictions in view-points from which the images are acquired. Diatoms are typically imaged on permanent microscope slides: samples are treated chemically in order to remove organic materials and the diatom suspension is allowed to settle out, which restricts each organism to lie either on its side or top. While in planktons, after appropriate sub-sampling by size-selective filtration, images of live samples are acquired using a submersible imaging flow-cytometer, which ensures that every processed organisms are analysed individually. Indeed due to imaging constraints, the images acquired using these microscopy methods result in discrete view-points. Examples of diatoms with inter-class similarity and intra-class variance are shown in Fig. 1. Figure 1(a) shows the images of diatoms from three different classes that have similar appearance and are often confused by the classification network. Figure 1(b) shows the images from a single class, but taken from the side and top view. Here, the network fails to identify all of them as belonging to the same class.

An intuitive approach to tackle this problem would be to separate the feature embeddings of different classes by a distance so that the network can better differentiate them. This is known as metric-learning [4,15] and the principle behind it is to bring closer the feature embeddings of the objects belonging to the same class while pushing apart the embeddings of the objects belonging to different classes. This is effective for inter-class similarity, but does not impose any constraints on the intra-class variance. Hence, in this paper, we propose an algorithm that automatically clusters the instances within the high variance classes. Then the generated clusters are considered as independent classes while training. The clustering is based on the learned visual features and so, each cluster contains similar feature embeddings. In this way, the variance within each class is reduced, and the network can learn fine-grained features specific to them. Our technical contribution is that our algorithm automatically chooses the classes to be clustered and the optimal number of clusters to be generated. Finally, to handle the problem of inter-class similarity, we use triplet loss to increase the distance between the inter-class features. Experimental results on a diatom and plankton dataset show that by reducing the impact of intra-class variance and inter-class similarity, the network learns finer-grained features that improves the classification performance.

Our contributions in this paper can be summarised as follows: (1) We propose a method to address the problem of inter-class similarity and intra-class variance in fine-grained visual classification, particularly in the setting where the images within a class have contrasting appearance changes. (2) We apply our method to a real-world problem of diatom and plankton classification and show that our method has improved performance over the existing state-of-the-art approaches.

2 Related Work

Early methods of plankton and diatom classification relied on hand-crafted methods to extract features for classification. [17] uses multiple kernel learning to perform plankton classification. [5] is a pilot study on using image processing techniques to perform automatic detection of diatoms. [2] analyses different morphological and statistical descriptors to classify the diatoms. Although the hand-crafted based methods have been proven to be successful in identification, it is time-consuming to choose the appropriate features. Thus, the recent focus is on using deep learning to extract features automatically.

[14] develops a deep network model to exploit the translational and rotational symmetry in plankton images. [8] compares the performance of various deep neural networks for plankton and coral classification. [10] develops a combination of unsupervised and supervised learning to classify plankton images. However, none of these works consider the influence of intra-class variance and inter-class similarity on the classification performance.

Few methods have been proposed in the computer vision literature to handle intra-class variance and inter-class similarity for visual recognition. [7] uses split-and-merge to handle high intra-image and intra-class variations for celiac disease diagnosis. [3] considers the instances contributing to high intra-class variance as outliers. They use triplet loss with a weighting scheme where each instance is given a weight based on how representative they are of their class. [13] uses a Hadamard layer to minimise the intra-class variance. The one closely related to ours is [6], where they cluster the instances within each class into a set of pre-defined sub-classes (K classes) using K-Means clustering. They calculate two sets of triplet losses: one for the broader class instances and the other for the sub-class instances. The drawback with this approach for our application is that since K-Means is applied to all the classes and K is pre-defined, it could result in over or under-clustering. Contrary to their approach, our algorithm uses X-Means [12] and decides the classes to be clustered and the optimal number of clusters during training. X-Means is a variant of K-Means that can automatically decide the number of clusters to be created based on certain conditions such as Akaike information criterion (AIC) or Bayesian information criterion (BIC) scores.

3   Method

The proposed method considers the two challenges of aquatic microorganism classification: (1) inter-class similarity and (2) intra-class variance.

3.1   Inter-class Similarity

Inter-class similarity results in the network learning similar feature embeddings for the classes with similar-looking images. During inference, this causes confusion in differentiating between them. Along with the cross-entropy loss commonly used for classification networks, we use triplet loss to separate the feature embeddings between each class. The triplet loss tries to minimise the distance between the objects belonging to the same class while maximising the distance between the objects belonging to different classes in the feature space. This can be formulated as follows: Let x_a, x_p and x_n be the anchor, positive and negative image. Here x_a and x_p belong to the same class while x_n is from a different class. Let f be the function to obtain the feature embeddings of the images. The triplet loss is given by

$$L_{triplet} = max\{||f(x_a) - f(x_p)|| - ||f(x_a) - f(x_n)|| + \alpha, 0\} \qquad (1)$$

where α is the margin to separate the positive and negative images in the feature space. Our final loss is the sum of the cross-entropy loss and the triplet loss.

$$L_{total} = L_{cross-entropy} + L_{triplet} \qquad (2)$$

3.2   Intra-class Variance

The classification network fails to identify all the images as belonging to the same class when there is a high variance of data within the class. Our proposed method clusters the classes with high variance into sub-groups and consider these sub-groups as independent classes for classification.

We use X-Means since it automatically decides the clusters to be generated. However, it can sometimes generate non-optimal number of clusters. When there is over-clustering, there will be overlap of visual features between two or more

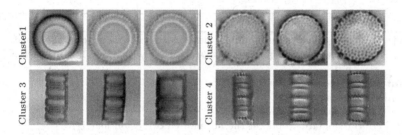

Fig. 2. Clusters generated based on the learned visual features for the diatom class *Aulacoseira pusilla*.

clusters. Considering these clusters as independent classes further aggravates the problem of inter-class similarity. Having a smaller number of clusters still doesn't solve the intra-class variance problem. Thus, the goal of our method is to find the optimal number of clusters to minimize both the inter-class similarity and intra-class variance. X-Means uses a parameter for the upper limit to the number of allowed clusters, and always generates clusters that are less than or equal to this value. Our algorithm decides this parameter for each class so that the optimal number of clusters is generated.

3.3 Training Algorithm

For every class in the data, we define a parameter `num-allowed-clusters`, which is the upper limit to the number of clusters that can be generated for that class. As the training progresses, `num-allowed-clusters` is adapted until it reaches the optimal value. There is a threshold to the maximum value that can be attained by `num-allowed-clusters` which is `max-clusters`. The overall training can be divided into the following steps and the process is repeated until the training converges: 1) Extract feature embeddings for the training images; 2) Cluster using X-Means; 3) Train the classification encoder network; 4) Perform validation and obtain the normalised confusion matrix; 5) Adjust `num-allowed-clusters` based on the confusion matrix.

In order to generate the clusters, we extract the feature embeddings of the images from the last fully-connected layer of a classification network pre-trained on the ImageNet dataset. X-Means uses these feature embeddings to cluster the images. At the beginning of training, we initialise `num-allowed-clusters` to 1 for all the classes, which is the same as training a standard classifier. However as the training progresses, we adapt `num-allowed-clusters` and X-Means generates clusters based on this value. These clusters are then considered as independent classes while training the network. Figure 2 shows an example of clusters generated for the diatom class *Aulacoseira pusilla*. The diatoms have been clustered based on the difference in view-point and the porosity. Since they are considered as independent classes, the network learns these intricate details which helps in fine-grained classification.

Algorithm 1: Training with clustering

Input: Training and validation data, `max-clusters`, `confusion-threshold`.
  Initialise number of clusters for each class with 1 and flag for each class
  with 0.
Output: Trained model
while *Not Converged* **do**
  Train the encoder network;
  Perform validation and get the normalised confusion matrix;
  Extract features of the images in the training data;
  for *each class* **do**
    if *false negative* > *confusion-threshold and flag=0* **then**
      Increase `num-allowed-clusters`. If the number of clusters reach the
      `max-allowed-clusters` set the flag to 1.
    else if *false negative* > *confusion-threshold and flag=1* **then**
      Decrease `num-allowed-clusters`. If the number of clusters reach 1
      then set the flag to 0.
    Generate the clusters and pseudo-labels using X-Means.

After every epoch of training, we obtain the normalised confusion matrix.
When the false-negative for a particular class is above `confusion-threshold`,
we increment `num-allowed-clusters` for that class. For our application, the
classification certainty of each class is important and so we use false-negatives to
optimize `num-allowed-clusters`. As the training progresses and when the false-
negatives is greater than the `confusion-threshold`, we increment `num-allowed`
`-clusters` until it reaches `max-clusters`. During the initial stages of the training, when the feature embeddings learned by the network are not fully refined,
the false negatives are relatively high for many of the classes. Thus the false
negatives of these classes will be above the `confusion-threshold` and the number of clusters may overshoot the optimal value. Thus we start decrementing
`num-allowed-clusters` until it reaches 1. This adaptation continues until the
optimal value is reached. The above process is repeated for every epoch until the
training converges. The summary of our algorithm is given in Algorithm 1.

4 Experiments

4.1 Datasets

We apply our method on two datasets:

Diatom Dataset. The diatom dataset consists of individual images of diatom
from three different public taxonomic atlases [1]. The dataset contains a total of
166 classes with a total of 9895 images.

WHOI-Plankton Dataset. [9] The WHOI plankton dataset consists of 3.4 million images spread across 70 classes. We considered only those classes that have at·least 50 images. Finally we obtained 38 classes and a total of 26612 images.

All the images were padded and resized to size 256 × 256. We used K-Fold cross-validation with K = 5.

4.2   Baselines

To evaluate our method we perform experiments on the following baselines:

1. **Standard Classification** - We use a state-of-the-art classification network pre-trained on ImageNet dataset and fine-tune to our dataset.
2. **Classification with triplet loss** - Along with the cross-entropy loss, we use the triplet loss. This method is done to study the impact of inter-class similarity on the classification performance.
3. **Classification with clustering** - This is our proposed clustering method, but using only the cross-entropy loss for classification. This is used to study the impact of intra-class variance on the classification performance.
4. **Classification with clustering and triplet loss** - This is our proposed method to minimise the impact of both the inter-class similarity and the intra-class variance.
5. **GS-TRS** [6] - This method uses K-Means to divide each class into K clusters and uses triplet loss for inter-cluster and inter-class objects.

We perform our experiments on two classification model architectures: ResNet50 and EfficientNet.

4.3   Evaluation Metrics

We evaluate the different approaches using the standard metrics used in classification, namely the classification accuracy, precision, recall, F-Score. A higher value of these metrics indicates a better performance. Additionally, we also calculate the variance of the per-class false-negatives and false-positives. The variance gives us a measure of how consistent the classification is and so a lower value is preferred.

4.4   Implementation Details

We use Adam optimizer and the learning rate is 0.0002 and we use a batch size of 128. The output feature embedding dimension from the network is 256. We trained our networks on GeForce GTX 1080 with 12 GB RAM. The value of `max-allowed-clusters` is set to 5. Our `confusion-threshold` is set to 0.3 based on hyper-parameter search.

Table 1. Quantitative metrics for classification on the diatom dataset.

Architecture	Method	Accuracy	Recall	Precision	F Score	Variance	
						FN	FP
ResNet50	Std. Classification	94.24	93.54	93.98	92.85	0.036	0.049
	Classification+triplet loss	96.06	95.86	95.97	95.33	0.022	0.023
	Classification+clustering	96.57	96.53	96.61	96.15	0.020	0.014
	Ours	**97.37**	**97.95**	**97.97**	**97.79**	**0.0059**	**0.0071**
	GS-TRS [6]	93.23	93.03	93.44	92.66	0.018	0.018
EfficientNet	Std. Classification	95.31	94.92	95.10	94.82	0.031	0.041
	Classification+triplet loss	96.67	96.52	96.68	96.50	0.021	0.021
	Classification+clustering	96.76	96.61	96.11	96.67	0.019	0.016
	Ours	**97.22**	**96.64**	**97.30**	**96.69**	**0.0047**	**0.0053**
	GS-TRS [6]	93.60	92.96	93.27	93.43	0.020	0.024

5   Results

5.1   Diatom Dataset

Table 1 shows the quantitative metrics for the diatom classification. Our results show that using both clustering and triplet loss consistently outperforms the other methods. One interesting conclusion from the results is that classification with clustering performs better than classification with triplet loss. This means that intra-class variance has a higher impact on the classification performance than the inter-class similarity. Finally, optimizing both the inter-class similarity and intra-class variance further improves the performance of the network. GS-TRS [6] is not well-suited for this application because the number of clusters generated are not optimal and over or under-clustering deteriorates the performance.

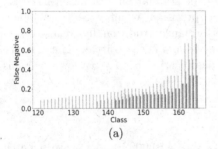
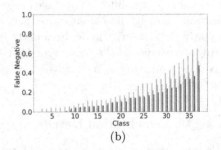

(a)   (b)

Fig. 3. Per-class false negatives of standard classification (cyan), classification with clustering (orange) and classification with clustering and triplet loss (green) for (a) diatom dataset and (b) WHOI-Plankton dataset with EfficientNet. *Note: The classes with 0 false negatives are not shown here.* (Color figure online)

Table 2. Quantitative metrics for classification on the WHOI-plankton dataset.

Architecture	Method	Accuracy	Recall	Precision	F Score	Variance	
						FN	FP
ResNet50	Std. Classification	88.54	84.90	85.82	84.71	0.022	0.136
	Classification+triplet loss	89.25	83.90	85.39	84.63	0.034	0.084
	Classification+clustering	88.17	**87.49**	83.25	84.52	**0.013**	0.095
	Ours	**89.48**	85.64	86.54	**85.50**	0.017	**0.034**
	GS-TRS [6]	87.53	78.75	**86.67**	80.81	0.035	0.156
EfficientNet	Std. Classification	88.82	86.51	82.21	81.67	0.030	0.125
	Classification+triplet loss	88.99	84.31	84.23	83.78	0.041	0.079
	Classification+clustering	88.71	85.96	81.65	81.49	0.015	0.103
	Ours	**90.53**	**88.91**	**87.13**	83.86	**0.013**	**0.024**
	GS-TRS [6]	87.66	82.25	82.35	82.03	0.033	0.147

For automatic classification of aquatic microorganisms, the certainty of prediction of a class is important which means that the false negatives should be minimal. Figure 3(a) shows a zoomed version of the false negatives with 3 methods: standard classification, classification with clustering, and classification with clustering and triplet loss overlaid onto a single graph. From the plots, 120 classes are perfectly classified when using a state-of-the-art classifier whereas 140 classes are perfectly classified when using clustering with triplet loss. Also, the overall magnitude of the false negatives is reduced when using clustering and triplet loss than when compared to the other methods. This is a significant improvement since the network can reliably be used to identify a larger number of classes than before.

5.2 WHOI-Plankton Dataset

Table 2 shows the quantitative metrics for classification on the WHOI-Plankton dataset. Similar to the diatoms, the clustering along with triplet loss outperforms the other methods. Figure 3(b) shows the overlay plot of the false negatives. In contrast to three classes that were perfectly identified by the state-of-the-art classifier, clustering and triplet loss improves it to seven perfectly identified classes. One could observe from Fig. 3(b) that when using only clustering and when using clustering along with triplet loss, the false negative magnitude does not change much. This is due to the relatively lower number of classes in the WHOI-plankton dataset, which reduces the impact of the inter-class similarity.

6   Conclusion

In this paper, we proposed a method to tackle the inter-class similarity and intra-class variance due to discrete image subsets, which is commonly found in microscopic images. Our method automatically identifies the classes to be clustered and the optimal number of clusters to be generated. Then these clusters are considered as independent classes while training a classification network. Finally, to deal with the inter-class similarity, we use triplet loss to separate out the features between each class. Using this approach, the network was able to learn finer-grained features that improved the classification performance. This was validated using quantitative metrics on a diatom and a plankton dataset.

References

1. Driee. atlas des diatomées. http://www.driee.ile-de-france.developpement-durable.gouv.fr/atlas-des-diatomees-a2070.html (2014)
2. Bueno, G., et al.: Automated diatom classification (part a): handcrafted feature approaches. Appl. Sci. **7**(8), 753 (2017)
3. Cacheux, Y.L., Borgne, H.L., Crucianu, M.: Modeling inter and intra-class relations in the triplet loss for zero-shot learning. In: Proceedings of the IEEE/CVF International Conference on Computer Vision, pp. 10333–10342 (2019)
4. Chen, W., Chen, X., Zhang, J., Huang, K.: Beyond triplet loss: a deep quadruplet network for person re-identification. In: Proceedings of the IEEE Conference on Computer Vision and Pattern Recognition, pp. 403–412 (2017)
5. Du Buf, H., et al.: Diatom identification: a double challenge called adiac. In: Proceedings 10th International Conference on Image Analysis and Processing, pp. 734–739. IEEE (1999)
6. Em, Y., Gag, F., Lou, Y., Wang, S., Huang, T., Duan, L.Y.: Incorporating intra-class variance to fine-grained visual recognition. In: 2017 IEEE International Conference on Multimedia and Expo (ICME), pp. 1452–1457. IEEE (2017)
7. Gadermayr, M., Uhl, A., Vécsei, A.: Dealing with intra-class and intra-image variations in automatic celiac disease diagnosis. In: Handels, H., Deserno, T.M., Meinzer, H.-P., Tolxdorff, T. (eds.) Bildverarbeitung für die Medizin 2015. I, pp. 461–466. Springer, Heidelberg (2015). https://doi.org/10.1007/978-3-662-46224-9_79
8. Lumini, A., Nanni, L., Maguolo, G.: Deep learning for plankton and coral classification. Appl. Comput. Inform. (2020)
9. Orenstein, E.C., Beijbom, O., Peacock, E.E., Sosik, H.M.: Whoi-plankton-a large scale fine grained visual recognition benchmark dataset for plankton classification. arXiv preprint arXiv:1510.00745 (2015)
10. Pastore, V.P., Zimmerman, T.G., Biswas, S.K., Bianco, S.: Annotation-free learning of plankton for classification and anomaly detection. Sci. Rep. **10**(1), 1–15 (2020)
11. Pedraza, A., Bueno, G., Deniz, O., Cristóbal, G., Blanco, S., Borrego-Ramos, M.: Automated diatom classification (part b): a deep learning approach. Appl. Sci. **7**(5), 460 (2017)
12. Pelleg, D., Moore, A.W., et al.: X-means: extending k-means with efficient estimation of the number of clusters. Icml. **1**, 727–734 (2000)
13. Pilarczyk, R., Skarbek, W.: On intra-class variance for deep learning of classifiers. Found. Comput. Decis. Sci. **44**(3), 285–301 (2019)
14. Py, O., Hong, H., Zhongzhi, S.: Plankton classification with deep convolutional neural networks. In: 2016 IEEE Information Technology, Networking, Electronic and Automation Control Conference, pp. 132–136. IEEE (2016)
15. Schroff, F., Kalenichenko, D., Philbin, J.: Facenet: A unified embedding for face recognition and clustering. In: Proceedings of the IEEE Conference on Computer Vision and Pattern Recognition (CVPR), June 2015

16. Zhao, F., Lin, F., Seah, H.S.: Binary sipper plankton image classification using random subspace. Neurocomputing **73**(10–12), 1853–1860 (2010)
17. Zheng, H., Wang, R., Yu, Z., Wang, N., Gu, Z., Zheng, B.: Automatic plankton image classification combining multiple view features via multiple kernel learning. BMC Bioinform. **18**(16), 1–18 (2017)

Semantic Interpretation

Measuring the Sim2Real Gap in 3D Object Classification for Different 3D Data Representation

Jean-Baptiste Weibel$^{(\boxtimes)}$ ⓘ, Rainer Rohrböck, and Markus Vincze ⓘ

Vision for Robotics Laboratory, Automation and Control Institute, TU Wien, Vienna, Austria
{weibel,vincze}@acin.tuwien.ac.at

Abstract. Perceiving the environment geometry is necessary for a robot to perform safe motions and actions. To decide upon meaningful actions, however, semantic understanding is also required. At the object level, this semantic classification task can directly be performed using the extracted object 3D data. While continuously improving, the performance of methods designed for this task still decrease on data captured by a robot because of input data differences [18], referred to as the Sim2Real gap. In this paper, we aim to better evaluate that gap for different 3D data representations and understand the impact of a variety of design choices through a set of specific experiments, performed both on the Model-Net dataset [20] to which a variety of alterations is applied and on the ScanObjectNN dataset [18]. Results indicate that occlusions plays an essential part in the gap and that their impact is mitigated by the use of hierarchical representation learned from the surface of the object itself.

Keywords: 3D object classification · Sim2Real gap · 3D data representation

1 Introduction

Understanding the geometry of the environment a robot is operating in is key to its safe operation. Whether it is to identify obstacles or to decide which elements of a scene are indeed objects that will be safely grasped and interacted with, the semantic information provided by 3D object classification is an essential element of this environment understanding.

The state-of-the-art of 3D object classification has continuously improved [11,16,19], but new methods are evaluated on standard CAD model datasets, like ModelNet [20]. This is not enough for robotic applications because data captured in the wild suffers from frequent occlusions, smoothed-out surfaces,

The research leading to these results has received funding from the Austrian Science Foundation (FWF) under grant agreement No. I3968-N30 HEAP and No. I3969-N30 InDex.

M. Vincze et al. (Eds.): ICVS 2021, LNCS 12899, pp. 107–116, 2021.
https://doi.org/10.1007/978-3-030-87156-7_9

and over- or under-segmentation. This difference in performance on artificial and on real data is partially demonstrated in [18], but exclusively for point-cloud based methods. Indeed, the evaluation of the Sim2Real gap is made more complex by the co-existence of different 3D data representation in the field.

The contribution of this paper is to complement this original study by evaluating the Sim2Real gap in multi-view, voxel grid and point cloud based methods. To do so, we select representative deep learning models based on different data representation and use their respective performance as a proxy to evaluate the Sim2Real gap in 3D object classification for each representation. Point clouds (using PointNet [10] and PointNet++ [11] as representatives), multi-view (using MVCNN [16] as representative) and voxel grids (using VoxNet [8] as representative) are the selected representation for evaluation as illustrated in Fig. 1. We train the deep learning models using a subset of the ModelNet [20] dataset (the entire dataset contains 12,311 artificial CAD models spread in 40 classes), and evaluate them using a subset of the ScanObjectNN dataset [18] (the entire dataset contains around 15,000 real objects spread in 15 classes, with 2902 unique object instances). In a second phase, we perform a set of experiments on modified artificial data to separately evaluate the impact of specific design elements from each deep learning model.

As a results of all these experiments, we formulate a set of design guidelines to improve performance on real-world data in the field of 3D object classification.

Fig. 1. 3D data representations: view-, grid and point-based representation

The remainder of the paper is organized as follows. After giving an overview of the relevant state-of-the-art methods in Sect. 2, Sect. 3 focus on the experiments performed on real data. Finally, Sect. 4 presents the results of the evaluation of specific design choices through experiments on artificial data modified adequately.

2   Related Work

We discuss methods for 3D object classification, subdivided into representations based on views, grid, and points.

2.1   View-Based Representation

The strengths of 2D convolution have first been demonstrated by AlexNet [6] for RGB images. This architecture also lends itself well to depth images, and can easily be applied to a set of views to perform 3D object classification. Research in the field focused on the most suitable way of combining the features of each view, starting with MVCNN [15] that combines them using a max-pooling layer creating a global object descriptor to learn from. This method has been improved in [16], which is the version we refer to as MVCNN here. Introducing groups of views as in [3], or ordering them to learn from a the sequence as in [4] improves performance. We choose to use MVCNN as the representative of this class as more recent works build on its architecture. Other directions designed specifically with the assumption of the complete object being present, like using a panoramic projection around the object [13] are not considered here.

2.2   Grid-Based Representation

For all the successes of 2D convolutions and view-based approaches, using 3D convolutions on voxel grids more naturally fits 3D data. This idea has been investigated early on in [8,20]. It was however limited by the exponential growth in memory and parameters of 3D grids and convolutions. This problem is tackled in [12] by using an octree-based learning architecture, and in [7] by using the same architecture as [8] but with less bits per voxels. Research is ongoing and better usage of computational resources can lead to efficient sparse 3D convolutions as in [2]. VoxNet [8] is chosen for its simplicity as it make the intrinsic strengths and weaknesses of voxel grid methods more visible.

2.3   Point-Based Representation

Finally, research is very active in 3D object classification from point clouds, as this representation is the closest to the output of depth sensors. The variable length of the point cloud and lack of explicit structure between data points requires specific architecture, the first of which was PointNet [10], improved by using a hierarchy of layers in [11]. More recent approaches learn directly from point neighborhood, using a more general definition of convolutions [21], or defining a set of kernel points spread around the point of interest to learn patterns depending on the presence of neighboring points [17]. Performance can be further boosted by defining points' neighborhood not only from point coordinates but also point features [19]. Notably, the Sim2Real gap in this subset of methods has been investigated in [18]. We choose PointNet and PointNet++ as representative for this set of methods because of the popularity of the architecture, which has been use in a variety of applications [5,14].

3   Measuring the Sim2Real Gap on ScanObjectNN

In this section, the experimental conditions used to measure the Sim2Real gap are first described, and an analysis of the results is then performed.

3.1   Experimental Setup

In this set of experiments, models are trained on the subset of 11 classes from ModelNet40 dataset that overlaps with the classes defined in the ScanObjectNN dataset, and then evaluated with objects from the same 11 classes from the ScanObjectNN dataset (as defined in [18]). However, to make the evaluation possible, both datasets have to be transformed.

First, the CAD models of the ModelNet dataset are rendered from multiple viewpoints and the obtained depth maps are used to reconstruct the object using a Truncated Signed Distance Function (TSDF) volume [9]. This step is done to remove artifacts, and more specifically, surfaces defined within the object itself (remnants of the human object modeling process), that would only affect PointNet and VoxNet, but not MVCNN. Object models are first scaled to the unit sphere, and 26 depth maps are created: 12 views in a circle slightly above the object, 12 views in a circle slightly below the object, and the top and bottom views. They are combined into a single TSDF volume from which the object mesh is extracted.

As the ScanObjectNN dataset was originally designed to evaluate point cloud-based object classification methods, a transformation is also necessary, because this format is not suitable for the view rendering necessary for the MVCNN. The surface of the object models is reconstructed from the dense point cloud with pre-computed normals using a ball pivoting method [1].

The transformations of both the train and test set make the results presented impossible to directly compare with those presented in [18], but were necessary to fairly compare the different methods evaluated in this paper.

PointNet [10] and PointNet++ [11] are used for point cloud representation, VoxNet [8] for voxel grids, and MVCNN [16] for multi-views. While these models might not reach the highest accuracy for their respective representation, the focus in this paper is on the relative change in performance, and their architectural simplicity makes them more representative of the behavior of other models based on the same representation. For every model, the authors' code is used, and the parameters of the paper are respected. MVCNN is evaluated using the VGG-11 backbone and 12 shaded views (in a circle slightly above the object), PointNet++ and PointNet use 1024 points, and VoxNet is trained on a $32 \times 32 \times 32$ grid.

3.2   Results and Analysis

Table 1 presents the results of evaluating the different deep learning models on the ScanObjectNN dataset and on the test set of the ModelNet dataset, when trained on the pre-defined training set of the ModelNet dataset. Two ScanObjectNN variants are evaluated: the OBJ_ONLY, where only points belonging to the actual object are considered, and the OBJ_BG where all points falling into the bounding box of the object are considered.

Overall, the MVCNN is the best performing approach, with a large gap when looking at the OBJ_ONLY variant. Because the MVCNN only relies on object views sampled on a circle slightly above the object, it is less affected than other

Table 1. Results when training on ModelNet and evaluating on ScanObjectNN, mean class accuracy and relative change is reported in percent

Model	ModelNet	OBJ_ONLY	OBJ_BG
VoxNet	90.08	49.77 (−44.8%)	54.36 (−39.7%)
MVCNN	93.49	62.69 (−33.0%)	58.58 (−37.3%)
PointNet++	93.31	52.49 (−43.8)	55.78 (−40.2%)
PointNet	90.31	54.22 (−40.0%)	55.71 (−38.3%)

methods by the absence of data at the bottom and under the object in the ScanObjectNN dataset.

The OBJ_ONLY variant tends to be over-segmented (parts of the objects are missing, for example, decorative cushion occludes parts of a sofa but would not be included), while the OBJ_BG is under-segmented (many background points are included, like the floor). MVCNN is clearly more affected by the under-segmentation than the over-segmentation, which is in line with the experiments in [16] suggesting that the model is sensitive to the object silhouette. On the other hand, VoxNet, PointNet and PointNet++ performs similarly on both variants. Looking further, results are significantly better on the OBJ_ONLY variant for the `table` class (relative improvement 122.2% for VoxNet, 82.4% for MVCNN, 47.6% for PointNet++ and 63.2% for PointNet) which often include the ground floor in the OBJ_BG variant. On the other hand, VoxNet (−10.7%), PointNet++ (−40.6%) and PointNet (−17.5%) performs worse on the `shelf` class. So removing the background points as in OBJ_ONLY seems only beneficial to certain classes while being detrimental on other classes, leading to similar overall performance on both variants for VoxNet, PointNet and Point++. We hypothesize that all methods are sensitive to the addition of background points, but VoxNet, Point-Net++ and PointNet are more sensitive to holes than MVCNN, as they break local patterns, whereas MVCNN better learns the overall object appearance from its silhouette.

4   Disentangling the Impact of Design Choices

In this section, objects from the ModelNet dataset are altered in specific ways to better understand the impact of design choices of each deep learning model evaluated in this paper and their consequences on the Sim2Real gap in 3D object classification. Those alterations are illustrated in Fig. 2. All deep learning models are trained on reconstructed objects models from the 40 classes of the ModelNet dataset and evaluated on the altered reconstructed test set, according to the experiment performed.

4.1   Hierarchical Learning from Object Parts

In this first set of experiments, the impact of hierarchy and subdivision of objects in deep learning models is investigated. Intuitively, learning from parts of the

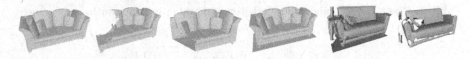

Fig. 2. Illustration of the alterations of artifical data. From left to right: complete sofa, with random occlusion (as in Fig. 3), with a cut (as in Table 3), with a bottom plane added (as in Table 3), an example sofa in the OBJ_BG and in the OBJ_ONLY variant of ScanObjectNN

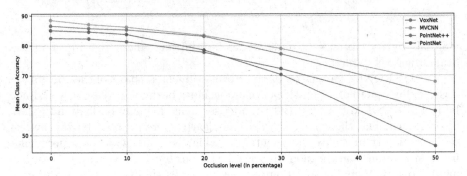

Fig. 3. Mean class accuracy for various levels of occlusion

object, and relations between these parts rather than the entire object at once should be more robust to objects occlusions. The performance of deep learning models under increasing amount of random occlusions is therefore evaluated and presented in Fig. 3. Occlusions here are generated by selecting a random face in the object mesh, and growing the region to be removed until a certain percentage of the object surface area is reached. PointNet performs the worst out of all models, which is consistent with the hypothesis, as it is the only model considering the entire set of points at once. PointNet++ performs the same operation at multiple levels, each level being applied on a larger subset of the object than the previous one. This design mitigates the issue as the performance degrades at the same rate as VoxNet, which also learns hierarchically thanks to the use of classic convolutions. MVCNN degradation relative to the level of occlusion is the slowest, as it benefits from both the hierarchical learning from convolutions in single views and the subdivision of the object in a set of views. We also noticed that while MVCNN performs better with multiple views, when using a single view of a clean artificial object (setting the other 11 to black), MVCNN performance only degrades by 13.8%, showing that MVCNN is quite robust to multiple corrupted views.

4.2   Impact of Surface-Based or Euclidean-Based Representation

MVCNN, because of its use of projection, only ever considers one side of an object surface at a time. On the other hand, PointNet++ considers local subset

Table 2. Impact of limited viewpoints during model reconstruction. Mean class accuracy and relative change in percent.

Model	Full	Half (Front)	Half (Back)	Quarter (Front)	Quarter (Back)
VoxNet	71.41	67.33 (–5.7%)	62.00 (–13.2%)	60.68 (–15.0%)	55.92 (–21.7%)
MVCNN	78.14	73.45 (–6.0%)	67.63 (–13.5%)	69.10 (–11.6%)	61.85 (–20.8%)
PointNet++	70.58	64.23 (–9.0%)	56.79 (–19.5%)	57.73 (–18.2%)	49.39 (–30.0%)
PointNet	75.27	67.45 (–10.4%)	64.10 (–14.8%)	51.62 (–31.4%)	49.14 (–34.7%)

of points defined by the Euclidean distance rather than the co-visibility of points. A robot operating in the wild can rarely observe a given object under every viewpoint. For example the top of the bottom of a table are unlikely to be both accessible. We hypothesize that patterns learned on subsets defined by the Euclidean distance will be more affected by viewpoints constraints than patterns learned on those defined by the object surface.

The impact of limited views is evaluated in Table 2. In this experiment, 12 views are generated all around the object on a horizontal circle at half the height of the object (the circle of views is therefore at a equidistant height to the two used to create the training set). We then report the performance on various subsets of views: the half-circle subsets include the 6 views of the front (respectively back) of the object, the quarter circle experiments report the average results when including the 3 left views and when including the 3 right views of the front (respectively back) of the object. The front, back, left and right are defined by the version of ModelNet where objects models are aligned.

PointNet++ performance and even more so, PointNet performance degrades faster than VoxNet and MVCNN. With more and more limited viewpoints available, the difference between surface and Euclidean neighborhood definition grows bigger. While VoxNet theoretically falls into the Euclidean type of representation, we attribute its relatively good performance here to the coarseness of its voxel grid. Indeed, in most situation, front and back surface of an object are likely to fall into the same voxel, mitigating this issue. For example, on the bathtub class, PointNet++ and PointNet show respectively a 85.4% and 87.1% decrease compared to –67.1% and –60.0% for the VoxNet and MVCNN respectively on the quarter (back) experiments. This implies a stronger reliance on the presence of both the outer (present) and inner (absent in this experiment) surface of the bathtub. Another example is the bowl class, where most models are barely affected, except the PointNet with an average decrease on all quarter experiments of 56.3%. While the class is discriminative enough thanks to its curvature that is uncommon in this dataset, PointNet reliance on both sides of the bowl being present leads to incorrect classification.

4.3 Impact of Over- and Under-Segmentation and Scale

Many CAD models like those provided in the ModelNet dataset do not have a reliable scale information, as the unit used to create them is not provided. It is

Table 3. Impact of scale, over- and under-segmentation. Mean class accuracy and relative change in percent.

Models	30% cut	30% cut scaled	50% cut	50% cut scaled	Bottom plane
VoxNet	73.5 (−18.4%)	73.0 (−19.0%)	73.0 (−19.0%)	45.2 (−49.8%)	66.5 (−26.2%)
MVCNN	83.1 (−11.1%)	86.0 (−8.0%)	71.0 (−24.1%)	72.7 (−22.2%)	78.3 (−16.2%)
PointNet++	84.3 (−9.7%)	83.3 (−10.7%)	71.1 (−23.8%)	68.8 (−26.3%)	25.3 (−72.9%)
PointNet	79.7 (−11.7%)	76.4 (−15.4%)	26.0 (−71.2%)	40.4 (−55.3%)	23.2 (−74.3%)

common to scale them to the unit sphere. As occlusions of objects will affect their bounding spheres, they affect the final scale of the object. To investigate further over- and under-segmentation and their connection with scale, a new type of occlusion is evaluated in Table 3. The object is cut vertically at a certain percentage of the unit sphere diameter, guaranteeing that the resulting object's scale will be changed when re-scaling the remaining points to the unit sphere. The reliance on the scale information of VoxNet is made clear, as the scaling and centering operation resulting from the occlusion strongly affects the voxel grid. PointNet and PointNet++, thanks to the fixed number of sampled points still extracts discriminative patterns from scaled up occluded objects, and MVCNN already scales every view around the object.

Under-segmentation is also evaluated in Table 3 by adding a ground plane under every object of the same width and length as the object. These experiments confirms MVCNN sensitivity to under-segmentation shown in Table 1, but also demonstrates the limits of the fixed number of points used in PointNet and PointNet++ representation. Not only does it add outlier point, but it also consequently limits the number of points that can be sampled on the object, forcing them to be further apart, and losing any discriminative local patterns in the process.

4.4 Application-Specific Considerations

While this paper focused so far on generally applicable guidelines for 3D object classification, knowledge about the end application can also inform the design of the classification method.

For example, the higher absolute performance of the MVCNN in this paper is partially attributed to its implicit use of surface normals, necessary to the creation of shaded images. They make classes with finer surface details easier to distinguish, making the method more robust to random occlusion. Looking at the difference between performance on complete reconstructed models and models with a 50% random occlusion, the benefit is noticeable for classes like keyboard (0% for MVCNN, −60.0% for VoxNet, −40.0% for PointNet++, −65% for PointNet) or curtain (−5.3% for MVCNN, −16.0% for VoxNet, −22.2% for PointNet++, −16.7% for PointNet). This benefit is tied to the availability of reliable surface normals in the end application.

The fixed set of viewpoints used by MVCNN can also be tuned to the application, but because of the projection process, it is less suitable to represent concave parts. Looking at the same experiments as before for the `sink` class, MVCNN (−36.8%) is performing worse than VoxNet (−9.3%), PointNet++ (17.6%) or PointNet (−20.0%).

5   Conclusion

The set of experiments presented here underlines the strengths and weaknesses of point cloud based, voxel grid based and multi-view based representation of 3D data. Through a set of experiments on both real and artificial data, design guidelines have emerged to further reduce the Sim2Real gap in 3D object classification. In particular, based on the results presented here, we advise to learn features hierarchically, as is already common, using object surfaces to define point neighborhood, rather than the Euclidean distance between points, and favoring data creation producing over-segmentation, especially when opting for a fixed number of points representation (which presents significant computational benefits). All these choices mitigate the impact of occlusions present in real data. Moreover, the application and the set of classes that will need to be recognised can further guide the design of the approach, as surface normal, and their implicit use in shaded images help differentiate finer details, but concave elements are harder to represent reliably using a set of views.

While this review focuses on 3D object classification, a natural extension of this work would be to look at multi-objects scenario and 3D object detection in general, and investigate the difference emerging, especially concerning the view selection for a model like MVCNN, that is made significantly less straightforward in this scenario.

References

1. Bernardini, F., Mittleman, J., Rushmeier, H., Silva, C., Taubin, G.: The ball-pivoting algorithm for surface reconstruction. IEEE Trans. Visual. Comput. Graph. **5**(4), 349–359 (1999). https://doi.org/10.1109/2945.817351
2. Choy, C., Gwak, J., Savarese, S.: 4D spatio-temporal convnets: Minkowski convolutional neural networks. In: Proceedings of the IEEE/CVF Conference on Computer Vision and Pattern Recognition, pp. 3075–3084 (2019)
3. Feng, Y., Zhang, Z., Zhao, X., Ji, R., Gao, Y.: Gvcnn: group-view convolutional neural networks for 3d shape recognition. In: Proceedings of the IEEE Conference on Computer Vision and Pattern Recognition, pp. 264–272 (2018)
4. Han, Z., et al.: 3d2seqviews: aggregating sequential views for 3d global feature learning by CNN with hierarchical attention aggregation. IEEE Trans. Image Process. **28**(8), 3986–3999 (2019)
5. He, Y., Lee, C.H.: An improved ICP registration algorithm by combining pointnet++ and icp algorithm. In: 2020 6th International Conference on Control, Automation and Robotics (ICCAR), pp. 741–745. IEEE (2020)

6. Krizhevsky, A., Sutskever, I., Hinton, G.E.: ImageNet classification with deep convolutional neural networks. Adv. Neural Inf. Proces. Syst. **25**, 1097–1105 (2012)
7. Ma, C., An, W., Lei, Y., Guo, Y.: Bv-cnns: Binary volumetric convolutional networks for 3d object recognition. In: BMVC. vol. 1, p. 4 (2017)
8. Maturana, D., Scherer, S.: Voxnet: A 3D convolutional neural network for real-time object recognition. In: 2015 IEEE/RSJ International Conference on Intelligent Robots and Systems (IROS), pp. 922–928. IEEE (2015)
9. Newcombe, R.A., et al.: Kinectfusion: Real-time dense surface mapping and tracking. In: 2011 10th IEEE International Symposium on Mixed and Augmented Reality, pp. 127–136 (2011). https://doi.org/10.1109/ISMAR.2011.6092378
10. Qi, C.R., Su, H., Mo, K., Guibas, L.J.: Pointnet: deep learning on point sets for 3D classification and segmentation. In: Proceedings of the IEEE Conference on Computer Vision and Pattern Recognition, pp. 652–660 (2017)
11. Qi, C.R., Yi, L., Su, H., Guibas, L.J.: Pointnet++ deep hierarchical feature learning on point sets in a metric space. In: Proceedings of the 31st International Conference on Neural Information Processing Systems, pp. 5105–5114 (2017)
12. Riegler, G., Osman Ulusoy, A., Geiger, A.: Octnet: Learning deep 3D representations at high resolutions. In: Proceedings of the IEEE Conference on Computer Vision and Pattern Recognition, pp. 3577–3586 (2017)
13. Sfikas, K., Pratikakis, I., Theoharis, T.: Ensemble of panorama-based convolutional neural networks for 3D model classification and retrieval. Comput. Graph. **71**, 208–218 (2018)
14. Shao, L., et al.: Unigrasp: learning a unified model to grasp with multifigured robotic hands. IEEE Robot. Autom. Lett. **5**(2), 2286–2293 (2020). https://doi.org/10.1109/LRA.2020.2969946
15. Su, H., Maji, S., Kalogerakis, E., Learned-Miller, E.: Multi-view convolutional neural networks for 3d shape recognition. In: Proceedings of the IEEE international Conference on Computer Vision, pp. 945–953 (2015)
16. Su, J.C., Gadelha, M., Wang, R., Maji, S.: A deeper look at 3D shape classifiers. In: Proceedings of the European Conference on Computer Vision (ECCV) Workshops (2018)
17. Thomas, H., et al.: Kpconv: flexible and deformable convolution for point clouds. In: Proceedings of the IEEE International Conference on Computer Vision (2019)
18. Uy, M.A., Pham, Q.H., Hua, B.S., Nguyen, D.T., Yeung, S.K.: Revisiting point cloud classification: a new benchmark dataset and classification model on real-world data. In: International Conference on Computer Vision (ICCV) (2019)
19. Wang, Y., Sun, Y., Liu, Z., Sarma, S.E., Bronstein, M.M., Solomon, J.M.: Dynamic graph CNN for learning on point clouds. ACM Trans. Graph. (tog) **38**(5), 1–12 (2019)
20. Wu, Z., et al.: 3D ShapeNets: a deep representation for volumetric shapes. In: Proceedings of IEEE Conference on Computer Vision and Pattern Recognition, pp. 1912–1920 (2015)
21. Xu, Y., Fan, T., Xu, M., Zeng, L., Qiao, Y.: Spidercnn: deep learning on point sets with parameterized convolutional filters. In: Proceedings of the European Conference on Computer Vision (ECCV), pp. 87–102 (2018)

Spatially-Constrained Semantic Segmentation with Topological Maps and Visual Embeddings

Christina Theodoridou(✉) , Andreas Kargakos , Ioannis Kostavelis ,
Dimitrios Giakoumis , and Dimitrios Tzovaras

Centre for Research and Technology Hellas, Information Technologies Institute,
6th Km Charilaou-Thermi Road, 57001 Thermi-Thessaloniki, Greece
{christtk,akargakos,gkostave,dgiakoum,Dimitrios.Tzovaras}@iti.gr
https://www.certh.gr/

Abstract. Semantic mapping has received much attention in the recent
years due to the fact that more and more robots need to operate in
complex environments and co-exist with humans or other robots. This
requires contemporary robots not only to be able to navigate safely in
their environment, but also to adopt a human-like understanding of their
surroundings i.e. to have a semantic apprehension of the mapped environment. This paper at hand, focuses on building successfully semantic
maps by combining spatial knowledge on the occupancy grid map with
deep learning and computer vision techniques. The presented method
exploits the vision based data captured by robot's perception system,
to ease its installation in the operational environment. Unlike previous
methods, the proposed one does not require any prior knowledge of the
environment concerning the semantics of places, as it is semi-supervised
and the labeling of the segmented areas is being performed manually
after the process is completed. The method has been evaluated in real
indoor environments by measuring the Jaccard and Dice indices for the
performed segmentation and exhibited remarkable performance.

Keywords: Semantic segmentation · Semantic mapping · Map
partitioning · Spatial segmentation · Visual embeddings · Robot
installation

1 Introduction

During the last decades, an abundance of personal [3,15] and professional [16]
service robots has been released into the market targeting operation in industrial
and domestic environments. Although experts estimated that by 2055, around
half of today's work activities could be automated by robots [18], the adoption
pace of the robotic technologies is still slow. On the one hand this is relied on the
fact that there are many challenges in real world environments that hinder contemporary robotic agents to work in unconstrained conditions given their current

© Springer Nature Switzerland AG 2021
M. Vincze et al. (Eds.): ICVS 2021, LNCS 12899, pp. 117–129, 2021.
https://doi.org/10.1007/978-3-030-87156-7_10

perception, cognition and mobility capacities. On the other hand, the deployment time and installation efforts are still very demanding, requiring each robot to preserve a detailed model of the operational environment, which is mostly performed with manual annotation, while at the same time the adaptation ability of the robots in environmental changes is poor [23].

It is evident that robots should be able to understand, interpret and represent their environment as humans do, and this is a condition sine qua non to allow their fast installation in realistic settings and the ambient human-robot interaction. For example, in an industrial environment, robots should adapt their planned motion and operation speed differently in the free space of the main corridor than in a packaging room, where multiple people or tools are more likely to be existent [26]. Similar examples can be found in home environments where service robots can operate safer and adaptively [15] when considering dynamic motions of people [14]. The latter requires increased perception and cognition capabilities that will enable future robots to apprehend concepts such as rooms, objects and their relations [11]. The so-called semantic mapping [27], introduced within the last years, steered the research endeavors towards the common human-robot apprehension of the environment. To enable robot's fast and efficient installation in domestic environments, the metric and semantic understanding of its surroundings is essential. Typically, during robot's first introduction in a new environment, a walk-through is performed by the mobile robot with a classic SLAM tool [1] to create a metric map, and the semantic annotation is performed subsequently either manually [13] or by employing a place categorization method [24] on top of the metric map to associate visual inputs obtained during robot exploration with the spatial recordings. However, such solutions are prone to errors like misclassification of the rooms due to unknown classes, and require manual annotation and tuning. In our method, no predefined semantic place categories are necessary as the annotation is done manually, and hence the method can be employed in totally new environments with unknown place categories.

This paper at hand aims to introduce a method that allows fast installation of a robot in a new environment by performing semantic mapping by processing the metric map to be organized in clusters of areas that share common spatial as well as semantic information. To this end, the main contributions of our work are summarized as follows: i) a spatial segmentation of the occupancy grid map using triangulation and topological map organization and ii) the optimization of the spatial segmentation with deep learning techniques.

The rest of the paper is organized as follows: Sect. 2 presents the existing work related to the semantic segmentation, Sect. 3 introduces our method, while report on experimental results is presented in Sect. 4. Conclusions and future works are drawn in Sect. 5.

2   Related Work

Semantic mapping methods can be split in two major categories: i) methods that find segments and label them simultaneously and ii) methods that firstly perform map/room segmentation and then place recognition [11]. Our algorithm is closer to the second category, as it spatially segments the occupancy grid map and then utilizes the semantics of the scene to perform the semasiological place partitioning.

In the first category, several researches have been published over the years. The work of Mozos et al. [20] segments maps using AdaBoost algorithm to create a classifier based on geometrical features extracted from range data. In [12] semantic maps are constructed by utilizing both place and object recognition in a supervised manner. More recently, the authors in [21] enhanced the occupancy grid map with semantic information using object point clouds to perform object recognition and label each room accordingly. A similar approach is described in [4] where CNNs are used to detect and recognize objects which are later mapped on the occupancy grid by utilizing the robot's localization. Later, they used a Bayesian probability framework combined with prior knowledge about objects and their associate rooms, in order to extract probabilities for the semantic label of each room.

In the second category, studies that aim to segment a map into rooms or areas often make use of the morphology of the building through point clouds or employ mathematical and/or computer vision tools to segment directly the occupancy grid map. In [5], room segmentation is performed directly on the point cloud, by using 3D mathematical operations, while in [10] the authors generate watertight floor maps by skeletonizing a 2D binary occupancy grid map and then label the separate rooms. In a different direction, the approach presented in [25], segments the occupancy grid map using quadtree and spectral clustering. The work in [19] presented a segmentation method for maps based on different modalities which can be applied in both robot-built maps and sketch maps. Hiller, Qiu et al. [7] generated topometric semantic maps from occupancy grids by creating a door hypothesis on the metric map using deep learning, and refined them using computer vision methods. Ambrus et al. [2] reconstructed floor plans from 3D point clouds using an energy minimization approach. More similar to our approach, authors in [17], extract a topological map from spatial graphs that represent areas and their passages, and cluster them using graph kernels.

Our method aims to semantically partition a map by creating an initial topological map from a Voronoi diagram and subsequently enhance it with semantic information, without requiring any prior knowledge of it. Unlike [17], we exploit both the visual coherence and the spatial continuity of the environment.

3   Methodology

The proposed pipeline for semantic mapping is graphically illustrated in Fig. 1. It starts with interpreting the occupancy grid map as a topological graph in order to apply a rough spatial segmentation of the environment and then improves it by using the inputs of the laser and camera sensors, along with an autoencoder network.

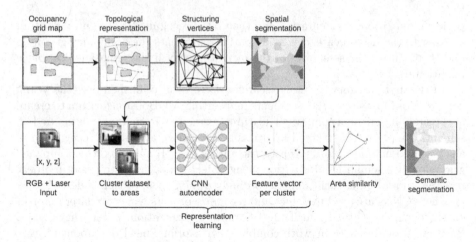

Fig. 1. Overview of the proposed method

3.1   Topological Representation

The 2D metric map of the environment is obtained through Gmapping [6] employing the robot's laser scanner. During robot's teleoperation in the mapping phase, RGB images of the visited places are also recorded and associated with the corresponding pose of the robot. Following the map generation and the data acquisition, the offline process of map partitioning starts by extracting the Voronoi diagram of the generated metric map. The map is encoded with vertices and edges, where vertices represent areas and edges represent their adjacencies. As vertices, we consider the junctions points in the Voronoi diagram. We reduce the number of the vertices acquired by pruning the graph under certain restrictions, adopted from the algorithm proposed in [9]. The first restriction concerns the removal of the edges that are in a shorter distance from occupied cells than a predefined threshold th_o. Since the vertices are expected to represent areas, vertices close to obstacles or walls are not likely to constitute a separate region. Then, we eliminate the vertices that are not dead-ends or junctions (vertices that are of *degree* = 2), and therefore we merge the edges connected to them with their respective paths, in an attempt to delete any vertex that is not informative. Finally, we also filter dead-ends that are shorter than a predefined length th_d, as they are too small to define a distinct area, and merge the vertices that have a smaller interval than a predetermined threshold th_{vm} as they most likely belong to the same area. An example of a generated topological graph and its respective occupancy grid can be seen in Fig. 2a, b. The topological representation does not consist a path for the robot but a graph showing the areas through vertices and their neighbors through edges. This explains the fact that in Fig. 2b the edges of the graph cross parts of the map that are not traversable.

3.2   Structuring Vertices

Upon the generation of the topological graph, we need to structure these vertices in polygons, in order to outline areas. Inspired by the A-shapes algorithm used in [9], we apply the constrained Delaunay triangulation using the map's outline. In our case, the graph $G(V, E)$ is consisted of centers of the areas detected from the above algorithm as vertices (V), and a polygon that approximates the outline of the occupancy grid map as edges (E). Extra vertices v are added on each corner of the map's border lines, in a way that the outline along with the vertices in the map, consist a valid graph $(V' = V + v)$. In the constrained Delaunay triangulation, the edges E of the graph are forced to be included in the triangulation of the vertices V (Fig. 2c, d).

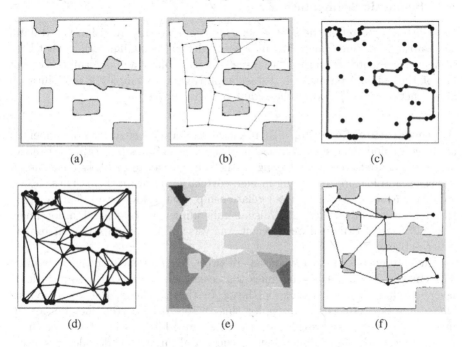

(a)   (b)   (c)

(d)   (e)   (f)

Fig. 2. (a) Occupancy grid map, (b) topological representation, (c) graph to triangulate, (d) constrained Delaunay triangulation, (e) initial segmentation generated and (f) topological graph from segmentation

3.3   Spatial Segmentation

At this point, the map is represented as a mesh of triangles that have as many points as the vertices V'. In order to create an initial segmentation, we prune these triangles' edges according to their length, which lies in an interval th_l. Then, we filter the generated polygons, according to the size of their area, assuming that a size under a certain threshold th_{sm} means that the polygon is too small to correspond to a separate region. In order to merge these parts in the neighboring segments we consider as region of each generated polygon, its bloated convex hull. This approach typically leads to an oversegmentation of the map and, thus, of the space. One important limitation is that the thresholds must be configured in a way, that no polygon in the resulting segmentation contains points that belong in more than one true area, but contain enough visual information for the refinement described in Sect. 3.4. The initial oversegmantation should provide rather many and enough small areas that can be merged later and approximate real area borders than few and bigger that possibly cross over to more than one real area. In the areas that polygons overlap, we split the overlapping area equally in all segments. An example of a generated segmentation and its corresponding graph is illustrated in Fig. 2c, d.

3.4   Semantic Segmentation

In an attempt to refine the spatial segmentation, we employ vision-based data, that captured during Gmapping, in order to define the similar regions that have been oversegmented from the spatial segmentation phase and determine whether or not they should be merged. To accomplish this, we employ a convolutional neural network (CNNs) over the acquired RGB images.

Representation Learning. To measure similarity between two segmented areas, we exploit the visual information of the surroundings. The captured images of the segmented areas that belong to the same room, most likely have similar structure and features, resulting in high correlation between them. These observations can be modelled by close relationships in the lower-rank feature space through visual embeddings [22]. Visual embeddings are, in general, a non-linear generalization of Principal Component Analysis (PCA), produced by an autoencoder network [8].

The autoencoder network consists of two CNNs, an encoder and a decoder. The encoder has 5 stacked modules that each one consists of a convolutional layer, a relu layer and a maxpool layer. In the last layer, the input's visual embedding is produced. In order for this vector to be a true encoding of the image, we engage a decoder, that takes the embedding as input and produces an image with the same dimensions as the initial input. The decoder has also 5 stacked modules that each one consists of a deconvolutional layer and a relu layer. The last layer produces the reconstructed image with the same dimensions as the input image. This way, the network is trained to encode the images of the current dataset. During the training of the autoencoder, Mean Squared Error (MSE) loss is used to measure the difference between the original and the retrieved image, for 30 epochs. Once the training is completed, we freeze the trained parameters, compute through the encoder a feature vector for each image, and combine them to extract the area embeddings, as described in the following section.

Area Similarity. For each area of the spatial segmentation, the *area embedding* is considered to be a feature vector of the averaged embeddings of the images that correspond to this area. This is achieved by taking the embedding vectors of all images that correspond to one particular area, as it is found by the robot's pose at the moment of recording, and averaging them. The images that belong to the same room are expected to have high similarity and similar features, so averaging them results in a characteristic vector for each room. It is evident that the more diverse the rooms are, the more distinctive these area embeddings will be. A critical constraint is that the particular method is vulnerable to the trajectory of the robot in the environment. The key assumption is that the images acquired in each area and depict neighboring areas are much less comparatively to the images that actually belong in it, and do not affect significantly the features of the specific area's data. These embeddings are then mapped in an even lower dimensional space through PCA, and their relationship is quantified by two metrics: the euclidean distance and the cosine similarity. Let $\mathbf{p}$, $\mathbf{q}$ be the n-length embedding vectors of each area then, the euclidean distance is defined as $d\left(\mathbf{p}, \mathbf{q}\right) = \sqrt{\sum_{i=1}^{n} \left(q_i - p_i\right)^2}$, where p_i, q_i correspond to the elements of vectors $\mathbf{p}$, $\mathbf{q}$ respectively, and the cosine similarity is expressed as $cos(\theta) = \frac{\mathbf{p} \cdot \mathbf{q}}{\|\mathbf{p}\|\|\mathbf{q}\|}$.

Upon the computation of metrics for the area embeddings, we proceed in the merging of the areas defined over the spatial and semantic segmentation. To decide which areas should be merged, we use a distance metric that combines both euclidean distance and cosine similarity and is defined as $Dist\_Metric = (1 - Cosine) + Euclidean$ and determine experimentally an upper threshold th_{merg}. Once the areas with distance lower than th_{merg} are joined, the final semantic map is generated. In this way, areas that share common semantic information e.g. office, and have been oversegmented during the spatial segmentation are now merged into the same area exploiting also the semantic coherence that stem from the embeddings comparison.

4   Experimental Results

This section demonstrates the performance of the proposed method in two real environments i.e. a domestic and an industrial one. The domestic environment has more bounded areas with clear differences between most of the rooms while the industrial environment is characterized by open spaces with soft margins and limits. The occupancy grid maps that are extracted from these environments, using Gmapping, are presented in Fig. 3a, d along with their approximate outlines, as they were provided by the polygon approximation of the outline of each map. The mobile robot used in the experiments is the Turtlebot2 by ROBO-TIS equipped with an Orbecc Astra Pro RGB-D sensor and a Hokuyo URG-04LX scanning laser rangefinder. The software system is implemented within

Table 1. The parameter tuning for the algorithm in Sect. 3.1.

	th_o (m)	th_d (m)	th_{vm} (m)	th_l (m)	th_{sm} (m²)
Domestic Env.	10	2	10	[20,40]	800
Industrial Env.	150	250	40	[30,300]	9200

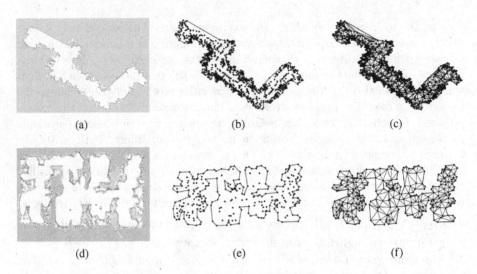

Fig. 3. Steps of the algorithm for the two environments: (a, d) the occupancy grid maps with their approximate outlines, (b, e) graphs after algorithm in Sect. 3.1 and (c, f) Delaunay triangulation. (a, b, c) correspond to the industrial environment while (d, e, f) to the domestic environment.

Fig. 4. Spatial segmentation produced in (a) industrial environment and (b) domestic environment

Robot Operating System (ROS) framework. For the extraction of the topological graphs, we experimentally set the thresholds concerning the steps of the algorithm in Sect. 3.1 as described in Table 1. For the refinement of the segmentation, we created a dataset from the surroundings of each environment. During images acquisition phase, we kept track of the robot's pose (during the Gmapping), in order to enable us partition them into clusters based on the initial spatial segmentation shown in Fig. 4. Each cluster consists of approximately 1000 sample images of resolution 640 × 480 pixels. Sample images of our datasets are shown in Fig. 5.

Fig. 5. Example images from datasets (up) in industrial environment and (down) in domestic environment

Table 2. The autoencoder's layer parameters

		Module1		Module2		Module3		Module4		Module5	
		Input	*Output*	*Input*	*Output*	*Input*	*Output*	*Input*	*Output*	*Input*	*Output*
Encoder		3	16	16	32	32	64	64	128	128	256
Filter size	(3,3)										
Padding	(1,1)										
MaxPool	(2,2)										
Decoder		256	128	128	64	64	32	32	16	16	3
Filter size	(2,2)										
Stride	(2,2)										

The utilized autoencoder has 5 modules in both the encoder and the decoder. The input is resized to 256×256 pixels, irrespectively of the original size of input images, to match the size of the network's input. The specific parameters of the layers are shown Table 2, where *input* and *output* represent the input and output channels of each module. *Filter size* refers to the convolutional and deconvolutional layer of each module in the encoder and the decoder, respectively. Also in the encoder, *Padding* refers to the convolutional layers and *MaxPool* represents the kernel of the MaxPool operation in every module. Stride of the deconvolutional layers of the decoder is reported as well, as *Stride*. The projection of the area embeddings in 2D space is depicted in Fig. 6 using the t-SNE algorithm.

To assess the relationship between these area embeddings, we computed their $Dist\_Metric$. Areas that are not adjacent cannot belong to the same area by default, so we only take into consideration measurements between areas that have common boundaries as defined in the topological graph from the spatial segmentation. Table 3 demonstrates the results, in accordance to which areas (A6, A7) in the domestic environment and (A1,A2), (A3,A2) in the industrial environment are merged. The th_{merg} threshold for these experiments was set equal to 0.17.

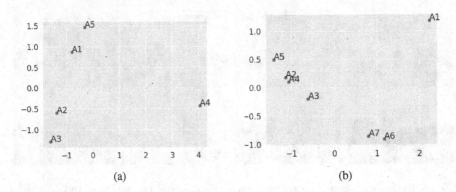

(a)   (b)

Fig. 6. Embeddings in 2D space in (a) industrial environment and (b) domestic environment

Table 3. Normalized euclidean distances and cosine similarities between embedding vectors of adjacent areas

	Area1	*Area2*	*Euclidean*	*Cosine*	*Dist_Metric*
Domestic environment	**A6**	**A7**	**0.0000**	**1.0000**	**0.0000**
	A3	A4	0.0836	0.8993	0.1843
	A3	A2	0.1270	0.8597	0.2673
	A4	A5	0.3734	0.7394	0.6339
	A3	A5	0.5644	0.3997	1.1647
	A1	A2	1.0000	0.0000	2.0000
Industrial environment	**A1**	**A2**	**0.0000**	**0.8316**	**0.1683**
	A3	**A2**	**0.0038**	**1.000**	**0.0038**
	A5	A4	0.7643	0.3357	1.4285
	A1	A4	0.8241	0.0523	1.7717
	A4	A2	0.8241	0.0000	1.8241
	A3	A4	1.0000	0.0722	1.9277

In Fig. 7 the final segmentation after the merging of areas is shown together with their ground truth segmentation. Each predicted segment corresponds to the segment in the ground truth with the biggest overlap. The segmentation accuracy of the semantic map is further evaluated by exploiting the Jaccard and Dice indices in the pixel-wise manner of the created maps, compared to the ground truth data. Table 4 indicates that the algorithm performs better in more constrained environments with higher diversity between the rooms, while it is less effective in open spaces. However, in all cases the automatic segmentation is achieved with significant accuracy proving the ability of the proposed method to semantically segment and annotate the environments in order to ease robot installation.

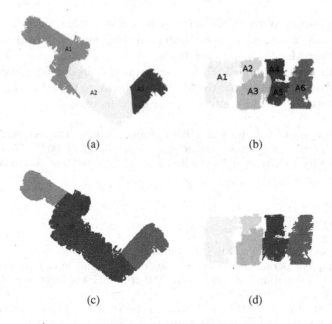

(a)   (b)

(c)   (d)

Fig. 7. (a, b) Final segmentation and (c, d) ground truth

Table 4. Jaccard and Dice index per area (%)

Domestic environment	Area	A1	A2	A3	A4	A5	A6	*Mean*
	J	98.6	90.2	90.3	89.5	77.6	97.0	**90.5**
	D	99.3	94.8	94.9	94.4	87.3	98.5	**94.9**
Industrial environment	**Area**	**A1**	**A2**	**A3**	*Mean*			
	J	61.1	85.0	89.2	**78.5**			
	D	75.9	91.9	94.3	**87.3**			

5   Conclusion and Future Work

In this paper, we have introduced a methodology that succeeds in arranging an
environment in clusters of areas, in order to facilitate robot installation and automate its deployment efforts. The proposed method represents a viable alternative
to semantic mapping methods that require environments with familiar objects
or rooms, or require doors to separate distinct areas. Although the limitation
of parameter tuning exists, our method manages to partition an occupancy grid
map based not only on the laser scans but also taking advantage of the spatial
continuity and visual coherence of the environment. The experiments were conducted with a real robot in diverse real environments. The experimental results
revealed that the method has satisfactory performance in segmenting both the
environments and as anticipated, and is more robust in better bounded environments with higher discrepancy between rooms. This is in complete agreement

with the philosophy of the CNN autoencoder, as it is expected to extract more representative features among areas with more distinguishing features. As future work, a strategy for the parameter tuning according to different metric map's characteristics can be applied. Further study is also needed for the preprocessing of the dataset in order for the method to be more trajectory independent, probably by the use of the depth sensor in the camera used.

Acknowledgments. This work has been supported from General Secretariat for Research and Technology under Grant agreement no. T6YB-00238 "Q-CONPASS: Dynamic Quality CONtrol on Production lines using intelligent AutonomouS vehicleS".

References

1. Abdelrasoul, Y., Saman, A.B.S.H., Sebastian, P.: A quantitative study of tuning ROS gmapping parameters and their effect on performing indoor 2D slam. In: 2016 2nd IEEE international symposium on Robotics and Manufacturing Automation (ROMA), pp. 1–6. IEEE (2016)
2. Ambruş, R., Claici, S., Wendt, A.: Automatic room segmentation from unstructured 3-D data of indoor environments. IEEE Robot. Autom. Lett. **2**(2), 749–756 (2017)
3. Bogue, R.: Domestic robots: Has their time finally come? Ind. Robot Int. J. (2017)
4. Fernandez-Chaves, D., Ruiz-Sarmiento, J.R., Petkov, N., Gonzalez-Jimenez, J.: From object detection to room categorization in robotics. In: Proceedings of the 3rd International Conference on Applications of Intelligent Systems, pp. 1–6 (2020)
5. Frias Nores, E., Balado Frías, J., Díaz Vilariño, L., Lorenzo Cimadevila, H.R., et al.: Point cloud room segmentation based on indoor spaces and 3D mathematical morphology (2020)
6. Grisetti, G., Stachniss, C., Burgard, W.: Improved techniques for grid mapping with rao-blackwellized particle filters. IEEE Trans. Robot. **23**(1), 34–46 (2007)
7. Hiller, M., Qiu, C., Particke, F., Hofmann, C., Thielecke, J.: Learning topometric semantic maps from occupancy grids. In: 2019 IEEE/RSJ International Conference on Intelligent Robots and Systems (IROS), pp. 4190–4197. IEEE (2019)
8. Hinton, G.E., Salakhutdinov, R.R.: Reducing the dimensionality of data with neural networks. Science **313**(5786), 504–507 (2006)
9. Hou, J., Yuan, Y., Schwertfeger, S.: Area graph: Generation of topological maps using the voronoi diagram. In: 2019 19th International Conference on Advanced Robotics (ICAR). pp. 509–515. IEEE (2019)
10. Jung, J., Stachniss, C., Kim, C.: Automatic room segmentation of 3d laser data using morphological processing. ISPRS Int. J. Geo-Inf. **6**(7), 206 (2017)
11. Kostavelis, I., Gasteratos, A.: Semantic mapping for mobile robotics tasks: a survey. Robot. Autonom. Syst. **66**, 86–103 (2015)
12. Kostavelis, I., Gasteratos, A.: Semantic maps from multiple visual cues. Exp. Syst. Appl. **68**, 45–57 (2017)
13. Kostavelis, I., Giakoumis, D., Malassiotis, S., Tzovaras, D.: Human aware robot navigation in semantically annotated domestic environments. In: International Conference on Universal Access in Human-Computer Interaction, pp. 414–423. Springer (2016). https://doi.org/10.1007/978-3-030-49108-6

14. Kostavelis, I., Kargakos, A., Giakoumis, D., Tzovaras, D.: Robot's Workspace enhancement with dynamic human presence for socially-aware navigation. In: Liu, M., Chen, H., Vincze, M. (eds.) ICVS 2017. LNCS, vol. 10528, pp. 279–288. Springer, Cham (2017). https://doi.org/10.1007/978-3-319-68345-4_25
15. Kostavelis, I., et al.: Understanding of human behavior with a robotic agent through daily activity analysis. Int. J. Soc. Robot. **11**(3), 437–462 (2019)
16. Lu, V.N., et al.: Service robots, customers and service employees: what can we learn from the academic literature and where are the gaps? J. Ser. Theor. Prac. (2020)
17. Luperto, M., Amigoni, F.: Predicting the global structure of indoor environments: a constructive machine learning approach. Autonom. Robot. **43**(4), 813–835 (2018). https://doi.org/10.1007/s10514-018-9732-7
18. Manyika, J., Chui, M., Miremadi, M., et al.: A future that works: AI, automation, employment, and productivity. McKinsey Global Institute Research, Tech. Rep. 60 (2017)
19. Mielle, M., Magnusson, M., Lilienthal, A.J.: A method to segment maps from different modalities using free space layout Maoris: map of ripples segmentation. In: 2018 IEEE International Conference on Robotics and Automation (ICRA), pp. 4993–4999. IEEE (2018)
20. Mozos, O.M., Triebel, R., Jensfelt, P., Rottmann, A., Burgard, W.: Supervised semantic labeling of places using information extracted from sensor data. Robot. Autonom. Syst. **55**(5), 391–402 (2007)
21. Qi, X., et al.: Building semantic grid maps for domestic robot navigation. Int. J. Adv. Robot. Syst. **17**(1), 1729881419900066 (2020)
22. Roweis, S.T., Saul, L.K.: Nonlinear dimensionality reduction by locally linear embedding. Science **290**(5500), 2323–2326 (2000)
23. Søraa, R.A., Fostervold, M.E.: Social domestication of service robots: the secret lives of automated guided vehicles (AGVs) at a Norwegian hospital. Int. J. Hum-Comput. Stud. **152**, 102627 (2021)
24. Sünderhauf, N., et al.: Place categorization and semantic mapping on a mobile robot. In: 2016 IEEE International Conference on Robotics and Automation (ICRA), pp. 5729–5736. IEEE (2016)
25. Tian, Y., Wang, K., Li, R., Zhao, L.: A fast incremental map segmentation algorithm based on spectral clustering and quadtree. Adv. Mech. Eng. **10**(2), 1687814018761296 (2018)
26. Tsamis, G., Kostavelis, I., Giakoumis, D., Tzovaras, D.: Towards life-long mapping of dynamic environments using temporal persistence modeling. In: 2020 25th International Conference on Pattern Recognition (ICPR), pp. 10480–10485. IEEE (2021)
27. Yue, Y., Zhao, C., Wu, Z., Yang, C., Wang, Y., Wang, D.: Collaborative semantic understanding and mapping framework for autonomous systems. In: IEEE/ASME Transactions on Mechatronics (2020)

Knowledge-Enabled Generation of Semantically Annotated Image Sequences of Manipulation Activities from VR Demonstrations

Andrei Haidu(✉) , Xiaoyue Zhang , and Michael Beetz

Institute for Artificial Intelligence, University of Bremen, Bremen, Germany
haidu@uni-bremen.de, xiaoy.zhang@jacobs-university.de,
beetz@cs.uni-bremen.de

Abstract. This work presents a cloud-to-edge framework capable of collecting and annotating synthetic images from human performances in virtual environments with the purpose of enabling the training and deployment of robot vision models. The virtual environment is capable of providing close-to-reality image data using state of the art rendering capabilities of game engine technologies. The human performances in the virtual world are fully recorded and segmented into meaningful motion phases of action models from cognitive science. The recorded performances are stored as fully re-playable episodes enabling multi-camera post-processing to acquire fully labeled vision data. The data is represented using KNOWROB acting as an extension of the robot's knowledge base, making it robot understandable and accessible using it's built in logic based query language.

1 Introduction

Image recognition is a core task in robot vision, as it enables robotic agents to navigate and manipulate objects in their surroundings. To equip robots with such capabilities multiple learning techniques are available, from which however deep learning algorithms have emerged as the most competitive ones. One of their major drawbacks though, is the large amount of annotated data that they require in order to successfully train their models. Collecting and annotating such large-scale image datasets is an expensive, time consuming process. Generating robot suitable datasets is not a trivial task due to the large variety of sensors available for robots, each with different parameters and capabilities. Datasets can thus become incompatible between robots, even if acting in the same environment, only because of the different sensing devices. As an example, most robotic systems require depth information in order to accurately understand scenes/ estimate 6D object poses. Due to these characteristics, most available computer vision datasets are not necessarily appropriate for robot vision.

One way to overcome these barriers is by creating custom-tailored synthetic image datasets by rendering and annotating scenes from virtual environments.

M. Vincze et al. (Eds.): ICVS 2021, LNCS 12899, pp. 130–143, 2021.
https://doi.org/10.1007/978-3-030-87156-7_11

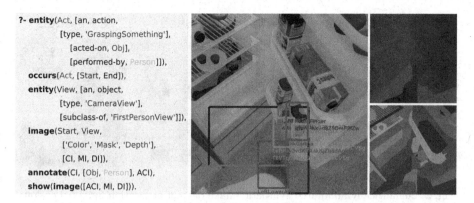

```
?- entity(Act, [an, action,
              [type, 'GraspingSomething'],
              [acted-on, Obj],
              [performed-by, Person]]),
   occurs(Act, [Start, End]),
   entity(View, [an, object,
              [type, 'CameraView'],
              [subclass-of, 'FirstPersonView']]),
   image(Start, View,
              ['Color', 'Mask', 'Depth'],
              [CI, MI, DI]),
   annotate(CI, [Obj, Person], ACI),
   show(image([ACI, MI, DI])).
```

Fig. 1. Query based image acquisition and annotation

This approach enables creating specific scenarios, thus providing: statistical variation in the data; the ability to study or correct for specific cases; address bias and class imbalance; and the ability to generate conditions that are challenging to re-create in reality, such as fragile setups or specific lighting conditions. Synthetic data gives the most controllable influence on simulating specific sensors parameters in order to obtain robot sensor approximated data, such as, resolution, field of view, lens distortions, noise, artifacts, etc. It further provides exclusive data annotation that is otherwise not available, such as the pixel-exact visibility information of the entities (occlusion and clipping). In [3,8–10] the authors showcase various similar advantages of using modern game engines with state of the art photo-realistic rendering capabilities in order to generate training datasets with pixel-accurate segmentation masks.

This work is built on top of the AMEvA (Automated Models of Everyday Activities) system [5], a special-purpose knowledge acquisition, interpretation, and processing framework, capable of recording and segmenting human performed manipulation activities in virtual environments. This work aims at providing robots and researchers with a framework capable of: (1) generating semantically annotated, sensor-specific synthetic image datasets from human performed tasks in virtual environments; (2) querying the dataset using specific action or visual scene parameters using the KnowRob query language [1]; and (3) providing a pipeline enabling training and deploying robot vision models from the acquired data. Figure 1 showcases a query example and the resulting images from the knowledge base. It starts by searching for human performed grasping actions, followed by the selection of the images' camera perspective (first-person view). Then, using the start time and the selected camera perspective, the color, mask and depth image data are requested, where the color image is further augmented with the bounds of the object acted on and the person performing the action.

The remainder of the paper is organized as follows: Sect. 2 gives an overview of the framework, describes the symbolic virtual environment and the structure

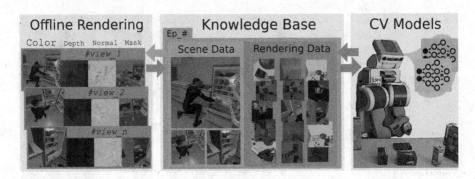

Fig. 2. Semantically annotated synthetic image dataset generation for robot vision

of the recorded episodes. Section 3 explains the image acquisition pipeline of replaying and post-processing recorded episodes and the 3D sphere scanning of entities or scenes. Section 4 gives various example queries for image acquisition and annotation, and a pipeline for automatically training a binary classifier from the requested image data. Finally Sect. 5 introduces various related works and Sect. 6 concludes the work and presents planned future work.

2   Overview

Figure 2 depicts the overview of the system, with KNOWROB at its core as a hybrid knowledge base consisting of *symbolic* and *subsymbolic* data. The symbolic data, represented using OWL [6], contains the shared ontology between the robot and the virtual environment, including the representation of all the entities and their properties (agents, objects, camera views, lights, articulations, partonomies, etc.), as well as the actions and events which can occur during the human's performance. The subsymbolic part contains the per-episode based world state information: poses of all the entities at every simulated frame (∼10 ms), the gaze of the user, forces and velocities used during execution, etc. Using the world state data, the episodes are visually re-enacted in order to extend the subsymbolic episode data with computer vision related information. The post-processing part is depicted in the left part of the figure, where the episode is re-rendered and processed from various given camera perspectives and sensor parameters. The resulting vision data is then integrated in the subsymbolic part of the corresponding episode and optimized for quick access by indexing it. The newly appended data can then be used in sync with the symbolic one in other to query for specific situations, events, or actions using KNOWROB's query language. The acquired image data can then be further prepared for training robot vision models on the fly.

2.1   Virtual Environment

The virtual environment used for data collection acts as a rendering of the robot's knowledge base, every entity with its properties has a representation in the

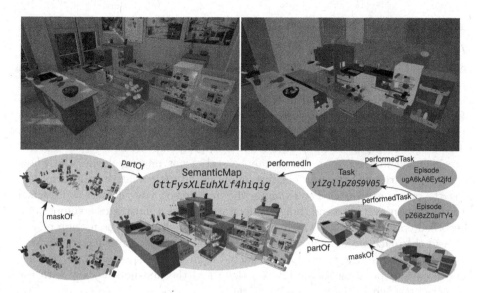

Fig. 3. A semantically annotated virtual environment in *color* and *mask* rendering mode (top) and the symbolic relations between episodes and the environment (bottom)

extended ontology of KNOWROB. The top part of Fig. 3 shows the level of detail of a semantically annotated kitchen environment, rendered in its default (color) and pixel based segmentation (mask) rendering mode. The bottom part illustrates the relations in the knowledge base between the executed tasks (episodes) and the virtual world in which the performance occurred (semantic map). Each episode is linked to a task description instance, which in turn is linked to the map instance in which it was performed. When generating a semantic map from a new virtual scene, each entity in the world will be appointed with a new unique identifier using UUID's. This guarantees uniqueness of all individuals across all previous and future semantic maps. The visible entities are then given unique pixel-based segmentation masks colors, with guaranteed uniqueness at the semantic map instance level, this limitation is due to the numerical limit of 8-bit RGB color combination (255^3) which cannot guarantee global collision free usage. If visual mask duplicates do arise, it is not an issue since they are never used in a global manner, they act as a property bound to the unique instance. When a new performance is to be executed in the virtual world, a semantic task description is created for it in the knowledge base, mostly consisting of the natural language description of the task to be executed. Once the semantic map in which it is to be performed is known, it is instantiated with a UUID and linked against the map instance. Therefore every performed instance will be further represented as an episode instance linked to the task description instance, which in its own links to the semantic map instance. This enables the actions and events performed in each episode to be directly linked to the entity instances in the virtual world representation.

2.2   Recorded Episodes

In order to be able to fully replay the human performance movements and their effects, during the execution the world state changes are continuously recorded into re-playable episodes bundled as *symbolic* and *subsymbolic* data. The symbolic representation is stored in KNOWROB containing the events and the performed actions, whereas the subsymbolic part is stored using NoSQL databases (MongoDB), containing the movement data of all the entities in the world. To be able to replay the episodes from multiple perspectives, virtual cameras are included in the world. These can be static, not moving during the whole episode, or attached to other entities, maintaining their relative transform during the whole execution. For example the first-person view camera is attached to the human avatar's head, pointing forward. Figure 4 illustrates a snippet of a recorded episode together with its underlying symbolic data: the motion phases of a fetch&place action, the various states of the entities, or the gaze information. In the figure the snippet is re-enacted from two perspectives: an overview static camera pointing at the kitchen (left) and the first-person view with the camera attached to the user's head (right).

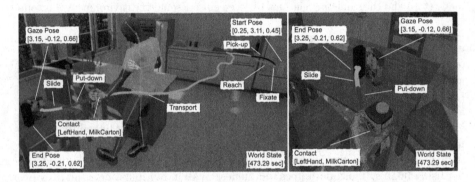

Fig. 4. Recorded episode snippet with symbolic annotations and the human gaze

3   Data Collection

This section presents the implementation details for collecting, annotating, and storing synthetic images from virtual environments. During its post-processing step, various types of render modes are used to acquire vision related data: *color*, *depth*, *normal*, *unlit*, and *mask*. The *color* mode represents the default shading technique, taking into account the direct/indirect lighting sources, reflections, etc. to render the scene. The *depth* mode renders the scene in a grayscale format using the rendering's engine built in depth buffer (z-buffer) data, thus providing a pixel based distance from the camera plane to the scene. The *normal* mode, renders the world-space normal vector values of the surfaces, useful for providing surface plane annotations. The *unlit* mode alters the visual entities materials to be emissive, this forces the materials to emit light uniformly across their surface, ignoring any external lighting, making them useful when the data is required to contain perfectly visible entities event in dark locations (e.g. back of a drawer). *Mask* applies the unique RGB color combination values for each entity to their materials and uses the *unlit* rendering mode to make sure the color distribution is uniform over the whole entity surface, thus providing a pixel-accurate segmentation of the scene.

The framework is equipped with two types of scan processes: one, where the recorded performances are replayed on frame by frame basis from all the requested custom camera perspectives; and two, where entities, or scenes, are re-enacted and then scanned from a given number of points on a sphere, thus capturing all possible angles of the given entity/scene. The two approaches come with different advantages and disadvantages. Replaying the recordings will provide the data with natural situations in the environments, useful for robot vision, since the images are not necessarily object centric. It however could miss various details due to the usage circumstances of the items (e.g. bottom of the milk carton is rarely visible). This, however, can be overcome using the second scanning process, namely, the 3D sphere based scan, capturing the entities from all angles. However, using only this approach could cause the trained models to overfit due to the abundance of very similar, or seldomly visible, data (e.g. bottom of the milk carton). Therefore, a combination of both would be a favorable approach.

Having the data connected to the knowledge base, specific queries can be written in order to acquire or generate specific situation data. If the detection of entities that are usually visible from any side in the real world is required (e.g. fruits), including their 3D scan data would be recommended. However, for entities usually found in stereotypical situations (e.g. milk in the fridge door) a more beneficial approach would be to re-construct the scene in their stereotypical format and provide a 3D scan of it. This can be either done manually, or using queries to selectively search and re-enact specific scenes from the episode data. By searching for contact events, such as between the fridge door and the milk container, then using the event's information (entity instances and timestamps) the scene can be specifically re-enacted and scanned.

During the scan process images and scene descriptions (visible entities in the frame) are constantly uploaded and amended to the corresponding episode in MongoDB. The data will eventually contain a full timeline of all the entity movements in sync with the rendered images and their scene descriptions. Once the scan process is complete, the data is re-indexed for quick access optimization. Every indexed field is organized in a `B-tree` data structure, reducing search time complexity to $\mathcal{O}(\log n)$. The vision data relevant index keys are: the `UUIDs` of the entities present in the scene, providing fast entity base image searches, such as "get all images including an apple". Other index keys are entity visibility related such as: percentage in the image, occlusion percentage, or if the entity is clipped or not (fully visible, or partially cut out of the image). This allows for further specific queries, such as including only images where the objects are fully

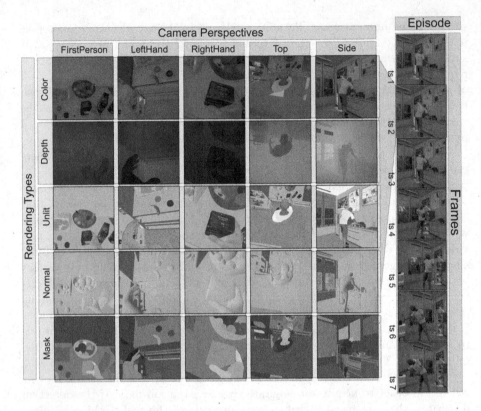

Fig. 5. Camera perspectives and rendering modes during episode frame processing

visible and occupy a large percentage in the image, or images which are partially occluded, but not clipped in the image, etc. Each providing various advantages when used as training data for building computer vision models.

3.1 Episode Replay

This subsection presents the image data processing and acquisition pipeline. The recorded episode world state movements are loaded and replayed from every given camera perspective. During this process the physics engine is disabled, thus the realtime factor and the update rates become irrelevant. This allows the rendering to be performed using the highest quality settings (detailed lighting, shadows, reflections, etc.). After every processed scene the acquired data is uploaded to the database and inserted in the corresponding part of the episode. Figure 5 shows an example of processing a frame from different camera perspectives and rendering modes.

Algorithm 1 presents an overview of the main simulation steps of the episode replay processing. The *episode* data acts as input and output, because of its updated state after every processed frame. The first step loads the requested

---

Algorithm 1: Episode processing

Input/Output: *episode*
ProcessEpisode
    SetRenderingParameters()
    foreach *frame* ∈ *episode* **do**
        SetEntityPoses(*frame*)
        foreach *view* ∈ *episode* **do**
            SetCameraPose(*view*)
            img_{color} ← **Render**('color')
            img_{depth} ← **Render**('depth')
            img_{unlit} ← **Render**('unlit''')
            img_{normal} ← **Render**('normal')
            img_{mask} ← **Render**('mask')
            scene ← **ProcessScene**(img_{mask})   // see alg. 2
            scene ← **ProcessOcclusion**(*scene*)   // see alg. 3
            Upload($img_{color}, img_{depth}, img_{unlit}, img_{normal}, img_{mask}$, *scene*)
        end
    end
    UpdateDatabaseIndexes()
  return

---

rendering parameters, such as resolution, lighting quality, lens effects, etc. Afterwards each episode frame is iterated through having their changes applied to the virtual world. Once the world state is set, the camera is moved into the requested perspectives using the virtual camera poses in the world. Once the camera pose is set, the rendering modes are iterated through and the resulting images are collected in bitmap format. After the *mask* render mode, the resulting segmentation image is further used to process the scene data in Algorithm 2 and the occlusion data in Algorithm 3. Once the scene has been processed, the images are compressed to a PNG format and uploaded together with the scene data to the database. After processing the last episode frame, the database is re-indexed on the new entries.

Algorithm 2 depicts the main steps for processing the scene using the rendered mask bitmap image as input. This step records all the entities and their visibility properties in the active scene. By iterating through the mask image pixel by pixel, the algorithm checks if the entity mapped to the given unique RGB color is already in the scene, if yes, its pixel count and bounding box is updated, if not, a new entry is created with an initial pixel count and bounding box. After finishing the iteration, the percentage of each entity in the image is calculated by dividing its pixel count with the image total.

Once the entity data is available in the *scene* the algorithm proceeds with the *occlusion* and *clipped* data calculation. The *occlusion* parameter will store the percentage of the entity overlapped by others in the image, where as *clipped* will flag if the entity is outside of the image bounds (partially cut out of the image). This additional information provides additional filtering options when requesting

---

Algorithm 2: Scene processing

Input: img_{mask}
Output: $scene$
ProcessScene
> $scene \leftarrow \emptyset$
>   **foreach** $pixel \in img_{mask}$ **do**
>> $uuid \leftarrow$ **GetEntityId**$(pixel)$
>> **if** $scene.$**Contains**$(uuid)$ **then**
>>> $\&entity \leftarrow scene.$**GetEntity**$(uuid)$
>>> $\&entity.num_{pixel} + +$
>>> $\&entity.bb.$**Update**$(pixel_x, pixel_y)$
>>
>> **else**
>>> $entity \leftarrow$ **Entity**$(uuid)$
>>> $entity.num_{pixel} \leftarrow 1$
>>> $entity.bb.$**Set**$(pixel_x, pixel_y)$
>>> $scene.$**Add**$(entity)$
>>
>> **end**
>
>   **end**
> $scene \leftarrow$ **CalcPerc**$(scene)$
return $scene$

---

image data. Images of barely visible entities or clipped by the image, can be avoided, or on the contrary, acquire images with entities within a given range of occlusion percentage. Algorithm 3 depicts the major steps of the occlusion processing. It starts by iterating all the entities in the scene. For each entity a custom occlusion ('x-ray') material (translucent with disabled depth pass) is applied which will force the rendering engine to draw it on top of everything else in the scene. After rendering the scene the resulting bitmap image is processed by counting the number of the pixels belonging to the custom material (white colored). The occlusion percentage is then calculated from the total number of visible pixels in the default scene divided with the total number of pixels visible using the occlusion material: $1 - \frac{num_{pixel}}{num_{occ}}$. During the pixel count the algorithm also checks if any of them are on the edge of the image in order to mark the entity as clipped or not. Once finished the mask material is re-applied to the entity. Resulting images from the process can be visualized in Fig. 6, where the white colored entities have the custom occlusion material applied to them, forcing them to be drawn on top of everything else.

3.2   3D Sphere Scan

The complementary approach for collecting robot vision data using virtual environments is the 3D sphere scans of entities or scenes. This generates n equidistant points on a sphere which will be used as camera poses pointing at the center of the scene. This approach provides perfectly visible images of scenes from numerous

---

Algorithm 3: Occlusion processing

Input/Output: *scene*
ProcessOcclusion
    foreach *entity* $\in$ *scene* **do**
        ApplyOcclusionMaterial(*entity*)
        $img_{occ} \leftarrow$ RenderView()
        $entity.num_{occ} \leftarrow$ CountPixels(img_{occ})
        $entity.clipped \leftarrow$ IsClipped(img_{occ})
        ApplyMaskMaterial(*entity*)
    end
  return *scene*

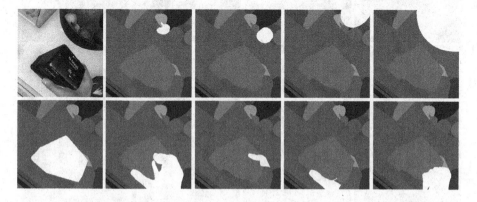

Fig. 6. Entity occlusion calculation with custom 'x-ray' material

angles, making a perfect candidate for providing base datasets for computer vision algorithms.

Figure 7 depicts examples of various 3D scanning processes including the scanning points ($n = 512$) on the sphere and some of the resulting images from the scan in their multiple render modes. There are two types of scan processes: one which iterates and scans all the classes in the semantically annotated virtual world, and a second one where custom scenarios are re-enacted from various events of human performances. On the left side of the image an entity scan is exemplified, in the middle a scenario scan is shown where the scene contains fruits in contact with a fruit bowl. The right side re-enact a scene from a human performance where a contact occurred with the human's foot and the handle of a drawer.

4   Experiments

This section presents various abridged KNOWROB queries accessing image related data from the knowledge base by combining symbolic data, such as

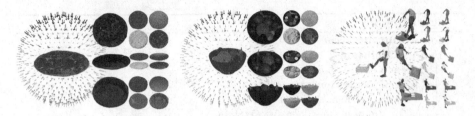

Fig. 7. 3D sphere scans of entities and scenes

Fig. 8. Images of a grasp action at the start and end (row 1&2) from multiple camera views, and images of the coffee package entity with various occlusion and clipping values (row 3&4) (Color figure online)

events and actions which occurred during the human performance, and sub-symbolic data from the rendered scene, such as the entities present in the scene and their visibility properties.

The following query searches and displays images from a particular event. It starts by searching in the pre-loaded episodes for grasping actions, namely grasping a coffee package. Once found, the *occurs* predicate will return (bound) the start and end time values of the action. Using the built in PROLOG predicate *findall* we iterate through all existing camera perspectives, request the associated *color* image and annotate it with the grasped objects' bounding box, class and id values. Figure 8 shows the result of such a query, depicting the start and the end of a grasp action, rendered from multiple camera perspectives (first and second row).

```
?- entity(Act, [an, action, [type, 'GraspingSomething'],
                [acted-on, [an, object, [type, 'CoffeePackage'], Obj]]]),
   occurs(Act, [Start, End]),
   findall(T, (entity(View, [an, object, [type, 'CameraView']]),
               image(Start, View, ['Color'], Img),
               annotate(Img, [Obj], T)), List),
   show(image(List)).
```

The next query searches for specific visibility parameters of the entities. It returns the images of the coffee package entity, where its given visibility properties, such as the occlusion percentage and the clipping property are met. The results of the query are visualized in the last two rows of Fig. 8 starting with fully visible, non occluded (green) images, followed by clipped and partially occluded (yellow), not clipped and partially occluded (blue), and not clipped and mostly occluded (red) images.

```
?- entity(Obj, [an, object, [type, 'CoffeePackage']]),
   findall(T, (image(Obj, [occlusion(0.1, 0.2), clipped(0)],
                          ['Color'], Img),
               annotate(Img, [Obj], T)), List),
   show(image(List)).
```

The next example query will search for specific events in the loaded episodes and re-enact the scene in order to trigger a 3D sphere scan. In this example the query searches for fruits in contact with a fruit bowl, collects the all the objects in contact in a scene and triggers a scan on it. Figure 7 depicts the resulting scene scan (middle) and a similar scene with a contact between the user's foot and the drawer (right).

```
?- entity(Bowl, [an, object,
                [type, 'Bowl'], [subclass-of, 'WoodenBowl']]),
   findall(T, (entity(Ev, [an, event, [type, 'ContactSituation'],
                          [in-contact, Bowl],
                          [in-contact, [an, object, [type, 'Fruit'], T]],
                          [during, [0.0, 0.1]]])), List),
   append(List, [Bowl], Scene),
   scan(Scene, 0.1, 512).
```

The following Fig. 9 shows the visualization of the training results using visdom[1] of a basic computer vision model trained from queried images from the knowledge base. This example implements a binary classifier using the VGG16 network as backbone with modified output layers. Two fully-connected layers are added with one dropout layer in between. The model receives input images with a resolution of 80×80 where the output is a probability score between 0 and 1. The data preparation, and training and deployment process is all done in one pipeline.

5   Related Work

Similar to the presented system, in [4,7] the authors present a system with the scope of collecting and annotating synthetic data form virtual environments.

---

[1] https://ai.facebook.com/tools/visdom/.

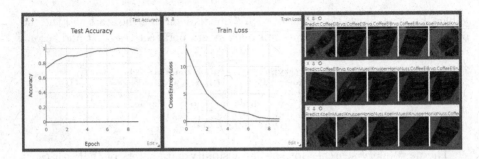

Fig. 9. Binary classifier model training pipeline

The main differences lays in the missing action segmentation capabilities and a built in robot understandable semantic data representation.

In the large-scale video dataset of EPIC-Kitchens [2] the authors store real world kitchen related performances from a first-person view perspective containing labeled item and action segments information. In comparison the presented system aims at recording scenes with a similar level of details in virtual environments, though capable of doing so from multiple camera perspectives, using custom sensor parameters and a fully automated action segmentation and image labeling tool.

6   Conclusion and Future Work

This work presents a framework capable of automatically collecting fully annotated vision data from human executed tasks in virtual environments. The data is stored in a hybrid knowledge base, combining symbolic and subsymbolic representation, making it understandable and accessible by robots. Technical details of the collection, annotation, and storage of the data are presented, with multiple example queries for searching and acquiring specific images are provided.

For future work the granularity of the collected data is planned to be extended to allow for scene specific occlusion queries, such as: *"get all images where the milk carton is occluded by the hand"*, for this the system would need to further extend the semantic data from the processed rendering scenes by including information about entities occluding each other. This can be done in the occlusion processing step (see Algorithm 3) by cross checking the masks segmentation pixels in the occlusion material area. This information can then be stored in a key value pair fashion to allow indexing in the database.

Another planned improvement tries to solve the similarity factor between the collected images. Because of the small increments when collecting the data, images can be very similar, or even almost identical. Currently this is avoided by querying for event-bound data, or using a large timestamp threshold, this however is far from an optimal approach. This could be solved using a database indexable similarity feature vector for each image. Once feasible approach would be to use the images scene information (camera and entity poses, visibility, etc.)

instead of its raw pixel data. This would make the feature vector's size comparably smaller. This similarity factor would then be integrated in the collected data providing access for queries to include a quantifiable similarity filter when querying for images.

Acknowledgements. This work was supported by the DFG as part of CRC #1320 "EASE - Everyday Activity Science and Engineering". The work was conducted in subproject R5.

References

1. Beetz, M., Beßler, D., Haidu, A., Pomarlan, M., Bozcuoglu, A.K., Bartels, G.: Know Rob 2.0 - a 2nd generation knowledge processing framework for cognition-enabled robotic agents. In: International Conference on Robotics and Automation (ICRA) (2018)
2. Damen, D., et al.: Scaling egocentric vision: the EPIC-KITCHENS dataset. In: European Conference on Computer Vision (ECCV) (2018)
3. Gaidon, A., Wang, Q., Cabon, Y., Vig, E.: VirtualWorlds as proxy for multi-object tracking analysis. In: IEEE Conference on Computer Vision and Pattern Recognition (CVPR) (2016)
4. Garcia, A., et al.: The RobotriX: an extremely photorealistic and very-large-scale indoor dataset of sequences with robot trajectories and interactions. In: IEEE International Conference on Intelligent Robots and Systems (IROS) (2018)
5. Haidu, A., Beetz, M.: Automated acquisition of structured, semantic models of manipulation activities from human VR demonstration. In: IEEE International Conference on Robotics and Automation (ICRA) (2021)
6. Horrocks, I., Patel-Schneider, P.F., Harmelen, F.V.: From SHIQ and RDF to OWL: the making of a web ontology language. J. Web Semant. **1**, 7–26 (2003)
7. Martinez-Gonzalez, P., Oprea, S., Garcia-Garcia, A., Jover-Alvarez, A., Orts-Escolano, S., Garcia-Rodriguez, J.: UnrealROX: an extremely photorealistic virtual reality environment for robotics simulations and synthetic data generation. Virtual Reality **24**(2), 271–288 (2019). https://doi.org/10.1007/s10055-019-00399-5
8. Müller, M., Casser, V., Lahoud, J., Smith, N., Ghanem, B.: Sim4CV: a photorealistic simulator for computer vision applications. Int. J. Comput. Vis. **126**, 902–919 (2018). https://doi.org/10.1007/s11263-018-1073-7
9. Richter, S.R., Vineet, V., Roth, S., Koltun, V.: Playing for data: ground truth from computer games. In: Leibe, B., Matas, J., Sebe, N., Welling, M. (eds.) ECCV 2016. LNCS, vol. 9906, pp. 102–118. Springer, Cham (2016). https://doi.org/10.1007/978-3-319-46475-6_7
10. Ros, G., Sellart, L., Materzynska, J., Vazquez, D., Lopez, A.M.: The SYNTHIA dataset: a large collection of synthetic images for semantic segmentation of urban scenes. In: IEEE Conference on Computer Vision and Pattern Recognition (2016)

Make It Easier: An Empirical Simplification of a Deep 3D Segmentation Network for Human Body Parts

Matteo Terreran[1]([✉]) [iD], Daniele Evangelista[1] [iD], Jacopo Lazzaro[2], and Alberto Pretto[1] [iD]

[1] Department of Information Engineering, University of Padova, Padova, Italy
{terreran,evangelista,alberto.pretto}@dei.unipd.it
[2] PlayCast Srl, Padova, Italy
jacopo@playcast.it

Abstract. Nowadays, computer vision is bringing benefits in different scenarios, such as home robotics, autonomous driving and healthcare. The latter is the main application scenario of this work. In this paper, we propose a simplified implementation of a state-of-the-art 3D semantic segmentation deep convolutional network used for automatizing the synthesis of orthopedic casts starting from 3D scans of patients' arms. The proposed network, based on the PointNet deep learning architecture, is capable of recognising and discriminating among several regions of interest on the scan of the patient's arm, like the regions around the thumb, the wrist and the elbow. Based on such segmented regions it is then possible to extract important measurements and features to synthesize a custom 3D printed cast. The aforementioned task is very specific and difficult to address with standard 3D segmentation algorithms, moreover it requires very specialized human intervention in data collection and preparation. Until now, semantic regions in human body parts are typically manually annotated by experts to ensure the required accuracy. Unfortunately, this process is time-consuming and, possibly, it may limit the amount of data available for data-driven approaches. In this work, we also investigate the usage of data augmentation to deal with such limited datasets and analyze the model performance by means of cross-validation, which highlights how the proposed architecture model can successfully, and with high accuracy, predict the regions of interest. This is an inspiring result for further research on deep models' adaptation to challenging applications, for which often clear and consistent data collections are not immediately available. Thus, an empirical approach based on pruning the network parameters and layers, together with a consistent data augmentation technique, could be really effective and prove to be the winning approach.

Keywords: 3D semantic segmentation · 3D data augmentation · Healthcare

© Springer Nature Switzerland AG 2021
M. Vincze et al. (Eds.): ICVS 2021, LNCS 12899, pp. 144–156, 2021.
https://doi.org/10.1007/978-3-030-87156-7_12

1 Introduction

Nowadays, computer vision is finding more and more real applications to simplify everyday life; for example in robotics, autonomous driving or to help people with visual impairments to autonomously navigate in unknown environments [18]. Furthermore, in healthcare scenarios, computer vision is becoming an important tool which enables novel applications, such as the possibility of obtaining a high-quality 3D scan of human limbs and the design of custom 3D printed casts as proposed by our industrial partner PlayCast[1] (See Fig. 1). 3D printed casts offer several advantages over traditional plaster casts widely used in orthopedics: they are lightweight, breathable and also both water and sweat resistant. Moreover, thanks to powerful 3D scanning systems, it is possible to obtain a complete and accurate scan in a few minutes. Thus, medical centers will be able to treat their patients even more effectively, more easily, and at a lower cost.

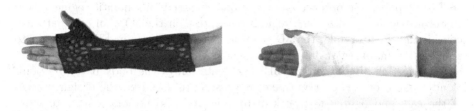

Fig. 1. Example of a 3D printed orthopedic cast (left), compared to the more traditional orthopedic cast made of plaster (right).

However, although an accurate scan of the part to be treated may be available, the design of orthopedic casts is currently performed by exploiting solid modeling Computer-Aided Design (CAD) programs, and creating such models is a time-consuming process that requires significant CAD experience [15]. The patient's anthropometric data must be gathered and processed, usually manually; this can generate many inaccuracies and requires many hours of advanced surface modeling in CAD systems [3,7]. Commercial CAD software are usually not easy to use for such geometries, due to their complex shape. Rich experience in CAD skills and long design time are required for an orthopaedist who may use commercial CAD software. Several CAD modeling approaches have been proposed for constructing cast models. The conventional cast model construction technique involves dozens of steps, and the total time required depends on the operator's CAD skills [8,10]. The various CAD modeling approaches can be classified into two main categories: direct modeling and parametric modeling. In the parametric modeling approach the required shape is built up by adding 3D features and defining relations and constraints among them, while the direct modelling approach focus on the direct manipulation of the 3D shape

---

[1] https://www.playcast.it/.

by pulling or pushing its faces. Despite being generally a slower procedure, the parametric modeling approach allows to define 3D models where every feature is controlled by dimensions; whenever some feature's dimensions are modified, the whole model is updated based on the relations between the features.

Following this approach, it is possible to develop a series of easy-to-use semi-automatic tools for the modelling of the medical device and ensure that they are ready to be manufactured [2, 7]. The developed procedure can be carried out by medical staff or clinicians for the most part, without the need of CAD expertise, thus solving the problem of production time and operator skills. In particular, the parametric modelling approach used by our industrial partner relies on some regions of interest manually localized on a 3D scan of a human limb. The patient cast is designed by analyzing the curves generated from the intersection of the 3D scan with some cutting planes passing through such regions of interest; these curves are measured and exploited to represent the patient anatomy in a suitable form to then automatically generate the custom 3D cast shape with edges and optimal ventilation patterns.

In this paper, we propose a novel approach based on semantic segmentation to automatically localize such regions of interest on the 3D scan of a patience; considering, for example, the 3D scan of a human arm as in Fig. 2, we aim to segment the main regions of the arm such as thumb, knuckles, wrist and elbow, and we do this directly on the 3D representation of the body part (3D point cloud). The proposed system makes it possible to speed up the design process of the cast and lighten the work of technicians, who no longer have to write down all the regions of interest on the scans by hand, but can limit themselves to check the regions proposed by the segmentation algorithm and, if necessary, correcting those regions that could be slightly misplaced. This allows to reach a complete automation of the entire process, leading to greater simplicity of the entire system, both for technicians and patients: only a 3D scan and one click from the scan to the real 3D printed model, customized for the patient.

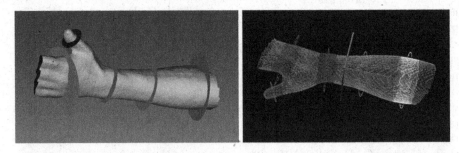

Fig. 2. Regions of interest considered for the parametric modelling approach on a sample 3D scan of a human arm.

Since the result of segmentation is directly used to derive the measurements and information needed to make the cast, it must be very accurate and precise.

Recently, deep learning networks have achieved very high performance in segmentation tasks when very large datasets are available. In our case, however, the regions of interest are system-specific and thus not present in other datasets publicly available in the literature; moreover, since each scan must be performed and annotated by an expert, only a small amount of data are available to appropriately train segmentation algorithms. This led us to investigate how to make the best use of the few data available: on one hand avoiding the use of too large and complex networks, and on the other hand exploiting various 3D data augmentation techniques. As demonstrated in our experiments, in such scenario a lighter network is capable of learning a more effective representation of the data while the use of data augmentation allows to further improve the model generalization performance.

To summarize, the paper presents 3 main contributions: (i) an application of 3D semantic segmentation in an healthcare scenario that automatizes the synthesis of a custom orthopedic cast for patients with fractures; (ii) a light deep learning network capable of recognizing specific regions of interest directly on a 3D scan (point cloud) of human limbs; (iii) the analysis of the impact of 3D data augmentation techniques for training a model on a very limited dataset. The rest of the paper is organized as follows. Section 2 reviews the literature about semantic segmentation on 3D data. In Sect. 3 we describe our proposed method, which is then thoroughly tested in Sect. 4 on a real scenario. Finally, in Sect. 5 conclusions are drawn and future research directions are illustrated.

2   Related Work

Several approaches have been proposed in the literature to analyze 3D data by means of deep-learning (DL) architectures, also due to the large number of formats that can be used to represent 3D data [1]: point clouds, meshes, volumetric grids or multi-view RGB-D images.

A first approach is to use architectures that work directly with volumetric or voxel grids inputs, as in VoxNet architecture [12] which relies on an occupancy grid. But voxelized inputs lose resolution compared to point clouds (since points very close end up in the same voxel), and sparse point clouds produce voxel grids with high memory usage (since all voxels are represented as occupied or free space). If the input data is a mesh, most approaches rely on graph-networks. Recently, in [5] authors proposed a CNN designed specifically for triangular meshes using specialized convolution and pooling layers that operate on the mesh edges. It is tested on mesh classification and mesh segmentation tasks.

Given a point cloud, different method paradigms are possible: projection-based, discretization-based, point-based and hybrid methods [4,11]. The first step of both projection and discretization based methods is to transform a point cloud into an intermediate regular representation (e.g. multi-view, spherical, volumetric), segment it and then project back the intermediate segmentation to the raw point cloud. In contrast, point-based methods directly work on irregular point clouds. Among the point-based methods, PointNet [16] represents the pioneer work which proposed to learn per-point features using shared MLPs and global features using symmetrical pooling functions. Based on PointNet, several point-based networks have been proposed in the literature. Given the limitations of networks based on volumetric representations, and the greater availability in the literature of networks using point clouds, in the end we chose to focus on this last type of networks to develop the DL architecture for extracting the cutting planes shown in Fig. 2, which represents our regions of interest.

Regarding the problem of recognizing several salient points or areas on a 3D scan, similar problems already tackled in the literature using deep-learning networks are 3D part segmentation [6,20] and hand-pose estimation [14,19] tasks. In 3D part segmentation tasks the network aims to decompose an object in its main parts; part segmentation is formulated as a per-point classification task, where each point in the input data is classified according to a set of classes representing the object parts. In hand-pose estimation tasks instead, the network aims to predict the position in the 3D space of particular points which represent the hand joints according to a given skeletal model. In the context of the project, we choose to exploit networks proposed for 3D part segmentation tasks in order to recognize and segment the areas around the cutting planes in Fig. 2. Once the areas are known, it is easy to define the cutting plane by computing the centroid and the principal components (e.g., PCA, SVD) of each area's points.

At the moment we do not consider hand-pose estimation networks, since the models found in the literature do not predict information on the forearm and wrist; we should then define a new skeletal model for the whole arm and a way to map the key points into parameters for the cutting planes. As a future research direction for the system, we will investigate how to take advantage of networks designed for hand pose estimation to refine the cutting planes estimated from the segmented parts.

3   Methods

To develop our automatic extraction method for the cutting planes we focus on deep learning architectures for 3D part segmentation tasks, capable of working directly with point cloud inputs. In this section, we describe the annotation algorithm developed to label the provided scans in a more convenient form for a semantic segmentation task; moreover, we present the deep learning architectures considered and further evaluated in our experiments described in Sect. 4.

3.1   Annotation Algorithm

The dataset provided by the industrial partner is composed of 21 scans of human arms. Each scan has been acquired using a 3D commercial sensor[2] with half millimeter resolution in depth estimation. All the scans have been manually annotated by experts that selected the cutting planes as shown in Fig. 2. The

---

[2] https://structure.io/structure-sensor-pro.

provided data are meshes in .OBJ format, which is not easy to be used as input for a deep learning network. Moreover, the planes annotated in the meshes consists of points outside the mesh itself and cannot be used directly to learn to segment the input data; each point of the scan should be annotated according to a set of labels.

Therefore, we developed an annotation algorithm to label the provided scans in a more convenient format to be handled by the deep-learning architecture. First the scans are converted to point clouds, by extracting the vertices from the mesh scans. Then, the information of the planes is used to annotate the points of the cloud. In particular, for each cutting plane:

1. Compute the corresponding plane equation in the 3D space;
2. Compute the parameters of its 3D circle (center, normal, radius) as shown in Fig. 2;
3. Based on the plane equation, select all the points with a distance from the plane less than a given threshold δ;
4. From the selected points, discards the points that have a distance from the center of the circle greater than its radius (this allows to avoid overlapping annotations, for example around the thumb);
5. Annotate the remaining neighboring points with the label associated with the plane.

With this procedure we labeled all the scans, considering a total of 6 classes, 5 classes for the different regions defined by the cutting planes, and 1 class (*Arm*) for the remaining points in the scan. Each plane is associated to a semantic label describing the region of the arm which it represents: *Thumb, Knucles, Wrist, Forearm* and *Elbow*. An example of the final labeled point cloud is depicted in Fig. 2, where we also show the original planes for reference. Once all the scans have been labeled with such annotation algorithm, the dataset has been divided in a train and test sets using a 80–20% division: the whole dataset of 21 labeled scans is divided in a training set of 16 scans, and a test set of 5 scans used only for evaluating each trained model; we rounded the number of scans in the training set to 16 to use multiples of 4 as batch size during training.

3.2   Segmentation Algorithm

Several architectures have been proposed in the literature, mostly derived from PointNet [16] architecture, such as PointNet++ [17], SO-Net [9], 3D-CapsNet [21]. However, such architectures are proposed and evaluated for very large dataset like ShapeNet-Part [13], which contains hundreds of scans for different types of objects. When considering a smaller and limited dataset like the one available (i.e., 21 scans of human arms), a large and complex architecture cannot be trained properly with a naive training (i.e., without proper data augmentation): from our experiments it generalizes very poorly on new data. Due to such considerations, we choose to develop our solution starting from Point-Net, which is the lightest among the state-of-the-art architectures selected, and we also consider a lighter version of PointNet (which we named *PointNet-light*) obtained by halving the number of convolutional filters used in each layer of the network. The result is an even lighter architecture in terms of parameters that from our experiments proved to be more efficient and accurate for very limited datasets.

In addition to propose and study the impact of reducing the number of parameters in a network for segmentation tasks with limited dataset, we also propose the use of data augmentation to make the model more robust when few data are available. Typically, in the case of images, the most commonly used data augmentation techniques consist of rotations, warping, scaling or color alterations. In the case of 3D data such as point clouds it is easy to use similar techniques, for example applying 3D rotations: the rotated point cloud will keep the same appearance and shape, but the spatial coordinates of its points will be very different, thus representing a new input for the network. In particular, we propose simple 3D data augmentation operations such rotation and reflection operations around the main axes of the point cloud (i.e. X, Y and Z axes) and jitter operations, where some Gaussian noise is added to the coordinates of the points forming the point cloud.

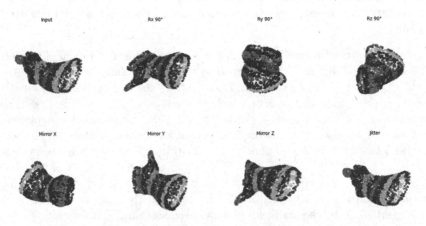

Fig. 3. Example of operations considered for our data augmentation. Top row: input point cloud and rotations about the main three axes. Bottom row: point cloud mirrored about the three main axes and jittered point cloud obtained adding Gaussian noise.

An example of the result of these various operations is represented in Fig. 3. Using such data augmentation techniques it is possible to greatly increase the cardinality of the training set when very few data are available (e.g., about 20 scans of our industrial partners), although it is not possible to reach the size of the datasets used to train state-of-the-art networks (about 1500 scans of different objects per category) where many distinct objects are available. Together with the proposed 3D data augmentation, our lightweight version of PointNet achieves very high accuracy in the given segmentation task, as demonstrated in our experiments.

4 Experiments

In this section, the results of our experiments are reported. In particular we first investigate which deep learning model performs better among the candidate architectures presented in Sect. 3. The best performing model is then optimized considering different data augmentation techniques and thoroughly evaluated with a 4-fold cross validation. All the experiments have been performed on a Dell XPS 8900, running Linux 18.04 and equipped with an Intel Core i7-6700CPU with 8 cores clocked at 3.40 GHz, a NVIDIA GeForce GTX 1070 graphics card and 16 GB of DDR3 RAM.

4.1 Model Selection

As a first step in the development of our automatic scan segmentation approach, we evaluated different state-of-the-art architectures proposed for semantic segmentation of point cloud data: Point-Net, 3D-PointCapsNet, SO-Net. All the models have been trained from scratch using the default hyper-parameters provided by the authors in their corresponding papers, using the train/test split described in Sect. 3.1. To evaluate the performance of each model, we used the metrics generally used in segmentation tasks: Global Accuracy and mean Intersection over Union. Global Accuracy (GA) describes the overall portion of correctly labeled points, while mean Intersection over Union (mIoU) is computed as the average value between the intersection of the prediction and ground truth regions over the union of them.

Table 1. Performance comparison of the considered architectures for 3D part segmentation on the limited dataset of the industrial partner.

Architecture	Global accuracy (%)	mIoU (%)
PointNet [16]	72.12	48.20
PointNet-light	**76.48**	**52.39**
3D-PointCapsNet [21]	45.02	7.89
SO-Net [9]	43.16	7.19

The results obtained for each candidate model are reported in Table 1. Large network such as SO-Net and 3D PointCapsNet perform very poorly on the provided dataset: the models predict only the class *Arm* for all the scan points giving a very low performance in terms of mIoU, since all the others regions of interest are misclassified. Compared to such architectures, PointNet is smaller and performs better on the test data, predicting almost all the classes considered; we obtain even better results when considering a lighter version of PointNet obtained by halving the number of kernels in each convolutional layer.

4.2   Data Augmentation

Although the light version of PointNet proved to be the best performing model among the one considered, its performance are not sufficient for an industrial application like the one in examination; indeed, we have a strong requirement on segmenting all the regions with high accuracy, otherwise the automatically generated cast can not adapt or even hurt the patient. As reported in Fig. 4, qualitative results are quite good. The network is able to correctly segment the main parts of the scan in most of the test data with good accuracy, especially for wrist, forearm and elbow areas. However, on some test data (e.g., third column in Fig. 4), the model fails completely to recognize the different areas. Moreover, the thumb area is never segmented and the model confuses it with the *Knuckles* class. Such problems are probably due to the limited number of scans in the dataset, which makes it difficult for the network to learn a robust description of each class to generalize on the test data.

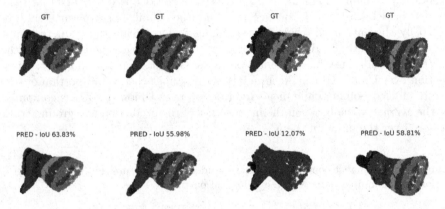

Fig. 4. Qualitative results obtained with the PointNet-light architecture. Top row, ground truth. Bottom row, model's predictions; note that the thumb region is never detected correctly.

Therefore, we investigated the possibility of applying data augmentation techniques to improve the performance of the chosen model on the limited dataset available. Using 3D data augmentation, we increase the number of samples in the training set to a total of 176 point clouds (11 times bigger than the original training set of 16 point clouds). The results obtained experimenting with different combinations of 3D data augmentation techniques are reported in Table 2, which highlight how data augmentation allows to significantly improve the model's performance. In our experiments, we also consider data normalization, in which the input point cloud is scaled in order to be represented inside a sphere of unitary radius. When used in conjunction with data augmentation, normalization further improves network's performance. Adding also jitter does not bring any particular improvement instead.

Table 2. Experimental results on the custom dataset using data augmentation. Baseline represents the performance of PointNet-light when trained on the train set of 16 scans.

Approaches	Global accuracy (%)	mIoU (%)
Baseline	0.76	0.52
Normalization	0.77	0.54
Augmentation	0.83	0.71
Augmentation + Normalization	**0.86**	**0.74**
Augmentation + Normalization + Jitter	0.85	0.72

Some qualitative results of the PointNet-light's predictions are shown in Fig. 3. Thanks to data augmentation we achieved more than 56% of IoU on all the test data, and the model correctly segments all the classes of interest including the thumb class. For most of the data the prediction accuracy is very high, about 80% in terms of IoU, which means that the predictions are really close to the scan annotations.

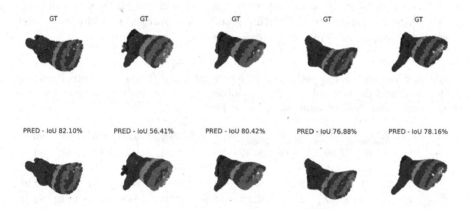

Fig. 5. Qualitative results obtained with the PointNet-light architecture and data augmentation. Top row, ground truth. Bottom row, model's predictions with IoU values.

4.3   Cross-Validation

From our experiments, we found out that a lighter PointNet architecture trained with data augmentation and normalization achieves the best results on the provided small dataset of 3D scans. To further investigate the performance of such approach we used a 4-fold cross validation technique, where the dataset is splitted into 4 groups of data; during the evaluation, in turn each group is used as a test set while the model is trained on the remaining groups. Cross-validation results are reported in Table 3, where we have also reported the results for Class

Accuracy and Class Precision metrics; Class Accuracy (CA) represents the average class recall, while Class Precision (CP) is computed as the average precision among the classes, which provides a measure of exactness, that is how many times the classifier's predictions are correct. For all the various folds, we can see that our PointNet-light models obtain good global performance in terms of accuracy, precision and mIoU; furthermore, our lighter version of PointNet predicts the various classes with a very high accuracy, a fundamental requirement for the application described in Sect. 1.

For comparison, in Table 3 we have also reported the results of cross-validation for the original PointNet architecture trained with the same augmented 3D data used for our PointNet-light. On each fold and for each class of interest our lighter version achieves better accuracy, especially for the *Thumb* class which remains a difficult category to predict for the original PointNet despite the introduction of 3D data augmentation. On average, our approach achieves +13% and +18% over PointNet in terms of class accuracy and mIoU. This result highlights that in the case of very limited datasets it could be not enough to use only data augmentation techniques, but also the network size must be considered: reducing the number of network parameters has proven to be successful in achieving better performance. In the end, we obtain a light and robust model capable of accurately recognize and segment all the main areas in a scan which correspond to the cutting planes; this represents an important step towards the automation of the of cutting planes extraction process.

Table 3. Class and global performances on the provided dataset for both PointNet-light (Ours) and the original PointNet architecture. First columns show accuracy per class on each fold. Last columns show global performance.

	Fold	Arm	Thumb	Knuckles	Wrist	Forearm	Elbow	GA	CA	CP	mIoU
Ours	1	90.69	75.00	73.48	84.15	89.85	86.84	86.78	83.33	88.69	74.15
	2	91.65	71.46	86.82	88.89	87.38	92.51	89.66	86.45	88.80	80.24
	3	89.94	89.49	86.79	90.30	92.82	95.27	90.64	90.77	88.84	82.24
	4	93.79	87.47	91.52	95.02	94.28	87.47	92.68	91.59	92.03	83.41
	Average	91.52	80.86	84.65	89.59	91.08	89.85	89.94	88.04	89.59	80.01
PointNet[16]	1	84.34	46.06	72.82	81.70	81.00	82.20	80.58	74.69	78.81	62.80
	2	81.32	7.07	79.49	76.97	89.75	91.14	79.99	70.96	75.09	57.11
	3	85.91	33.14	73.66	82.61	93.39	91.57	84.01	76.71	77.06	64.91
	4	87.04	29.05	82.40	86.23	93.54	88.42	85.31	77.78	84.04	66.69
	Average	84.65	28.83	77.09	81.88	89.42	88.33	82.47	75.04	78.75	62.88

5   Conclusion

In this paper, we propose a novel approach based on semantic segmentation of 3D data to automatically localize particular regions of interest on 3D scans of a human body part. In particular, we demonstrated how the proposed method is capable of segmenting with high accuracy the point cloud of a body arm; the relevant regions of the point cloud are correctly localized and segmented, and this information is helpful to automatize the synthesis of a custom 3D printed cast for the patient. To develop our approach we investigated various strategies to address the problem of training deep learning networks on very limited datasets, a common situation in the case of system-specific real-world applications. On one hand we simplify the network by reducing the number of parameters, on the other hand we propose the use of 3D data augmentation to make the network learn a more robust representation of the few data available. Experiments have been performed on a limited dataset acquired by an industrial partner, showing how the proposed 3D data augmentation approach can cope with the lack of larger and more comprehensive data collections. Moreover, by means of cross-validation, we demonstrated that a lighter version of PointNet can learn a more effective and robust representation of the training data, achieving better generalization performance. This is an inspiring result for further research on deep models' adaptation to challenging applications, especially when only very limited datasets are available or difficult to be acquired. Thus, an empirical approach based on simplifying the network parameters and layers, together with a consistent data augmentation technique, could represent an interesting and effective approach. Future works are based on the acquisition and annotation of additional data to further test the generalization capabilities of the proposed method; moreover we will investigate new different operations for the 3D data augmentation and their impact on the model's performance.

References

1. Ahmed, E., et al.: A survey on deep learning advances on different 3d data representations (2019)
2. Buonamici, F., et al.: A practical methodology for computer-aided design of custom 3D printable casts for wrist fractures. Vis. Comput. **36**(2), 375–390 (2020)
3. Górski, F., Wichniarek, R., Kuczko, W., Żukowska, M., Lulkiewicz, M., Zawadzki, P.: Experimental studies on 3D printing of automatically designed customized wrist-hand orthoses. Materials **13**(18), 4091 (2020)
4. Guo, Y., Wang, H., Hu, Q., Liu, H., Liu, L., Bennamoun, M.: Deep learning for 3d point clouds: a survey. In: IEEE Transactions on Pattern Analysis and Machine Intelligence (2020)
5. Hanocka, R., Hertz, A., Fish, N., Giryes, R., Fleishman, S., Cohen-Or, D.: Meshcnn: a network with an edge. ACM Trans. Graph **38**(4) (2019)
6. Huang, Z., Wang, X., Huang, L., Huang, C., Wei, Y., Liu, W.: CcNet: Criss-cross attention for semantic segmentation. In: 2019 IEEE/CVF International Conference on Computer Vision (ICCV), pp. 603–612 (2019)
7. Li, J., Tanaka, H.: Feasibility study applying a parametric model as the design generator for 3D-printed orthosis for fracture immobilization. 3D Print. Med. **4**(1), 1–15 (2018)
8. Li, J., Tanaka, H.: Rapid customization system for 3D-printed splint using programmable modeling technique-a practical approach. 3D Print. Med. **4**(1), 1–21 (2018)

9. Li, J., Chen, B.M., Lee, G.H.: So-net: Self-organizing network for point cloud analysis. In: Proceedings of the IEEE Conference on Computer Vision and Pattern Recognition, pp. 9397–9406 (2018)

10. Lin, H., Shi, L., Wang, D.: A rapid and intelligent designing technique for patient-specific and 3D-printed orthopedic cast. 3D Printing in Med. 2(1), 1–10 (2016)

11. Liu, W., Sun, J., Li, W., Hu, T., Wang, P.: Deep learning on point clouds and its application: a survey. Sensors 19(19), 4188 (2019)

12. Maturana, D., Scherer, S.: Voxnet: A 3D convolutional neural network for real-time object recognition. In: 2015 IEEE/RSJ International Conference on Intelligent Robots and Systems (IROS), pp. 922–928 (2015)

13. Mo, K., et al.: Partnet: a large-scale benchmark for fine-grained and hierarchical part-level 3D object understanding. In: Proceedings of the IEEE/CVF Conference on Computer Vision and Pattern Recognition, pp. 909–918 (2019)

14. Moon, G., i Yu, S., Wen, H., Shiratori, T., Lee, K.M.: Interhand2.6m: a dataset and baseline for 3D interacting hand pose estimation from a single ROP image (2020)

15. Mulders, M.A., Rikli, D., Goslings, J., Schep, N.: Classification and treatment of distal radius fractures: a survey among orthopaedic trauma surgeons and residents. Eur. J. Trauma Emerg. Surg. 43(2), 239–248 (2017)

16. Qi, C.R., Su, H., Mo, K., Guibas, L.J.: Pointnet: Deep learning on point sets for 3D classification and segmentation. In: Proceedings of the IEEE Conference on Computer Vision and Pattern Recognition (CVPR), July 2017

17. Qi, C.R., Yi, L., Su, H., Guibas, L.J.: Pointnet++: deep hierarchical feature learning on point sets in a metric space. In: NIPS, pp. 5105–5114 (2017)

18. Terreran, M., Tramontano, A.G., Lock, J.C., Ghidoni, S., Bellotto, N.: Real-time object detection using deep learning for helping people with visual impairments. In: 2020 IEEE 4th International Conference on Image Processing, Applications and Systems (IPAS), pp. 89–95 (2020)

19. Xiang, D., Joo, H., Sheikh, Y.: Monocular total capture: Posing face, body, and hands in the wild. In: Proceedings of the IEEE/CVF Conference on Computer Vision and Pattern Recognition (CVPR), June 2019

20. Zhao, J., Li, J., Cheng, Y., Sim, T., Yan, S., Feng, J.: Understanding humans in crowded scenes: deep nested adversarial learning and a new benchmark for multi-human parsing. In: 26th ACM International Conference on Multimedia, pp. 792–800, October 2018

21. Zhao, Y., Birdal, T., Deng, H., Tombari, F.: 3D point capsule networks. In: Proceedings of the IEEE/CVF Conference on Computer Vision and Pattern Recognition, pp. 1009–1018 (2019)

Video and Motion Analysis

Video Popularity Prediction Through Fusing Early Viewership with Video Content

Alexandros Vrochidis[1]([✉]) [iD], Nikolaos Dimitriou[1] [iD], Stelios Krinidis[1] [iD],
Savvas Panagiotidis[2], Stathis Parcharidis[2], and Dimitrios Tzovaras[1] [iD]

[1] Center for Research and Technology - Hellas, 57001 Thessaloniki, Greece
avrochid@iti.gr
[2] Inventics - Hellas, 57001 Thessaloniki, Greece

Abstract. In this paper, an approach for video popularity prediction is proposed, by combining two different methods, video content analysis, and early viewership. Firstly, a multi-modal framework is used, which analyses video content features such as the number of presented people, poses, emotions of presenters and attendants, and an audio events detection algorithm to detect claps, pauses, and speech. Afterwards, all these features feed a linear regression model that predicts each video's views. In parallel is utilized, a second method that uses interaction metrics such as early viewership to predict popularity. Viewership is crawled through an online tool developed based on Google Analytics. In order to go one step further, a fusion methodology of the views is proposed coming from the video content, with early viewership, while comparisons between models are investigated. The experimental results were based on real-life data, demonstrating that the proposed system is a promising tool for the prediction of the video popularity, having a Mean Absolute Error of less than 7.5.

Keywords: Video views prediction · Audience analysis · Popularity prediction · Content analysis · User interaction · Video content analysis

1 Introduction

Video popularity prediction is a subject of great interest as its importance in applications is growing day by day. This is partly due to the constant growth of videos available online but also for commercial and marketing purposes. Online conference attendance has increased in recent years and when a conference is held, a few people are present at the conference room while there are much more who attend it online. In this paper, a methodology is presented aiming at popularity prediction of online videos while the videos that are analyzed, are coming from lecture conferences. There is an evolution of the recent method of [1], by combining early viewership of conference videos with the video content in order to forecast mid-term popularity. More accurate results can be produced by examining different tradeoffs between user interaction and content analysis. The performance of this methodology on conference videos from one to seven days is also evaluated in order to find which model is better and the difference between an early data model with a model based only on video content.

M. Vincze et al. (Eds.): ICVS 2021, LNCS 12899, pp. 159–168, 2021.
https://doi.org/10.1007/978-3-030-87156-7_13

Video recommendation systems have the capability of filtering information coming from videos and selecting items that are likely to be attractive and interesting to a user. Tavakoli et al. [2] suggested a novel method to help learners see relevant educational videos according to market needs. Meng et al. [3], proposed a recommendation system that uses football videos to collect football data from players, and then it can propose players to managers according to their characteristics. Zhu et al. [4] proposed a method that uses video content to detect its topic and then generates recommendations to users according to their topic interests. Another similar system created by Deljoo et al. [5], uses content analysis to extract stylistic visual features such as color, motion, and lighting and recommends videos according to them.

Most of the recommendation systems are based on user profiling, keeping track of user's preferences, and providing similar recommendations. Obviously, such approaches raise privacy concerns as they rely on logging and storing user's activity. Another drawback stems from their limited applicability in thematically similar videos as in the case of scientific conferences or workshops. In such events, recommendations should be based not so much on user preferences but on viewership. Of course, an obvious issue for this approach is the cold start problem. In this work, a hybrid method is proposed that fuses video content analysis and early viewership data to predict video popularity. In this way predictions are provided before any view is recorded by analyzing the audience. Then, after finding the most interesting and popular videos, they are recommended to users that want to see the most interesting videos of the conference.

The contribution of this paper is a fusion of two novel methodologies for predicting views that conference videos will gain by increasing the final result accuracy this way. In this fusion, early viewership is combined with video content analysis. Users who attend a common conference will have similar interests, so recommendations which are based on those are difficult to be created. When a user wants to see on-demand a conference and doesn't have time to see the whole event, it is important to find the most important videos of it as recommended. They will probably be the most important for him too and by finding them his experience is improved. This framework also solves some privacy issues that the other models have by using only content for predicting video views.

The rest of this paper is organized as follows. In Sect. 2, the related work on both view prediction and audience analysis methods is presented. In Sect. 3 the methodology of predicting the views of online conference videos is presented and explained with the experimental evaluation following in Sect. 4. Then in Sect. 5 conclusions are presented followed by some future improvements.

2   Related Work

Predicting the popularity of a video has attracted wide attention in recent years, due to the large volume of videos uploaded each day on the internet. Researchers try to predict how many views a video will get by analyzing the features, such as likes or dislikes. This will help users to see videos that will be the most popular and probably the most interesting ones. By finding them, users will not spend so much time searching for the most interesting videos because they will be presented as suggested videos.

To tackle this problem Wu et al. [6], proposed a system that can predict engagement according to the videos. After predicting the engagement of a video, these metrics can be used to predict its popularity. Li et al. [7], presented an initial study about the popularity prediction of videos propagated in online social networks along with friendship links while Trzciński and Rokita [8] proposed a regression method that predicts the popularity of online videos measured by their numbers of views. Hoiles et al. [9], proposed that meta-level features can be useful for estimating the popularity of a video. Pinto et al. [10], in their research work, created a method for predicting video popularity from early view patterns, while a methodology developed at Stanford University by Li et al. [11] examined features such as time, category, description, likes, dislikes, comments but they finally used only the first three for predicting the popularity. In their future work, they wanted to examine the content of the video in order to see if it can help in predicting the views.

This is something that Vrochidis et al. [1] tried to do in their methodology. Their system uses only content features to predict the popularity of videos coming from conference lectures. They analyzed the audience that is appeared on those videos. Through audience analysis, it can predict the online views and can be used to approach the problem of cold-start which appears when a video is just uploaded and cannot have statistics such as early views or likes and comments.

Video content analysis is the capability of analyzing automatically videos to determine and detect events that are either temporal or spatial. They are used in a wide range of domains such as healthcare [12], vehicles, homes. Predicting views is one of those domains and this is the reason that these methods should be analyzed. In such methods, computer vision techniques are implemented. Jacob et al. [13] proposed an innovative approach for aerial video surveillance by analyzing video content. Zhu et al. [14] designed a video evaluation system that can grade a cataract surgery performance in terms of three metrics such as spatiality, duration, and motion. Aljarrah and Mohammad [15] created a methodology that can help in producing a searchable text file that summarizes the video content.

A computer vision technique that is widely used in video content analysis is motion segmentation. It refers to the partitioning of a video into a set of trajectories according to the moving object they correspond to. Dimitriou and Delopoulos [16] proposed a method that can improve motion segmentation by using locally sampled subspaces. They also proposed a novel approach [17] of motion-based segmentation, in which video sequences are divided in time windows and then motion segmentation is performed respectively on each window. Video segmentation techniques are also used in human activity recognition tasks to distinct the activities that people do on videos [18]. Human activity recognition is the task of identifying the specific actions of a human based either on sensors or on video content analysis [19].

Another technique that Abbas and Li [20] used is keyframe extraction for event detection and classification that enable a user to classify a cricket video into different events. Sun et al. [21] proposed a method that could be applied in multi-type videos and uses texture and information complexity features to find the keyframes of a video. Another technique that is used for video content analysis is face detection. Zheng and Xu [22] proposed a method that can efficiently detect faces and track them in video sequences based on deep learning.

In this paper there is an expansion of [1], by fusing early viewership with content analysis, to predict how many views will each video get. This method can be applied in conference event videos that are thematically similar and it is impossible to recommend videos according to user's interest topics.

3 Proposed Video Popularity Prediction Approach

The framework starts by taking a conference video as input and analyzing its content. The main computer vision techniques that are used in this multi-modal system are keyframe extraction, face detection, pose estimation, emotion estimation, and audience event detection. The first module extracts the keyframes of each video and only those frames are analyzed later on. By using them computer costs and space are reduced. Then a face detection module is used for finding the faces in those frames. After finding them it passes the bounding boxes to the pose estimation module which examines the orientations of each participant's face.

The emotion estimation module is the next one and it uses a neural network model called JAA-Net [23]. It estimates action units and then based on the Facial Action Unit Coding System [24] the emotion of each individual can be estimated separately. After examining all image features the framework continues to the audio event detection. This module tries to detect whether there are claps, speech, pauses in the conference's audio. Based on those features, the framework creates a prediction for each video's popularity in terms of views, using a linear regression model. More details about the content analysis features can be found in [1] and can be seen in Fig. 1.

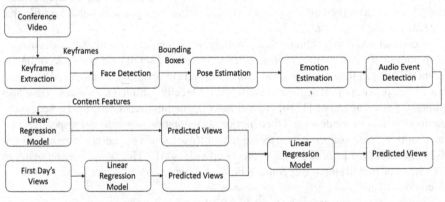

Fig. 1. Flowchart of the fused prediction methodology.

Wanting to enhance this model with features coming from the interaction that each user had with that uploaded conference video, features automatically crawled were examined using analytics. Such features were the views that the video had the first seven days of its existence examined day by day. There were also experiments with the time spent on every video by each user but through correlation analysis, it proved that it has limited impact in predicting views.

All video events used are stored in the cloud. For these experiments, there was a focus on 3 different events belonging to the medical sector. More details about the dataset can be found in Sect. 4.1. Their views can be crawled on their first days, after developing a service that uses Google Analytics [25]. Each video in the database has a unique id, the number of views, the number of unique views which doesn't count users who re-projected a video, and also includes average time on each video. After collecting the views that each video had in its first seven days, the data was given as input together with the views that the video had in its first six months to a linear regression model to predict future videos. The linear regression model was used since a strong linear correlation was found and also because it can lead to a comparison between the new methodology and the previous one which included the same type of model. Besides this, it can lead to an investigation about how the weights of early views and content analysis are changing as the days pass by. Different prediction models were created, having only as input the views of the first one day, three days, etc. Seven new models were created and they had as input content views prediction together with the prediction made by early views.

After examining the differences between the model that works only with content and the one working only with viewership, there was a fusion of the results from the early views model together with those from the content model using a linear regression model. Besides creating a better prediction model there was an investigation about the difference between the weights of the two models as the days pass by. The equation used in the linear regression model is given by:

$$V = a * Q1 + b * Q2 \tag{1}$$

where V is the total predicted views, while a and b are constants. Q1 stands for content predicted views, while Q2 stands for early viewership predicted views.

The system architecture of the fused framework is presented in Fig. 2. Content features coming both from the audience and presenter analysis make up the prediction model that uses only the video without any metadata to estimate its views. Then, there is a model that uses only online viewership to estimate the views that each video will have. The fusion model is a third one that uses the content predicted views together with the online viewership predicted views. Those outputs are given to a linear regression model and then the popularity of each video is predicted. The framework then sorts the videos of each conference according to popularity and then the top videos are recommended to users who want to see the most popular videos of a particular conference.

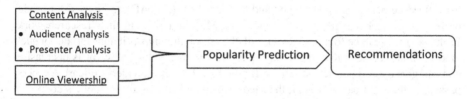

Fig. 2. System architecture diagram

4 Experimental Results

4.1 Datasets

The neural network used for emotion estimation was JAA-Net [23]. This network was trained with DISFA [26], which is a dataset consisted of videos together with facial action units of people presented on them. The training dataset had a total of 101.744 frames, while the testing set had 29.070. The audio event prediction model is defined in [27] and was trained with a custom-created dataset which is consisted of 403 videos taken from the LiveMedia platform [28]. All of these videos were taken from conference events. For this model 2.187 audio samples were used for training and 547 for testing. The model was trained with spectrograms produced, by these samples.

The content prediction model was also created with videos coming from the same platform. For the new created models, 50 videos were used, that were coming from 3 different conferences which took part in different periods during the year and all of them belong to the medical sector. They were crawled through a tool that is analyzed in Sect. 3. A total number of 40 videos was used for training the early prediction model and 10 of them coming from a different conference which was excluded from training were given as a testing set. An example of how views are growing for 5 typical videos of the used dataset, in 6 months period can be seen in the left part of Fig. 4.

4.2 Evaluation

After crawling the data that came up after users interacted with each video, there was an investigation about which metrics should be measured and how important is each one of them. To do so, the correlation between metrics and the video views on their first six months was calculated. Besides having the views in the first days of video access, there was also a metric that gave the total time users watched each video. This metric didn't have a high correlation with the final views number so it was excluded. As for the first days' views, it seemed that as the days pass by, the correlation was increasing and can be seen in Fig. 3. The views on the first day started with a correlation number of 0.58 and on the seventh day, they reached 0.89. This shows that they can be proved valuable for the prediction system.

After examining the correlation numbers, the model with only input the early views was created. The days which were examined were the first, the third, the fifth, and the seventh. The metric used was the mean absolute error (MAE) which represents the average number of errors made by the model. Error is calculated as the absolute value of the difference between the predicted and the actual value. MAE can be used for model performance error according to Willmott and Matsuura [29]. In their research work, further analysis can be found, together with the reason that makes it appropriate for such models. It can be seen that as the days pass by, the mean absolute error is decreasing and can give a good prediction score after the first days of the video's release has been passed. In the right part of Fig. 4, the Mean Absolute Error of all the models created is presented.

When the early views model was completed, there was an analysis made only from video content. The presenters and the audience presented in the conferences were analyzed so that metrics can be created. Those metrics are used in a previously made

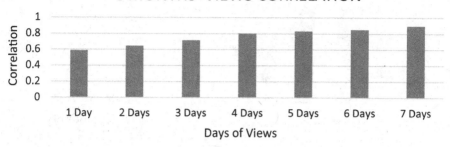

Fig. 3. Correlation between early views and 6 months' views.

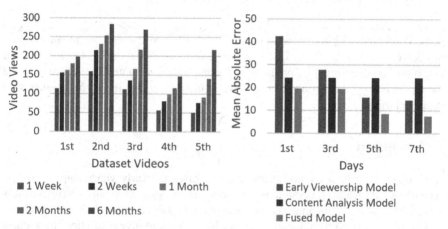

Fig. 4. Mean absolute error of the three linear regression models.

prediction model [1] which was compared with the new one. The mean absolute error of the content model was 24.3, which means that it can be more useful in the first three days of the video existence as it has a lower error than the corresponding models. This model works only with video content and therefore, it can be used exactly after the video is uploaded and can provide the prediction of the video views early.

Wanting to evolve the model from [1], it was made a fusion of the content predicted views with the ones predicted from the early viewership. Both of them were given as input to a linear regression model. In this way except for examining if the model improved, there could be an examination about how the weights of the model are changing according to which early views model will be used as input. The combined linear regression models had no intercept and their weights could be seen in the left part of Fig. 5. Except for the final model, all others showed a decrease in the weights of the content predicted views and an increase in those of early viewership. In the final model, there was an increase in the content weights, while the early showed a slightly decreasing trend.

When the two models' outputs were combined the results showed improvement and in the last model which came from early views of the first seven days of the video's

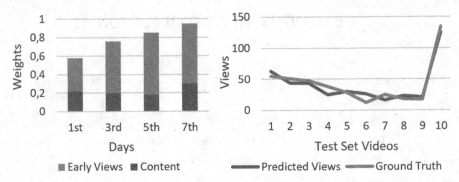

Fig. 5. The regression weights of content and early views for each model (left). Ground truth correlated with the predicted values of the combined model (right).

release combined with the views coming from the video content, the mean absolute error decreased most, reaching 7.5. As it can be seen in left part of Fig. 4, as views from more days become available, predictions become more accurate. The results that the final model had for the testing set are shown in the right image in Fig. 5, together with the ground truth values.

5   Conclusion

In this paper there is a method proposed, that fuses the early viewership of conference videos with features, coming from the content analysis. Through experiments, it is showed that video content analysis is critical in the first three days of the video's release and that it can solve the cold-start problem. It is critical to give prediction the soonest possible because after some time users will just select the most popular, so predictions will not be as useful as on video's early days. After the first three days, working with early views give better results. When the views coming from content and the views coming from early data are combined, there are much better results, and the model predicts the values close to the ground truth. Weights for content and early views follow a dis-proportional distribution when those two features are given to a linear regression model to predict conference video popularity. The limitation of this study is that this model isn't applicable for other formats than conference videos. As future work, there is a deployment of this system on a larger scale, including more features that can help the model's prediction and exploration of other state-of-the-art methodologies as alternatives to the proposed one. Focusing on video highlights – key moments and analyzing those specific frames are also in future plans.

Acknowledgments. This research has been financed by the European Regional Development Fund of the European Union and Greek national funds through the Operational Program Competitiveness, Entrepreneurship and Innovation, under the call RESEARCH–CREATE–INNOVATE (project code: LiveMedia++, T1EDK-04943). This support is gratefully acknowledged.

Conflicts of Interest. The authors declare no conflict of interest. The funders had no role in the design of the study; in the collection, analyses, or interpretation of data; in the writing of the manuscript; nor in the decision to publish the results.

References

1. Vrochidis, A., Dimitriou, N., Krinidis, S., Panagiotidis, S., Parcharidis, S., Tzovaras, D.: A multi-modal audience analysis system for predicting popularity of online videos. In: Iliadis, L., Macintyre, J., Jayne, C., Pimenidis, E. (eds.) EANN 2021. PINNS, vol. 3, pp. 465–476. Springer, Cham (2021). https://doi.org/10.1007/978-3-030-80568-5_38
2. Tavakoli, M., Hakimov, S., Ewerth, R., Kismihók, G.: A recommender system for open educational videos based on skill requirements. In: IEEE 20th International Conference on Advanced Learning Technologies, pp. 1–5 (2020)
3. Meng, X., et al.: A video information driven football recommendation system. Comput. Electr. Eng. **85** (2020)
4. Zhu, Q., Shyu, M., Wang, H.: VideoTopic: content-based video recommendation using a topic model. In: IEEE International Symposium on Multimedia, pp. 219–222 (2013)
5. Deldjoo, Y., Elahi, M., Cremonesi, P., Garzotto, F., Piazzolla, P., Quadrana, M.: Content-based video recommendation system based on stylistic visual features. J. Data Semant. **5**, 99–113 (2016)
6. Wu, S., Rizoiu, M.A., Xie, L.: Beyond views: measuring and predicting engagement in online videos. In: Proceedings of the International AAAI Conference on Web and Social Media, vol. 12, no. 1 (2018)
7. Li, H., Ma, X., Wang, F., Liu, J., Xu, K.: On popularity prediction of videos shared in online social networks. In: Proceedings of the 22nd ACM International Conference on Information & Knowledge Management (2013)
8. Trzciński, T., Rokita, P.: Predicting popularity of online videos using support vector regression. IEEE Trans. Multimedia **19**(11), 2561–2570 (2017)
9. Hoiles, W., Aprem, A., Krishnamurthy, V.: Engagement and popularity dynamics of YouTube videos and sensitivity to meta-data. IEEE Trans. Knowl. Data Eng. **29**(7), 1426–1437 (2017)
10. Pinto, H., Almeida, J.M., Goncalves, M.A.: Using early view patterns to predict the popularity of YouTube videos. In: Proceedings of the sixth ACM International Conference on Web Search and Data Mining, pp. 365–374 (2013)
11. Li, Y., Eng, K., Zhang, L.: YouTube Videos Prediction: Will this Video Be Popular? Stanford University (2019)
12. Loukas, C.: Video content analysis of surgical procedures. Surg. Endosc. **32**(2), 553–568 (2017). https://doi.org/10.1007/s00464-017-5878-1
13. Jacob, J., Sudheep Elayidom, M., Devassia, V.P.: An innovative approach for aerial video surveillance using video content analysis and indexing. In: Chen, J.Z., Tavares, J., Shakya, S., Iliyasu, A. (eds.) ICIPCN 2020. AISC, vol. 1200, pp. 574–583. Springer, Cham (2021). https://doi.org/10.1007/978-3-030-51859-2_52.
14. Zhu, J., Luo, J., Soh, J.M., Khalifa, Y.M.: A computer vision-based approach to grade simulated surgeries. Mach. Vis. Appl. **26**, 115–125 (2015)
15. Aljarrah, I., Mohammad, D.: Video content analysis using convolutional neural networks. In: 9th International Conference on Information and Communication Systems (2018)
16. Dimitriou, N., Delopoulos, A.: Improved motion segmentation using locally sampled subspaces. In: 19th IEEE International Conference on Image Processing, pp. 309–312 (2012)
17. Dimitriou, N., Delopoulos, A.: Motion-based segmentation of objects using overlapping temporal windows. Image Vis. Comput. **31**, 593–602 (2013)

18. Moniruzzaman, M., Yin, Z., He, Z.H., Qin, R., Leu, M.: Human action recognition by discriminative feature pooling and video segmentation attention model. IEEE Trans. Multimedia (2021)

19. Vrochidis, A., et al.: A recommendation specific human activity recognition dataset with mobile device's sensor data. In: Maglogiannis, I., Macintyre, J., Iliadis, L. (eds.) AIAI 2021. IAICT, vol. 628, pp. 327–339. Springer, Cham (2021). https://doi.org/10.1007/978-3-030-79157-5_27

20. Abbas, Q., Li, Y.: Cricket video events recognition using HOG, LBP and multi-class SVM. In: Journal of Physics: Conference Series, vol. 1732, no. 1 (2021)

21. Sun, Y., Li, P., Liu, Y., Jiang, Z.: Feature extraction and clustering for static video summarization (2021)

22. Zheng, G., Xu, Y.: Efficient face detection and tracking in video sequences based on deep learning. Inf. Sci. **568**, 265–285 (2021)

23. Shao, Z., Liu, Z., Cai, J., Ma, L.: JAA-Net: joint facial action unit detection and face alignment via adaptive attention. Int. J. Comput. Vis. **129**, 321–340 (2021)

24. Ekman, P., Rosenberg, E.L.: What the Face Reveals: Basic and Applied Studies of Spontaneous Expression Using the Facial Action Coding System (FACS). Oxford Un. Press (1997)

25. https://analytics.google.com

26. Mavadati, S.M., Mahoor, M.H., Barlett, K., Trinh, P., Cohn, J.F.: DISFA: a spontaneous facial action intensity database. IEEE Trans. Affect. Comput. **4**(2), 151–160 (2012)

27. Vafeiadis, A., et al.: Acoustic scene classification: from a hybrid classifier to deep learning. In: DCASE Workshop, Munich, Germany, pp. 123–127 (2017)

28. https://www.livemedia.gr

29. Willmott, C.J., Matsuura, K.: Advantages of the mean absolute error (MAE) over the root mean square error (RMSE) in assessing average model performance. Climate Res. **30**, 79–82 (2005)

Action Prediction During Human-Object Interaction Based on DTW and Early Fusion of Human and Object Representations

Victoria Manousaki[1,2]([✉]) [ID], Konstantinos Papoutsakis[2] [ID],
and Antonis Argyros[1,2] [ID]

[1] Computer Science Department, University of Crete, Heraklion, Greece
[2] Institute of Computer Science, Foundation for Research and Technology - Hellas
(FORTH), Heraklion, Greece
{vmanous,argyros,papoutsa}@ics.forth.gr

Abstract. Action prediction is defined as the inference of an action label while the action is still ongoing. Such a capability is extremely useful for early response and further action planning. In this paper, we consider the problem of action prediction in scenarios involving humans interacting with objects. We formulate an approach that builds time series representations of the performance of the humans and the objects. Such a representation of an ongoing action is then compared to prototype actions. This is achieved by a Dynamic Time Warping (DTW)-based time series alignment framework which identifies the best match between the ongoing action and the prototype ones. Our approach is evaluated quantitatively on three standard benchmark datasets. Our experimental results reveal the importance of the fusion of human- and object-centered action representations in the accuracy of action prediction. Moreover, we demonstrate that the proposed approach achieves significantly higher action prediction accuracy compared to competitive methods.

Keywords: Action prediction · Early action classification · Dynamic Time Warping (DTW) · Soft DTW · Global Alignment Kernel (GAK)

1 Introduction

The capability to foresee and predict future outcomes is a very important human ability as it enables us to plan our next moves and actions and articulate with the environment. Likewise, prediction is an important capability of several technical systems. For example, home assisting robots need to be able to predict user actions and intentions in order to plan ahead their own actions and provide fast and accurate assistance to the user [9,10]. In another example, autonomous

The research work was supported by the Hellenic Foundation for Research and Innovation (HFRI) under the HFRI PhD Fellowship grant (Fellowship Number: 1592).

M. Vincze et al. (Eds.): ICVS 2021, LNCS 12899, pp. 169–179, 2021.
https://doi.org/10.1007/978-3-030-87156-7_14

cars [23] need the ability to predict the movement of pedestrians and other vehicles to plan a safe route and avoid accidents.

In this paper, we investigate the specific problem of vision-based action prediction in human-object interaction scenarios. Action prediction is the capability of inferring the class label of an *ongoing* (i.e., partially executed, incomplete) action [37]. Thus, our input consists of trimmed video recordings, from which time series of 3D skeletal data can be extracted using a number of methods (e.g., [30])[1]. The observed part of the action depends on the observation ratio which is in the range (0, 100%]. An observation ratio of 100% signifies a fully observed action; in that case, action prediction is equivalent to full action classification.

2   Related Work

Vision-based prediction is a rising topic in the field of computer vision [28]. From pedestrian trajectory prediction [33] to pose prediction [22] to accident anticipation [5], prediction has become the focus of several investigations [32]. Ryoo et al. [37] were the first to define the problem of vision-based action prediction as "an inference of unfinished activities given temporally incomplete videos". Action prediction methods can be on trimmed or untrimmed videos [20].

Action Prediction in Trimmed Videos: Action prediction on trimmed videos focuses on recognizing the label of a video given incomplete observations at each point in time [4,12]. Wang et al. [41] created a teacher-student network where the teacher part of the network recognizes the action while the student part takes as input a partial video and predicts the action. The method in [3] uses a 3D convolutional neural network to extract spatio-temporal features and perform short-term action prediction by using multiple binary classifiers. In [19] the action label is predicted by distinguishing video pairs of different classes that are difficult to discriminate. In [9] everyday actions are predicted by using motion trajectory prediction and taking into account the objects and their affordances.

Action Prediction in Untrimmed Videos: This is performed on non-trimmed videos and its goal is to recognize early (a) all the action labels that are present in a video and (b) their anticipated duration [16,25,26]. Since action boundaries are not known, Liu et al. [20] used a scale selection network to select the right window size with the use of convolution layers. The method presented in [11] predicted the future actions with two ways: recursively using an RNN network and in one-pass by using a CNN network. Recursive prediction of actions can accumulate errors. For this reason, Ke et al. [17] predicted actions in an one-shot fashion. The method presented in [13] recognizes the actions of the ongoing video along with their duration by inferring information about the verbs and the objects that are present in the scene through aligning video segments.

---

[1] In our work the terms "video recordings" and "skeletal data" are used interchangeably.

Video Alignment: Video alignment is gaining increasing popularity in the confrontation of different tasks. The work in [14] uses a variant of DTW with a *smoothMin* approximation as loss in their network to achieve 3D pose reconstruction and fine-grained audio/visual retrieval. The work in [15] solves the problems of action phase classification, action phase progression, and fine-grained frame retrieval by using temporal alignment and regularization loss. As their temporal alignment loss they employ Soft Dynamic Time Warping (Soft DTW). DTW has been used in the past in relevant contexts. The work in [42] uses DTW for intention prediction based on eye gaze and fixation time-series for autonomous vehicles. In [2] action prediction is based on time-series of features extracted from flow with the use of CNN networks. However, DTW has not been used before for short-term action prediction in the context of human-object interaction scenarios.

Our Contribution: We cast the problem of short-term action prediction as a problem of time series alignment and comparison. Video recordings of actions are represented as multidimensional time series through feature extraction mechanisms. The employed features encode the temporal behavior of both the action-related humans and objects. Given a time series representation of an incomplete action, we seek for its best alignment and match with a set of time series corresponding to prototype executions of a variety of actions. The predicted action label is the label of the best matching prototype action execution. For the alignment task, we investigate three DTW variants [38], called OpenEnd-DTW [39], Soft Dynamic Time Warping [8] and Global Alignment Kernel [7]. Our approach is evaluated quantitatively on the skeletal data of three standard benchmark datasets, namely MSR Daily Activities [40], CAD-120 [18] and MHAD [27]. Our results reveal (a) the impact of the used DTW variant and (b) the importance of the fusion of human- and object-centered action representations in the accuracy of action prediction. Moreover, we demonstrate that the proposed approach achieves significantly higher action prediction accuracy compared to competitive methods.

3   DTW-Based Action Prediction

We assume that a video recording of an action (full or incomplete) can be represented as an N-dimensional time series through some appropriate feature extraction mechanism (see Sect. 3.1).

Let Q be such a time series representation of an incomplete action. We are interested in inferring the unknown action label $L(Q)$ of Q. We also consider a set of C time series P^i, $1 \leq i \leq C$, corresponding to known, prototype action executions with labels $L(P_i)$. Our approach compares Q with each of the time series P_i through Dynamic Time Warping-based alignment (DTW). Let $DTW(X,Y)$ denote the DTW alignment cost of time series X and Y. Then, action prediction can be formulated as:

$$L(Q) = L\left(arg\ min_{1 \leq i \leq C}\left(DTW(Q, P^i)\right)\right). \tag{1}$$

Essentially, the proposed method predicts that the action label of Q is that of the prototype action P^i which can be aligned with Q at a minimum DTW-based alignment cost.

3.1   Feature Extraction

Given a video, we represent each of its frames as a multidimensional vector of action-related features. Depending on the employed scenario, such features encode the human body pose, the class and the pose of the involved object, or both. Section 4 presents different sets of extracted features for the standard benchmark datasets employed in this work.

3.2   DTW-Based Time Series Alignment

Dynamic Time Warping (DTW): Let X and Y be two time series with $X = (x_1, \ldots x_l) \in \mathbb{R}^{n \times l}$ and $Y = (y_1, \ldots, y_m) \in \mathbb{R}^{n \times m}$. We define the distance matrix $D(X, Y) = [d(x_i, y_i)]_{ij} \in \mathbb{R}^{l \times m}$, where $d(x, y)$ is the Euclidean distance between x and y. We also define Π, the set of all path-based alignments of X and Y, connecting the upper-left to the lower-right of the matrix D. Finally, let $\pi \in \Pi$ be one of all those alignments. The inner product $\langle \pi, D(X, Y) \rangle$ yields the alignment score associated with π.

DTW [38] is a dynamic programming algorithm that estimates the minimum-cost alignment of two time series. On the basis of the above notation, this is $DTW(X, Y) = min_{\pi \in \Pi} D(X, Y)$. For the partial alignment, a variant of the original DTW [38] is employed, called open-end DTW [39]. The alignments can end at any point at the last column of the D matrix. The alignment score is normalized by the number of diagonal steps of the calculated optimal alignment path. Open-end DTW is defined as:

$$DTW_{oe}(X, Y) = min_{j=1,\ldots,m} DTW(X, Y_j). \tag{2}$$

Soft DTW: Soft-DTW [8] builds upon the original and popular dynamic time warping (DTW) measure and considers a generalized soft minimum operator applied to the distribution of all costs spanned by all possible alignments between two time series of variable size. Given the following generalized minimum operator, subject to a smoothing parameter $\gamma \geq 0$,

$$min\,\gamma(\pi_1, \ldots, \pi_k) = \begin{cases} min_{i \leq k}\, \pi_i, & \gamma = 0, \\ -\gamma \log \sum_{i=1}^{k} e^{\pi_i/\gamma} & \gamma > 0, \end{cases} \tag{3}$$

the soft-DTW score is defined as:

$$SDTW_\gamma(X, Y) = min^\gamma \{\langle \pi, D(X, Y) \rangle, \pi \in \Pi\}. \tag{4}$$

The original DTW score is obtained by setting $\gamma = 0$.

Global Alignment Kernel: Global Alignment Kernel (GAK) [7] measures the similarity between two multidimensional time series X, Y. On top of $D(X, Y)$, the GAK is computed as:

$$GAK(X, Y) = \sum_{\pi \in \Pi} \exp \left(\frac{-\langle \pi, D(X, Y) \rangle}{\gamma} \right). \tag{5}$$

In comparison to DTW, in order to find the alignment score of two time-series, instead of using the operators (min, +) on the $\langle \pi, D(x, y) \rangle$ GAK uses the (+, X) operators. According to [7], the GAK considers the full spectrum of the $\langle \pi, D(X, Y) \rangle, \pi \in \Pi$, while the DTW distance considers only the minimum score.

3.3   Early Fusion of Human and Object Representations

The aforementioned variants of DTW operate on the distance matrix $D(X, Y)$ of time series X and Y, which, for notational convenience, will be denoted with D. In the human-object interaction scenario we are considering, this distance matrix is defined as follows. First, we construct a distance matrix D_H which results from the frame-wise comparison of the part of the representation that contains the information regarding the human. We also construct an analogous distance matrix D_O which results from the frame-wise comparison of the part of the representation that contains the information regarding the object with which the human interacts. Then, the distance matrix D on which DTW operates is defined as:

$$D = \alpha_H D_H + \alpha_O D_O. \tag{6}$$

In the above equation, α_H and α_O are weighting factors that may be dataset-dependent, but have been defined experimentally and commonly for all employed datasets. If the two compared actions involve objects of the same class, then $\alpha_H = \alpha_O = 0.5$. If the two compared actions involve objects of different classes, then $\alpha_H = 0.7$ and $\alpha_O = 0.3$. The intuition behind this choice is that the same action can be performed by using different objects (e.g., reach, move, etc.). Therefore, actions can still be compared, but with giving emphasis on the part of the representation concerning the humans rather than the objects. If no objects are present in the scene, then $\alpha_H = 1$ and $\alpha_O = 0$. Finally, in the case that one of the actions involve an object and the other does not, $\alpha_H = 3$ and $\alpha_O = 0$. Essentially, the two actions are again compared on the basis of the human performance, but the mismatch on the presence of objects is penalized by a large α_H value.

In the observed scene, several objects may be present. From those, we consider the one that is closest to and/or manipulated by the actor. One limitation of this choice is that we cannot take into account actions involving more than one object. However, ongoing research beyond the scope of this paper indicates that the extension of our approach towards handling more that one manipulated objects is feasible. Another limitation and future extension of our work lies in the need to know the start frame of an action. The generalization of our approach towards handling unsegmented actions is another topic of ongoing research.

4 Experiments

Datasets: The proposed framework is evaluated on 3 standard datasets with different characteristics.

MHAD Dataset [27]: Contains 11 actions (jumping in place, jumping jacks, bending, punching, waving one hand, waving two hands, clapping, throwing a ball, sit down and stand up, sit down, stand up) performed by 12 subjects. The majority of the actions do not involve objects (with the exception of the action "throwing a ball"). The database provides motion capture data containing the 3D positions of 43 LED markers, which have been processed to obtain 3D skeletal data of 30 joints. The standard evaluation split is used as in [27].

Features: The MHAD [27] dataset contains the 3D positions of skeletal joints. Based on these 3D positions, we build a human body representation as proposed in [35] and also used in [21,29]. Specifically, a human pose is represented as a $30 + 30 + 4 = 64D$ vector. The first 30 dimensions encode angles of selected body parts with respect to a body-centered coordinate system. The next 30 dimensions encode the same angles in a camera-centered coordinate system. The representation is augmented with the 4 angles between the fore- and the back-arms as well as the angles between the upper- and lower legs.

MSR Daily Activity 3D Dataset [40]: Consists of 16 actions (drinking, eating, reading a book, speaking on cellphone, writing on paper, using a laptop, using a vacuum cleaner, cheering up, sitting still, tossing paper, playing a game, lie down on the sofa, walking, playing the guitar, standing up and sitting down) performed by 10 subjects. Every subject performs each action twice, once sitting on a sofa and once standing. We followed the experimental settings of [34,43].

Features: The dataset contains the 3D skeletal joint positions for all the human joints. We consider only the 9 upper body joints due to the fact that the data for the lower body are quite noisy. The 3D upper skeletal joint positions are calculated to be invariant to the body center. The invariant 3D joint positions are concatenated with the 3D joint angles. The 3D joint angles are represented as a 30D vector. The 30 dimensions encode angles of selected body parts with respect to a body-centered coordinate system [35] but we are taking into account only the angles that correspond to the upper body. For the objects in this dataset, we employed the YoloV4 [6] trained on ImageNet in order to acquire fast and accurate labels and 2D positions of the objects in the scene. We densely annotated the training part of the MSR-Daily dataset and re-trained the YoloV4 [6] on the MSR Daily Activities dataset. The invariant 3D upper skeletal joint positions are 27D and the 3D joint angles that correspond to the upper body are 18D. The positions of the objects are 2D. Thus, each frame of a video is represented as a $27 + 18 + 2 = 47D$ vector.

CAD-120 Dataset [18]: Contains activities performed by 4 subjects, which can be subdivided into 10 sub-activities. The subjects perform the activities with different objects. Activities are observed from different viewpoints. The sub-activity labels are: reach, move, pour, eat, drink, open, place, close, clean, null.

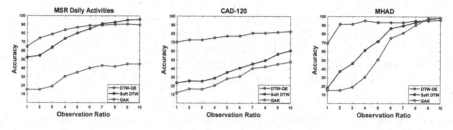

Fig. 1. Comparison of DTW_{oe}, SDTW and GAK on the MSR (left) CAD-120 (middle) and MHAD (right) datasets.

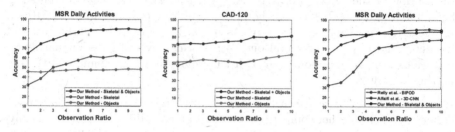

Fig. 2. Action prediction results for different representations. (Left) MSR Daily Activities Dataset, (Middle) CAD-120 Dataset. (Right) Action prediction accuracy of our method in comparison to state of the art methods on the MSR Daily Activities Dataset.

We are experimenting on the sub-activity labels using the standard 4-fold cross validation as in [18]

Features: We used a set of features based on [18]. Specifically, to represent human motion we use the location of each of 8 joints (24D), the distance moved by each joint (8D) and the displacement of each joint (8D).

For representing objects we used their 3D centroid location, the distance moved by the object's centroid (1D), the displacement of the object's centroid (1D) and the distance between each joint location and the object centroid (8D). In total, a frame of a sequence is represented as a 53D vector.

Performance Metrics: We measure the action prediction accuracy as a function of the observation ratio, i.e., the percentage of the part of the action that has been observed and compared to action prototypes. In our experiments, the observation ratio ranged from 10% to 100% in steps of 10%.

Evaluation of DTW Variants: We evaluated the three DTW variants presented in Sect. 3.2 with respect to their action prediction accuracy on all three datasets. During testing, every query sequence is compared to all sequences in the training set. We employed a publicly available [1] implementation of DTW_{oe} and the implementations of the DTW variants that reside in the Tslearn toolkit [36]. The parameter γ was experimentally set equal to 0.1 for the (MHAD, MSR) datasets and to 0.01 for the CAD120 dataset. As it can be observed in Fig. 1, DTW_{oe} outperforms SDTW by a great margin in the MHAD and CAD120 datasets. In turn, SDTW clearly outperforms GAK. This holds true for all three datasets, regardless of whether they involve humans in interaction with objects (MSR, CAD120) or not (MHAD). Moreover, the superiority of DTW over the rest two variants is dominant especially in lower observation ratios. This shows the potential of the method for accurate and early action prediction.

Evaluation of Alternative Representations: We evaluated the impact of action representations on action prediction. More specifically, we investigated three different experimental conditions, (a) representations that involve only the joints of the human actor (b) representations that involve only the class and the motion of the involved objects and (c) their early fusion, as presented in Sect. 3.3. Figure 2 (left, middle) shows the results we obtained in the MSR and the CAD120 datasets[2], respectively. As it can be verified, the early fusion of the actor and object representations outperforms any of the individual representations in predictive power, by a vast margin (from a minimum of 10% to a maximum of 40%).

Comparison to the State of the Art: Figure 2 (right) presents a comparison of our approach to other competitive methods on the MSR dataset. Specifically, we are comparing to the work of Reily et al. [34] and to that of Alfaifi et al. [3]. As it can be observed, we outperform [34] at all observation ratios and [3] for all observation rations greater than 40%.

To the best of our knowledge, there are no reported quantitative results for action prediction on the CAD120 dataset. We only report action classification results from the very recent method of Mavroudi et al. [24] that achieves an action classification accuracy of 90.4%) which can be compared to the action prediction results of our method in the case of an observation ratio of 100%.

Similarly, there are no reported quantitative results for action prediction on the MHAD dataset. For action classification, the very recent method of Qin et al. [31] achieves an accuracy of 100%, compared to the action classification accuracy of 96% of our method, for an observation ratio of 100%. Interestingly, an action prediction accuracy of more than 90% is achieved by our method, even when a small portion of the activity has been observed (observation ratio of 20%).

5 Summary

We approached the problem of predicting the actions of humans interacting with objects as a problem of aligning fused, frame-based action representations of humans and objects. Specifically, actions are represented as multidimensional time-series. Then, their alignment and the assessment of their similarity is performed with a DTW-based approach. On this task, three DTW variants have been evaluated in three well-known datasets. We also investigated and assessed quantitatively the importance of the fusion of human- and object-based action

---

[2] MHAD is not included in this investigation as the vast majority of its actions do not involve human-object interactions.

representations. The obtained results suggest that DTW_{oe} outperforms all tested variants and that the proposed fusion of representations increases considerably the predictive capability of our framework, which performs considerably better than recently published competitive action prediction methods.

References

1. https://github.com/statefb/dtwalign
2. Afrasiabi, M., Mansoorizadeh, M., et al.: DTW-CNN: time series-based human interaction prediction in videos using CNN-extracted features. Vis. Comput. **36**, 1127–1139 (2019)
3. Alfaifi, R., Artoli, A.: Human action prediction with 3D-CNN. SN Comput. Sci. **1**, 1–15 (2020)
4. Arzani, M.M., Fathy, M., Azirani, A.A., Adeli, E.: Skeleton-based structured early activity prediction. Multimedia Tools Appl. **80**(15), 23023–23049 (2020). https://doi.org/10.1007/s11042-020-08875-w
5. Bao, W., Yu, Q., Kong, Y.: Uncertainty-based traffic accident anticipation with spatio-temporal relational learning. In: ACM International Conference on Multimedia (2020)
6. Bochkovskiy, A., Wang, C., Liao, H.: YOLOv4: optimal speed and accuracy of object detection. arXiv:2004.10934 (2020)
7. Cuturi, M.: Fast global alignment kernels. In: ICML 2011 (2011)
8. Cuturi, M., Blondel, M.: Soft-DTW: a differentiable loss function for time-series. arXiv:1703.01541 (2017)
9. Dutta, V., Zielinska, T.: Predicting human actions taking into account object affordances. J. Intell. Robot. Syst. **93**, 745–761 (2019)
10. Dutta, V., Zielińska, T.: An adversarial explainable artificial intelligence (XAI) based approach for action forecasting. J. Autom. Mob. Robot. Intell. Syst. (2021)
11. Farha, A., Richard, A., Gall, J.: When will you do what?-anticipating temporal occurrences of activities. In: IEEE CVPR (2018)
12. Gammulle, H., Denman, S., Sridharan, S., Fookes, C.: Predicting the future: a jointly learnt model for action anticipation. In: IEEE ICCV (2019)
13. Ghoddoosian, R., Sayed, S., Athitsos, V.: Action duration prediction for segment-level alignment of weakly-labeled videos. In: Proceedings of the IEEE/CVF Winter Conference on Applications of Computer Vision, pp. 2053–2062 (2021)
14. Hadji, I., Derpanis, K.G., Jepson, A.D.: Representation learning via global temporal alignment and cycle-consistency. arXiv preprint arXiv:2105.05217 (2021)
15. Haresh, S., et al.: Learning by aligning videos in time. arXiv preprint arXiv:2103.17260 (2021)
16. Ke, Q., Bennamoun, M., Rahmani, H., An, S., Sohel, F., Boussaid, F.: Learning latent global network for skeleton-based action prediction. IEEE Trans. Image Process. (2019)
17. Ke, Q., Fritz, M., Schiele, B.: Time-conditioned action anticipation in one shot. In: IEEE CVPR (2019)
18. Koppula, H., Gupta, R., Saxena, A.: Learning human activities and object affordances from RGB-D videos. Int. J. Robot. Res. **32**, 951–970 (2013)
19. Li, T., Liu, J., Zhang, W., Duan, L.: HARD-Net: hardness-aWaRe discrimination network for 3D early activity prediction. In: Vedaldi, A., Bischof, H., Brox, T., Frahm, J.-M. (eds.) ECCV 2020. LNCS, vol. 12356, pp. 420–436. Springer, Cham (2020). https://doi.org/10.1007/978-3-030-58621-8_25

20. Liu, J., Shahroudy, A., Wang, G., Duan, L., Kot, A.: Skeleton-based online action prediction using scale selection network. IEEE PAMI **42**, 1453–1467 (2019)

21. Manousaki, V., Papoutsakis, K., Argyros, A.: Evaluating method design options for action classification based on bags of visual words. In: VISAPP (2018)

22. Mao, W., Liu, M., Salzmann, M.: History repeats itself: human motion prediction via motion attention. In: Vedaldi, A., Bischof, H., Brox, T., Frahm, J.-M. (eds.) ECCV 2020. LNCS, vol. 12359, pp. 474–489. Springer, Cham (2020). https://doi.org/10.1007/978-3-030-58568-6_28

23. Mavrogiannis, A., Chandra, R., Manocha, D.: B-GAP: behavior-guided action prediction for autonomous navigation. arXiv:2011.03748 (2020)

24. Mavroudi, E., Haro, B.B., Vidal, R.: Representation learning on visual-symbolic graphs for video understanding. In: Vedaldi, A., Bischof, H., Brox, T., Frahm, J.-M. (eds.) ECCV 2020. LNCS, vol. 12374, pp. 71–90. Springer, Cham (2020). https://doi.org/10.1007/978-3-030-58526-6_5

25. Miech, A., Laptev, I., Sivic, J., Wang, H., Torresani, L., Tran, D.: Leveraging the present to anticipate the future in videos. In: IEEE CVPR Workshops (2019)

26. Ng, Y., Basura, F.: Forecasting future action sequences with attention: a new approach to weakly supervised action forecasting. IEEE Trans. Image Process. **29**, 8880–8891 (2020)

27. Ofli, F., Chaudhry, R., Kurillo, G., Vidal, R., Bajcsy, R.: Berkeley MHAD: a comprehensive multimodal human action database. In: IEEE Workshop on Applications of Computer Vision (WACV) (2013)

28. Oprea, S., et al.: A review on deep learning techniques for video prediction. IEEE PAMI (2020)

29. Papoutsakis, K., Panagiotakis, C., Argyros, A.: Temporal action co-segmentation in 3D motion capture data and videos. In: CVPR (2017)

30. Qammaz, A., Argyros, A.: Occlusion-tolerant and personalized 3D human pose estimation in RGB images. In: 2020 ICPR. IEEE (2021)

31. Qin, Y., Mo, L., Li, C., Luo, J.: Skeleton-based action recognition by part-aware graph convolutional networks. Vis. Comput. **36**, 621–631 (2020)

32. Rasouli, A.: Deep learning for vision-based prediction: a survey. arXiv:2007.00095 (2020)

33. Rasouli, A., Yau, T., Rohani, M., Luo, J.: Multi-modal hybrid architecture for pedestrian action prediction. arXiv:2012.00514 (2020)

34. Reily, B., Han, F., Parker, L., Zhang, H.: Skeleton-based bio-inspired human activity prediction for real-time human-robot interaction. Auton. Robots **42**, 1281–1298 (2018)

35. Rius, I., Gonzàlez, J., Varona, J., Roca, F.: Action-specific motion prior for efficient Bayesian 3D human body tracking. Pattern Recogn. **42**, 2907–2921 (2009)

36. Tavenard, R., et al.: Tslearn, a machine learning toolkit for time series data. J. Mach. Learn. Res. **21**, 1–6 (2020)

37. Ryoo, M.: Human activity prediction: early recognition of ongoing activities from streaming videos. In: IEEE ICCV (2011)

38. Sakoe, H., Chiba, S.: Dynamic programming algorithm optimization for spoken word recognition. IEEE Trans. Acoust. Speech Signal Process. **26**, 43–49 (1978)

39. Tormene, P., Giorgino, T., Quaglini, S., Stefanelli, M.: Matching incomplete time series with dynamic time warping: an algorithm and an application to post-stroke rehabilitation. Artif. Intell. Med. **45**, 11–34 (2009)

40. Wang, J., Liu, Z., Wu, Y., Yuan, J.: Mining actionlet ensemble for action recognition with depth cameras. In: IEEE CVPR (2012)

41. Wang, X., Hu, J., Lai, J., Zhang, J., Zheng, W.: Progressive teacher-student learning for early action prediction. In: IEEE CVPR (2019)
42. Wu, M., et al.: Gaze-based intention anticipation over driving manoeuvres in semi-autonomous vehicles (2020)
43. Xia, L., Aggarwal, J.: Spatio-temporal depth cuboid similarity feature for activity recognition using depth camera. In: IEEE CVPR (2013)

GridTrack: Detection and Tracking of Multiple Objects in Dynamic Occupancy Grids

Özgür Erkent[1,2]([✉]), David Sierra Gonzalez[1], Anshul Paigwar[1] [iD],
and Christian Laugier[1]

[1] Chroma Team, INRIA, Rhône-Alpes, Grenoble, France
{ozgur.erkent,david.sierra-gonzalez,anshul.paigwar,
christian.laugier}@inria.fr
[2] Department of Computer Engineering, University of Hacettepe, Ankara, Turkey
ozgurerkent@hacettepe.edu.tr

Abstract. Multiple Object Tracking is an important task for autonomous vehicles. However, it gets difficult to track objects when it is hard to detect them due to occlusion or distance to the sensors. We propose a method, "GridTrack", to overcome this difficulty. We fuse a dynamic occupancy grid map (DOGMa) with an object detector. DOGMa is obtained by applying a Bayesian filter on raw sensor data. This improves the tracking of the partially observed/unobserved objects with the help of the Bayesian filter on raw data, which has a powerful prediction capability. We develop a network to track the objects on the grid and fuse information from previous detections in this network. The experiments show that the multi-object tracking accuracy is high with the usage of the proposed method.

Keywords: Tracking · Autonomous vehicles · Occupancy grids

1 Introduction

The ability of the autonomous vehicles (AVs) to navigate safely depends on their comprehension of the environment. For this reason, Advanced Driver Assistance Systems (ADAS) require reliable information about the locations and motion of the obstacles around the AV. Multiple Object Tracking (MOT) is one of the essential tasks for ADAS to estimate the poses of multiple objects for a given time interval. Due to recent advancements in object detection by using a variety of sensors, tracking algorithms heavily rely on object detection; either they use the output of a detection algorithm or integrate a detection algorithm into the tracking method. However, when the tracked object cannot be detected by the object detector, such as due to occlusions or distance to the sensor, the tracking cannot be achieved accurately.

In this work, we aim to increase the accuracy of the tracking performance by tracking objects that cannot be detected by the object detector due to poor observability. To be able to achieve this, we use Dynamic Occupancy Grid Maps (DOGMas) which are constructed by applying Bayesian filters on raw sensor data. Bayesian filters have

This work was supported by Toyota Motor Europe.

M. Vincze et al. (Eds.): ICVS 2021, LNCS 12899, pp. 180–194, 2021.
https://doi.org/10.1007/978-3-030-87156-7_15

a high capacity of predicting the occupancy and motion states of the grids, which are not directly observable by the sensors [22]. In MOT, when Bayesian filters are used, they are generally applied on the object detections to predict the next location of the detected object [5,6,28]. We are proposing a new approach for MOT by integrating the Bayesian filter on raw sensor data with different off-the-shelf precise object detectors [13,26]. This will also result in enriched occupancy grid by integrating tracked object information into the grid.

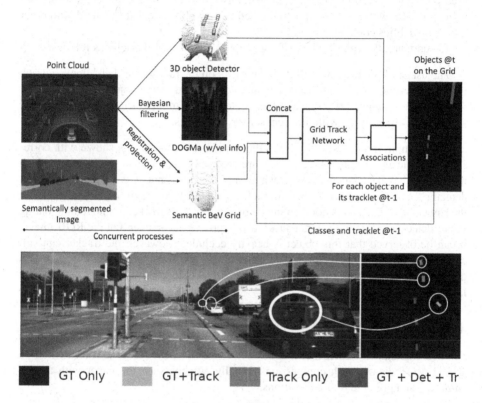

Fig. 1. On top, the general overview of our approach. In the bottom, tracked objects for the given image. GT: Ground truth, Track: Tracked object output from Grid Track Network (GTN), Det: Object output from Object Detector. The circles show the corresponding tracked objects.

The proposed framework is shown in Fig. 1. The GTN takes the input from processed data DOGMa, projected Semantic Bird's eye View (BeV) and output from the previous time step. In addition, the outputs of the GTN are associated with an object detector. The association performs three operations: a) it associates the detected objects from the object detector with the tracked objects from GTN; b) creates new objects; and c) represents tracked objects from GTN even if no corresponding object detection exists. The output of the framework consists of the poses of each object together with their instance id's in the previous frame and their class type. For illustration, we used pointcloud as input for DOGMa construction, but other sensor modalities such as stereo cameras or radar can also be used as input. We use Conditional Monte Carlo Dense Occupancy Tracker (CMCDOT) to obtain DOGMa which can predict the occupation and motion states of each cell on the grid map [22]. To obtain the projected semantic BeV, we semantically segment RGB images with an off-the-shelf method whose details are given in the Sect. 3, and register the points with the point cloud and project them onto the grid. It should be noted that it is also possible to use other sensor modalities to obtain the semantic grid [9]. The losses are used during training while association is used only during testing. We have evaluated two different object detectors which use pointclouds; however, it should be reminded that an object detector method with other sensor modalities could also be used.

In summary, the contributions of our proposal can be listed briefly as follows:

- The usage of the Bayesian filter via DOGMa on the raw sensor data allows to track the objects that are heavily occluded and not detected by the object detector
- Integration with an off-the-shelf object detector as a module allows it to be used for different object types with different sensor modalities

An example is shown in Fig. 1. On the bottom right, the grid is shown with corresponding tracked objects. Three objects are detected as *car* and shown in green which means that they have labels in GT, Det and Tr. The truck is not detected since the object detector recognizes only cars; therefore it has only GT label. A circled object (pink) on the right side of the grid is not recognized by detector, it is tracked without anticipating the re-detection of the object. GT label also approves our tracker. On the RGB image, it can be observed that this object is heavily occluded; however, the tracker can still estimate its location on the grid. The same is true for two circled (yellow) *cars* at a distance. Note that these two objects are correctly tracked; however, their GTs are not labeled.

We evaluate our method on KITTI MOT dataset. It is shown both qualitatively and quantitatively that the method is capable of achieving high accuracy results.

In Sect. 2, we shortly review the literature related to MOT. In Sect. 3, we give a detailed explanation of our method. In Sect. 4, we show the results of our method on KITTI MOT dataset with comparisons. Finally, we conclude the paper with a brief summary and possible future directions.

2   Related Work

We discuss here the recent progress on MOT studies. Although 3D MOT is more relevant to our approach for AVs, we will cover both 2D and 3D MOT methods, since 3D methods are generally based on ideas from 2D MOT.

Early object trackers used hand-crafted features as points of interest and achieved a fast and robust performance for problems where the cues were evident such as corners, edges, etc. [1,25]. For a detailed list of features used in trackers, interested readers are referred to [20]. However, these approaches were lacking in performance when the objects did not have sufficient features. As powerful deep learning object detectors emerged, instead of tracking the features, the objects were tracked. These methods, which are called as *tracking-by-detection*, use the output of the object detector and predict the location of the object through time by associating the outputs of the object detector. One of the earliest works is SORT [4], which used the output of the object detector and a Kalman filter to predict the next state of the tracked object. The object association through time was achieved by Hungarian algorithm. DeepSORT [28] used deep learning re-identification network to distinguish similar appearances of the objects to overcome the Id switch (Ids) problem. Ids can be explained as the miss-switch of the instances of the objects at different time steps. If the object detector can detect the objects accurately for a given domain, the performance of *tracking-by-detection* can also be sufficient [5, 15]; however, the object detector cannot always be accurate for partially observed objects.

In a number of other studies, Bayesian filters, such as the Kalman filter, have been replaced by recurrent neural networks (RNNs). The main reason is the end-to-end training capability of RNNs. An early work is by Sadeghian *et al.* [23] where a separate RNN is used for appearance, motion and re-identification. The advantage is that no extra network training is necessary such as an extra re-identification network and possible implementation difficulties of a Bayesian filter are avoided. Again, although they achieved a superior performance in certain domains [19], they are limited by the accuracy of the object detector.

Tracking-by-detection approaches have also been used in 3D MOT and they are similar to 2D MOT methods. They use a 3D object detection method and make a relation in between detections through time with an association method [11, 27]. As mentioned, again the temporal data is not used for detection and if an object instance cannot be detected in a few number of frames (e.g. due to heavy occlusion), it is lost.

To be able to overcome the problem of using a single frame without any temporal information for object detection, recent studies focused on joint *detection-and-tracking*. In these approaches, generally more than one frame is provided as input and the detection is not independent of the tracking. In one of the early works, Feichtenhofer *et al.* [10] used two separate convolutional neural networks (CNNs) and multiple frames as input and then associated the outputs. Bergmann *et al.* [2] used a neural network for association of detected objects in a similar method. Center track [30] is one of the recent successful methods which achieved high performance results on benchmarks; however, one of the problems of this approach is that when an object is not detected for any reason, it is initialized as a new object when it is re-detected.

After the successful performance of joint detection-and-tracking in 2D images, a similar approach has been followed for 3D MOT. Early work by Luo *et al.* [18] used pointclouds from different frames similar to [10] and associated the outputs. In another similar study, Guo *et al.* [14] used keyframes instead of using all frames. Recently, Center Point [29] is inspired from the success of center track [30]. There are two main problems with these methods. The first one is that since they are data dependent, their training requires a long time for each new domain and object type. Secondly, if the objects are not detected due to any reason such as heavy occlusion or small scale at a distance, these methods cannot predict the location of the objects.

Finally, we will mention the methods where the grid based approach is used for tracking. Engel *et al.* [7] uses DOGMa as input and predicts the objects and their associations in time. However, the objects cannot be estimated precisely due to the noisy nature of the occupancy grids.

Our proposal is different from the aforementioned approaches in the sense that we continue tracking of the objects, even if the observability is poor due to occlusion or distance, by using the Bayesian filters on the raw sensor data to obtain DOGMa and integrate with a precise object detector for tracking on BeV.

3 Method

We formulate the detection and tracking of multiple objects in the grid as follows. We receive information from each sensor S_m at time t, detect objects for a given class type such as *car, cyclist* or *pedestrian* with respect to our ego vehicle and track this object instance for the given time interval $[t, t + T]$ while the object is in the perception range of the ego vehicle. The total number of class types will be denoted with N_c. Each object $o^i_{t+\delta t}$ is defined by its class type c, location $x = (x_1, x_2)$, dimension $d = (w, l)$, orientation θ and its unique instance id i at time $t + \delta t$. Initially, objects are recognized by the detection method; after initialization they are tracked as explained in this section. Time depends on acquisition time of data from the sensors and will be annotated as discrete afterwards. The range of the tracking is equal to that of the occupancy grid map, which is selected by the user. The tracklet $g(t-k, t) = \{x(t-k), x(t-k+1), \cdots, x(t)\}$ is defined as the location information of an object in the time interval $[t - k, t]$ in this study. The approach is online as it does not use future information. An illustration is shown in Fig. 2 for clarification. An object is shown at three different time steps o_{t-2}, o_{t-1} and o_t. It has three possible tracklets: $g(t - 1, t)$; $g(t - 2, t)$ and $g(t - 2, t - 1)$ (trajectory from time step $t - 1$ to t; $t - 2$ to t; and $t - 2$ to $t - 1$ respectively).

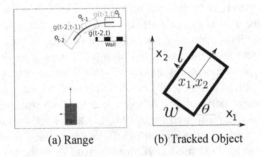

(a) Range   (b) Tracked Object

Fig. 2. On the left, the object is shown in the range of the ego vehicle on the grid for three different time steps: $\{t-2, t-1, t\}$ with all three possible tracklets. On the right, the location, dimension and orientation of the tracked object is illustrated.

The sensor data is processed to obtain a dynamic occupancy grid map, semantic representation of the grid and object detection in the grid. First, we will explain these processes briefly, then how we track objects with this data.

3.1 Bayesian Occupancy Grids

To obtain dynamic occupancy grid maps, we use a Bayesian Filter method. The occupancy probability of each cell of the grid is computed by using the sensor measurements and the previous states of the cells. We will very briefly explain the steps to compute the probability by using CMCDOT [22], which is a successful DOGMa approach. The state of each cell is defined as {*free, statically occupied, dynamically occupied, unknown area*}. First, the current state of the cell is predicted by using the probabilities from the previous states with transition probabilities. Transition probability is a value that represents the probability of transition of a state from one to another. Next, the probabilities from first step are evaluated with a probabilistic sensor model as the observation model. One of the advantages of the sensor models is that they can be used with a variety of sensors including LIDAR, radar, RGB cameras, etc. Once the evaluation is completed, the state distributions are estimated and the cycle is completed with a particle re-sampling step which assigns new particles to new dynamically occupied regions. For each cell with a high dynamic probability, a velocity related information of the motion state is also computed. The output consists of 4 channels for occupancy states and 2 channels for motion states. It should be noted that, although DOGMa does not have explicit object definition, it contains predictions for all grid cells regardless of their occlusion or distance.

3.2 Semantic Grid

Occupancy grids don't contain semantic information. To achieve this, we semantically segment the RGB images by using a deep learning method MobileNetV2 [24] which is adapted for KITTI dataset [8], register each pixel with a point in the pointcloud which is obtained from LIDAR data and project this information onto the grid. Although the data is sparse, it is a fast approximation of semantic grids. It should be noted that semantic grids can also be obtained in a dense manner and they would not require a specific sensor type as shown in [9]. The semantic grid is converted to a 1-hot vector to be used as input by the GTN. It consists of $N_c + 2$ channels where N_c is total number of classes, 1 additional channel to represent cells with no points and 1 channel for cells with unclassified points.

3.3 3D Object Detection

We use two different off-the-shelf 3D object detectors for estimating the 3D poses of the objects in the grid. Both of them use point clouds as input [13,26]. We require the following outputs from the detector: the class type of the detected object, its center location on the grid, dimension (width and length) and orientation. It should be reminded that the detector can use any sensor type as long as it provides the required outputs.

Furthermore, we use it as an independent module in our framework so that it can be interchanged if necessary, such as to detect another object class, or interchange it with another sensor modality in another data domain.

3.4 Grid Tracking Network

An overview of the method is given in Fig. 3. As explained above, our method is not dependent on a specific sensor modality. Here we illustrate with LIDAR and RGB camera sensor types, which are available in most of the current datasets. Semantic grid is transformed into a 1-hot vector depending on the class types we will use. We use the *car*, *bike* and *pedestrian* classes. DOGMa, semantic grid maps, the class estimations on the grid and the tracklets $g(t-2, t-1)$ from the previous time step $t-1$ are concatenated and they are fed into a ResNet-34 backbone to extract the features. During training, the tracklets from previous steps are provided from the ground truth. The class estimation on the grid is simply the rendered tracking estimation where each cell contains information about the occupying object class type. The class estimations and tracklets have both $N_c + 1$ (class types and background) number of channels. Therefore, ResNet-34 has an input of $3 \times N_c + 10$ channels.

The features are processed by a feature pyramid network (FPN). We omit the details of FPN and refer the interested reader to [17]. The output of FPN is first input to the class convolutions. It has 5 layers each consisting of a convolution with a batch normalization with the corresponding channel sizes, $(192, 64, 16, 16, N_c)$. The output of class convolution is used to find the cross entropy loss for the class estimation on the grid $\mathcal{L}_C$ (Class loss). Then, for each object instance output at time step $t - 1$, the output of the class convolution is concatenated with the binary grid estimation at $t - 1$ where the cells that contain the corresponding object instance are 1, and 0 otherwise. The instance convolution has 12 convolution layers. The initial convolution layers consist of 8 channels. The instance convolution is applied for each instance at $t - 1$ and N_I outputs are obtained for time step t where N_I is the number of instances at $t - 1$. Therefore, for each object instance at $t - 1$, their new location prediction is obtained at t. Finally, an instance loss (Object ID loss) is computed as the binary cross entropy loss for each instance estimation, $\mathcal{L}_I = \sum_i^{N_I} \mathcal{L}_i$; therefore the total loss is defined as $\mathcal{L} = \mathcal{L}_C + \mathcal{L}_I$.

This output provides the coarse estimations at t for each instance from time step $t - 1$. Finally, an association algorithm is applied that fuse coarse estimations with the outputs of the 3D Object detector at t.

3.5 Association

We perform three operations in association; a) starting a new instance seed from 3D detection; b) associating an existing instance with the 3D detection; c) tracking the object detected by GTN but not by the object detector. Note that association is not used during training.

The algorithm is given in Algorithm 1. For each object detected by object detector and by GTN, the centers are found by simple morphological operations, ct_{est} and ct_{GTN}. A similarity matrix is obtained which represents the distance between the distances of the object detector and GTN detections. For association of the objects, we use

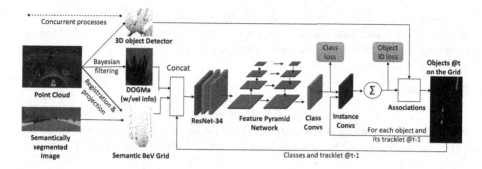

Fig. 3. Overview of the proposed framework.

Algorithm 1: Object Association

Definitions: $ct_{tr}(i)$: Estimation center of ith object from association, $ct_{est}(i)$: Estimation center from detection network, $ct_{GTN}(i)$: Estimation center from GTN, τ_d: Distance threshold; $Id(i)$: Id of object i

Initialize $M = |ct_{GTN}|$; $N = |ct_{est}|$;

create simmat:

for $m = 1, \cdots, M$ do

    for $n = 1, \cdots, N$ do

        if $||ct_{GTN}(m) - ct_{est}(n)|| > \tau_d$ then

           $simmat(m, n) = \infty$

        else

           $simmat(m, n) = ||ct_{GTN}(m) - ct_{est}(n)||$

apply Hungarian algorithm:

$assoc = H(simmat)$

for $n = 1, \cdots, N$ do

    if $ct_{est}(n) \in assoc$ then

        $m = assoc(n)$

        $ct_{tr}(m) = ct_{est}(n)$

        $Id(m) = m$

    else

        $ct_{tr}(max(Id) + 1) = ct_{est}(n)$

        $Id(max(Id) + 1) = max(Id) + 1$

for $m = 1, \cdots, M$ do

    if $ct_{GTN}(m) \notin assoc$ then

        $ct_{tr}(m) = ct_{GTN}(m)$

        $Id(m) = m$

return ct_{tr}, Id

Hungarian algorithm with a parameter which asserts that the distance between the centers of the associated objects should be smaller than a threshold τ_d. If the object found by the object detector is not associated with the detection from GTN, then it is initiated as a new instance. If GTN detection is not associated with an object detector detection, then it is included in the tracked objects list with the location found by GTN. The final output is the centers of the tracked objects with their Ids.

Removing of instances is automatic due to instance convolution layer of the proposed network which outputs no objects for objects that are not in the grid anymore; therefore, we don't have a specific algorithm for removal process.

3.6 Training

During training, we use the Ground Truth object locations instead of the 3D Object detector. For the semantic segmentation, we use the output of the off-the-shelf segmentation algorithm. We use SGD with a learning rate of 0.001 for optimization.

4 Experiments

We have evaluated our approach on KITTI MOT dataset training data which is collected by using a vehicle equipped with various sensors [12]. We have used 15 sequences, 6523 frames, 20199 instances of car, 8304 instances of pedestrians and 1088 instances of cyclists for training; 6 sequences, 1481 frames, 7093 instances of car, 3166 instances of pedestrians and 850 instances of cyclists for validation. It has RGB camera, LIDAR and corresponding calibration parameters for the sensors and GPS data for the vehicle localization. The training and validation is made on Nvidia GTX 1080Ti. First, we give our qualitative results. Then, in the second part, we provide comparative results against other methods.

4.1 Qualitative Results

We show two sequences of images through time in Fig. 4 and Fig. 1 - bottom. On the left, RGB images are shown with circles for some of the detected objects to show their corresponding labels on the grid. On the right, the grids are shown with object labels. "GT only" means that the object is neither detected nor tracked but a GT label is provided in the dataset. "GT+Track" means that the object has a GT label and it is tracked by GTN although it was not detected by the object detector. "Track only" means there is a track of an object but there is no detection or GT label. "GT + Det + Tr" means that the object is in GT and it is detected and tracked while "Det + Tr" means that it is not given in GT, but an object is detected and tracked at that location.

On top image, 4 objects have correct common detection and tracking with a GT ("GT+Det+Tr"). A car on the lower left which is partially observable is tracked, but its location is estimated wrong. Two objects on the left and one on the upper right of the grid are detected and tracked, but they have no GT. The van is not detected; therefore it is not tracked yet. The top image is four time steps before $(t - 4)$ the image in the *middle*.

The *middle image* has 5 common GT+Track+Detections. As it can be seen, one of the cars which was detected in the $t - 4$ frame is now also given in the GT. Two cars on the left and right side of the grid are not detected, but they are still tracked since they were detected in the $t - 4$ frame. The van is tracked since it was probably detected as a car in between frames t and $t - 4$. A car has GT, but it has not been detected yet on the right side of the grid.

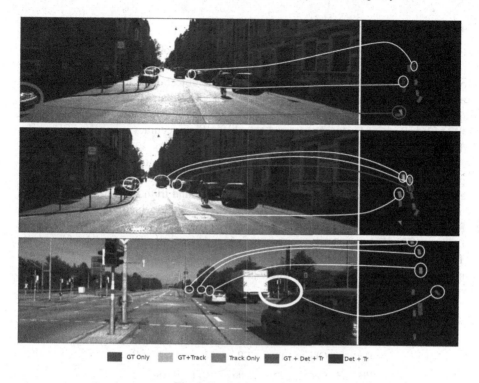

GT Only   GT+Track   Track Only   GT + Det + Tr   Det + Tr

Fig. 4. Qualitative analysis.

In the bottom, two previous time steps $t - 2$ of the image in the bottom of Fig. 1 is given. Here, the car on the far away right is observable and it is detected, tracked with a GT. The circled far away three cars are tracked even if they are not detected by the object detector. The most far away object is not tracked anymore on frame t in Fig. 1 since it is out of view. The truck is not detected nor tracked since the object detector is not trained for trucks.

These images help us to visualize that the objects can be tracked even if they are not detected due to heavy occlusion, distance, or any other reason. We attribute this mainly to the Bayesian filter process on the raw data, which has a strong predictive capacity for unobserved regions. However, as it can be seen, the ground truth of KITTI MOT dataset does not contain all the labels for the cars, cyclists and pedestrians available in the environment as it has been reported by other studies [21,27]. When the algorithm is used directly on this dataset, the false positives increase tremendously. To overcome this problem, we include an additional condition in our algorithm. We keep track of all object centers in Algorithm 1, but report only the ones whose centers are close to the estimated tracked instance in the previous frame, $||ct_{tr}^t - ct_{tr}^{t-1}|| < \tau_{det}$ if it is not a new seed. This reduces false positives significantly.

4.2 Quantitative Results

For quantitative analysis, we have compared two different object detection methods, different grid sizes for our proposal and another tracking method on KITTI MOT for three object types; cars, pedestrians and cyclists. For the object detection, we have included two 3D object detection methods; one of them is GridPillars (GP) which uses a modified version of PointPillars [16] for occupancy grids [13]. The other one is PointRCNN (PR) [26]. Both of them are reported to achieve high accuracy results for 3D object detection.

The results for the object detection without tracking is given in Table 1. Here, we project the 3D bounding boxes onto the grid and assume that an object is correctly estimated if the projected bounding boxes of the ground truth and estimation overlaps more than 50%. The results are given for a single threshold which gives the best result for AB3DMOT tracking method [27]. Here, we give the TP (True Positive), FP (False Positive), FN (False Negative) and precision and recall results for each object type. These will be useful in interpreting the results for tracking. One of the largest performance differences is in Cyclists, where [26] is more successful for both precision and recall.

Table 1. Object detection accuracy

Det.	Object	TP	FP	FN	Prec	Recall
PR [26]	Car	6022	1007	1071	0.8567	0.8490
GP [13]	Car	5799	383	1294	0.9380	0.8176
PR [26]	Ped.	1830	41	1336	0.9781	0.5780
GP [13]	Ped.	2470	402	696	0.8600	0.7802
PR [26]	Cyclist	720	84	130	0.8955	0.8471
GP [13]	Cyclist	363	80	487	0.8194	0.4271

Next, we compare two tracking methods with two object detection methods and two different grid sizes as shown in Table 2, 3 and 4 for Cars, Pedestrians and Cyclists respectively.

We include Multi-object tracking accuracy (MOTA) which is defined as $MOTA = 1-(FP+FN+IdS)/GT$ and Id switches (IdS) [3]. An object is correctly tracked only if it is correctly detected with the correct ID; therefore, MOTA also includes accuracy for location, dimension and orientation of the objects. The size depicts the number of grids. The range of the grid is same for both grid size ($92 \times 62\,\mathrm{m}^2$), only the resolution doubles which is 0.15 m and 0.3 m respectively. The ego vehicle is in the middle lower edge of the grid. Size is Not Applicable (NA) for AB3DMOT [26] since it directly uses the exact location of the objects. For our method, after we detect and track the object on the grid, we find its center and bounding box, and convert it to the coordinates of the KITTI MOT for comparison. Since we find the objects in the grid, which is discrete, we have some error due to this. For small objects, the results are expected to improve on larger sized grids since the effect of the grid discretization will reduce.

First, we consider the cars. The MOTA measure for GridTrack is slightly higher for both object detection methods. It should be noted that AB3DMOT is a traditional tracking method and its success is limited by the detection accuracy. As it can be observed, the tracking performance of AB3DMOT is already close to object detection accuracy. For example for object detection method [13], the number of TPs is already 5790 for tracking, which is very close to 5799 TPs of the original object detection. It also reduces FPs. However, GridTrack has the capacity of increasing the number of TPs which reduces the FNs. Although the IdS and FP is higher for GridTrack, due to its increased performance in TPs, MOTA also increases. GridTrack achieves this higher TP number by estimating objects even when they are not detected by using the GTN. The high IdS and FP values can be related to the track predictions of instances which have very close centers for different instances in consecutive frames. Another point of evaluation is the size of the grid. The value of MOTA is slightly higher for smaller grid size, which shows that for large objects such as cars, a smaller grid size can be selected without losing performance in the accuracy.

Table 2. Tracking methods for car in KITTI MOT

Tracker	Size	MOTA	TP	FP	FN	IdS
GridTrack + [26]	207×307	**0.7609**	5754	325	1339	32
GridTrack + [26]	415×615	0.7555	5760	329	1333	72
AB3DMOT + [26]	NA	0.7545	5970	618	1123	0
GridTrack + [13]	207×307	**0.7751**	5998	474	1095	26
GridTrack + [13]	415×615	0.7736	6015	462	1078	66
AB3DMOT + [13]	NA	0.7727	5790	308	1303	1

Next, we consider the pedestrians. The pedestrians are much smaller than the cars. The TPs are increased for [26] object detection. The MOTA increase is slightly higher in this case. The results are improved for the larger grid size in this case, which is expected since the pedestrians have a small size and a larger grid size reduces the errors in discretization. TPs are increased in PR-based detection [26] with the usage of GTN.

Table 3. Tracking methods for pedestrian in KITTI MOT

Tracker	Size	MOTA	TP	FP	FN	IdS
GridTrack + [26]	207×307	0.5648	1879	49	1287	42
GridTrack + [26]	415×615	**0.5774**	1936	93	1230	15
AB3DMOT + [26]	NA	0.5442	1762	39	1404	0
GridTrack + [13]	207×307	0.6412	2261	195	905	36
GridTrack + [13]	415×615	**0.6652**	2328	214	838	8
AB3DMOT + [13]	NA	0.6595	2383	294	783	1

Table 4. Tracking methods for cyclist in KITTI MOT

Tracker	Size	MOTA	TP	FP	FN	IdS
GridTrack + [26]	207 × 307	0.7576	686	38	164	4
GridTrack + [26]	415 × 615	**0.7659**	688	36	162	1
AB3DMOT + [26]	NA	0.6471	618	68	232	0
GridTrack + [13]	207 × 307	0.3294	362	80	488	2
GridTrack + [13]	415 × 615	**0.3294**	363	80	487	3
AB3DMOT + [13]	NA	0.2929	322	73	528	0

Finally, we consider the cyclists. Their MOTA performance improves significantly, probably due to less number of cyclists in the scenes. The approach does not confuse the cyclists with each other and achieves a high performance. The size of the cyclists is also large; therefore, the performance is similar for both grid sizes. GTN successfully detects cyclists even if they are not detected by detection algorithm.

From these results it can be stated that GridTrack approach can be used with an object detector to achieve a SOTA performance on the multi-object tracking task.

5   Conclusion

In this study, we have proposed a method which obtains a DOGMa by applying a Bayesian filter on raw sensor data and we integrated this information with a precise 3D object detector to track the objects even when they were hardly observable. We have used point clouds and RGB images to realize the framework; however, as it has been mentioned, other sensor modalities can also be used. The results suggest that the framework is capable of detecting partially observed objects even when they are not detected by an object detector. As part of the future work, we plan to integrate appearance classification into our framework so that the number of ID Switches are reduced. Another interesting direction would be to test the method with other sensor modalities.

Acknowledgment. We thank Gabriel Othmezouri, Jérôme Lussereau and Lukas Rummelhard for their assistance in this study. Parts of the experiments presented in this paper were carried out using the Grid'5000 testbed, supported by a scientific interest group hosted by Inria and including CNRS, RENATER and several Universities as well as other organizations (see https://www.grid5000.fr).

References

1. Babenko, B., Member, S., Yang, M.H., Member, S.: Robust object tracking with online multiple instance learning. IEEE Trans. Pattern Anal. Mach. Intell. **33**(8), 1619–1632 (2011)
2. Bergmann, P., Meinhardt, T., Leal-Taixe, L.: Tracking without bells and whistles. In: ICCV (2019)

3. Bernardin, K., Stiefelhagen, R.: Evaluating multiple object tracking performance: the CLEAR MOT metrics. Eurasip J. Image Video Process. **2008** (2008). https://doi.org/10.1155/2008/246309

4. Bewley, A., Ge, Z., Ott, L., Ramos, F., Upcroft, B.: Simple online and realtime tracking. In: ICIP, pp. 3464–3468. IEEE (2016)

5. Chandra, R., Bhattacharya, U., Randhavane, T., Bera, A., Manocha, D.: RoadTrack: realtime tracking of road agents in dense and heterogeneous environments. In: ICRA, pp. 1270–1277 (2020)

6. Ebert, J., Gumpp, T., Münzner, S., Matskevych, A., Condurache, A.P., Gläser, C.: Deep radar sensor models for accurate and robust object tracking. In: ITSC, pp. 8–13 (2020)

7. Engel, N., Hoermann, S., Henzler, P., Dietmayer, K.: Deep object tracking on dynamic occupancy grid maps using RNNs. In: ITSC (2018)

8. Erkent, O., Laugier, C.: Semantic segmentation with unsupervised domain adaptation under varying weather conditions for autonomous vehicles. IEEE Robot. Autom. Lett. **5**(2), 3580–3587 (2020). https://doi.org/10.1109/LRA.2020.2978666

9. Erkent, O., Wolf, C., Laugier, C., Gonzalez, D., Cano, V.: Semantic grid estimation with a hybrid Bayesian and deep neural network approach. In: IEEE IROS, pp. 888–895 (2018)

10. Feichtenhofer, C., Pinz, A., Zisserman, A.: Detect to track and track to detect. In: ECCV, vol. 14, pp. 709–736 (2017)

11. Frossard, D., Urtasun, R.: End-to-end learning of multi-sensor 3D tracking by detection. In: ICRA, pp. 635–642 (2018)

12. Geiger, A., Lenz, P., Urtasun, R.: Are we ready for autonomous driving? The KITTI vision benchmark suite. In: CVPR, pp. 3354–3361. IEEE (2012)

13. González, D.S., Paigwar, A., Erkent, Ö., Dibangoye, J., Laugier, C.: Leveraging dynamic occupancy grids for 3D object detection in point clouds. In: 16th IEEE International Conference on Control, Automation, Robotics and Vision (ICARCV) (2020)

14. Guo, X., Huang, K.: 3D object detection and tracking on streaming data. In: ICRA, pp. 8376–8382 (2020)

15. Khalkhali, M.B., Vahedian, A., Yazdi, H.S.: Vehicle tracking with Kalman filter using online situation assessment. Robot. Auton. Syst. **131**, 103596 (2020)

16. Lang, A.H., Vora, S., Caesar, H., Zhou, L., Yang, J., Beijbom, O.: PointPillars: fast encoders for object detection from point clouds. In: CVPR, pp. 12697–12705 (2019)

17. Lin, T.Y., Dollár, P., Girshick, R., He, K., Hariharan, B., Belongie, S.: Feature pyramid networks for object detection. In: CVPR, pp. 2117–2125 (2017)

18. Luo, W., Yang, B., Urtasun, R.: Fast and Furious: real time end-to-end 3D detection, tracking and motion forecasting with a single convolutional net. In: CVPR (2018)

19. Maksai, A., Fua, P.: Eliminating exposure bias and loss-evaluation mismatch in multiple object tracking. In: CVPR, pp. 4639–4648 (2019)

20. Miah, M., Pepin, J., Saunier, N., Bilodeau, G.A.: An empirical analysis of visual features for multiple object tracking in urban scenes. In: ICPR (2020)

21. Pöschmann, J., Pfeifer, T., Protzel, P.: Factor graph based 3D multi-object tracking in point clouds. In: IROS, pp. 10343–10350 (2020)

22. Rummelhard, L., Nègre, A., Laugier, C.: Conditional Monte Carlo dense occupancy tracker. In: ITSC, pp. 2485–2490. IEEE (2015)

23. Sadeghian, A., Alahi, A., Savarese, S.: Tracking the untrackable: learning to track multiple cues with long-term dependencies. In: ICCV (2017)

24. Sandler, M., Howard, A., Zhu, M., Zhmoginov, A., Chen, L.C.: MobileNetV2: inverted residuals and linear bottlenecks. In: CVPR, pp. 4510–4520 (2018)

25. Shi, J., Tomasi, C.: Good features. In: CVPR, pp. 593–600 (1994)

26. Shi, S., Wang, X., Li, H.: PointRCNN: 3D object proposal generation and detection from point cloud. In: CVPR, pp. 770–779 (2019)

27. Weng, X., Wang, J., Held, D., Kitani, K.: AB3DMOT: a baseline for 3D multi-object tracking and new evaluation metrics. In: IROS, pp. 10359–10366 (2020)

28. Wojke, N., Bewley, A., Paulus, D.: Simple online and realtime tracking with a deep association metric. In: ICIP, pp. 3645–3650 (2017)

29. Yin, T., Zhou, X., Krähenbühl, P.: Center-based 3D object detection and tracking. In: CVPR (2021)

30. Zhou, X., Koltun, V., Krähenbühl, P.: Tracking objects as points. In: Vedaldi, A., Bischof, H., Brox, T., Frahm, J.-M. (eds.) ECCV 2020. LNCS, vol. 12349, pp. 474–490. Springer, Cham (2020). https://doi.org/10.1007/978-3-030-58548-8_28

An Efficient Video Desnowing and Deraining Method with a Novel Variant Dataset

Arezoo Sadeghzadeh[1], Md Baharul Islam[1,2]([✉])[ID], and Reza Zaker[3][ID]

[1] Department of Computer Engineering, Bahcesehir University, Istanbul, Turkey
arezoo.sadeghzadeh@bahcesehir.edu.tr
[2] College of Data Science and Engineering,
American University of Malta, Cospicua, Malta
[3] Department of Electrical Engineering,
Azarbaijan Shahid Madani University, Tabriz, Iran
zaker@azaruniv.ac.ir

Abstract. Video desnowing/deraining plays a vital role in outdoor vision systems, such as autonomous driving and surveillance systems, since the weather conditions significantly degrade their performance. Although numerous approaches have been reported for video snow/rain removal, they are limited to a few videos and did not consider the variations that occurred for the camera and background in real applications. We build a complete snow and rain dataset to overcome this limitation, consisting of 577 videos with synthetic snow and rain, quasi-snow, and real snow and rain. All possible variations of the background and the camera are considered in the dataset. Then, an efficient pixel-wise video desnowing/deraining method is proposed based on the color and temporal information in consecutive video frames. It is highly likely for a single pixel to be a background pixel rather than a snowy pixel at least once in the consecutive frames. Inspiring from this fact along with the color information of the snow pixels, we extract the background pixels from different consecutive frames by searching for the minimum gray-scale intensity. Experimental results demonstrate and validate the proposed method's robustness to illumination and high-performance static background and camera.

Keywords: Desnowing · Deraining · Temporal information · Snow and rain dataset · Static/dynamic background · Synthetic/quasi snow

1 Introduction

Weather conditions such as rain, snow, fog, and haze have a negative effect on the perceptual quality of the videos/images captured from outdoor video/image processing or vision systems such as video/movie editing, vision-based navigation, autonomous driving, and video surveillance [4]. Consequently, the performance of the related video/image processing tasks such as object tracking and detection [17] and disparity estimation [9] is significantly degraded. Providing

© Springer Nature Switzerland AG 2021
M. Vincze et al. (Eds.): ICVS 2021, LNCS 12899, pp. 195–208, 2021.
https://doi.org/10.1007/978-3-030-87156-7_16

an example, the falling snowflakes in Fig. 1 severely distort the results of the static image-based object detection [5, 17] (Fig. 1(a)) and the video-based stereo matching for disparity map estimation (Fig. 1(b)) [9]. Thus, it is vital to remove these weather conditions from the input images and videos as a pre-processing step, which has attracted much attention among researchers in the computer vision field.

Earliest rain removal approaches were mostly based on the correlation between pixels in consecutive frames [2], and physical characteristics of rain such as shape, appearance, brightness, etc. [3]. However, these methods cannot achieve good performance in complex scenes since no prior knowledge of videos is employed. Later, this limitation was overcome by considering the prior knowledge of the rain in [18]. Recently, various deep learning-based approaches have been proposed for rain removal using deep convolutional neural networks (CNNs) or deep recurrent convolutional neural networks (RCNNs).

One of the main challenges in the field of video-based snow and rain removal is the lack of appropriate dataset. In earlier works, some rainy scenes of the movies [2] or real snowy videos from YouTube [9, 11] have been employed for the implementations. However, using these kinds of datasets cannot be suitable for quantitative analysis due to the lack of ground-truth information. In some other approaches, synthesis snow and rain have been added to the clean videos [11]. The characteristics of the snowflakes and rain streaks in these datasets are limited. At the same time, there can be varieties of scenarios for them with different sizes, velocities, and densities of snowflakes and rain streaks with different states (static and dynamic) for the cameras and the background. Additionally, these videos with synthetic snow and rain are not entirely the same as the real snowy, and rainy videos as their movement and scattering patterns may differ from the real ones.

Object detection in presence of snow   Object detection from the scene without snow

Left image   Right image   Disparity map

Fig. 1. The negative effects of snow on the performance of computer vision applications, a) object detection based on YOLOv3 [5, 17], b) stereo disparity map estimation [9].

Another challenge in the video-based snow removal approaches is the performance degradation of the video rain removal techniques applied to the snowy videos. Complicated characteristics of snow such as sparse scattering, uneven density, multi-scale shapes, and irregular transparency make video-based snow removal more challenging and inapplicable than video-based rain removal. Thus, applying rain removal techniques on snowy videos cannot remove the large bright snowflakes. Moreover, these algorithms cause severe blurring artifacts even for static backgrounds when the camera slightly shakes or moves while capturing the videos.

To address the aforementioned challenges, we build a complete dataset of snow and rain videos that are employed in our implementations. Then, a simple but efficient video desnowing/deraining method is proposed based on the temporal information of the adjacent frames and the intensity of the corresponding pixels in consecutive frames. Our dataset can be used in future research to have a complete evaluation and comparison of the proposed method. Overall, the main contributions of the this work can be summarized as follows:

- A new snow and rain videos dataset is provided for the first time. This dataset consists of 577 videos in which there are three types of particles: synthetic snow and rain, quasi snow, and real snow and rain. All variations of background (static and dynamic) and the camera (static and dynamic, e.g., translation, zooming, illumination changes, and rotation) are considered. The ground-truth information in the synthetic snow and rain videos allows the researchers to evaluate their methods in different scenarios. This dataset can be useful for all future video snow/rain removal approaches.
- A simple but very efficient video desnowing/deraining method is proposed based on the temporal information and the color of the pixels in consecutive frames of the video. This pixel-wise method can successfully remove the snow and rain for static background and camera even if there is heavy snow with high density while its computational cost is low. It is also robust to illumination changes and camera shaking.

2   Related Works

In this section, a brief review of the reported approaches in the literature for rain and snow removal is presented. These approaches can be mainly categorized into two groups: 1) image-based methods, and 2) video-based approaches. In both groups of the approaches, two major types of techniques have been applied, i.e. conventional computer vision techniques, and techniques based on deep neural networks (DNNs). Some of the main recent works are discussed in the following subsections.

2.1   Image-Based Snow/Rain Removal

Considering a video in frame-by-frame manner, the image-based approaches can also achieve satisfying performance for video-based rain/snow removal. However, due to the lack of the temporal information in image-based techniques, video-based methods achieve significantly better performance for video rain/snow removal. As the first attempts in the field of image-based atmospheric-particle-removal approaches, several priors, e.g. sparsity prior, patch-rank prior, have been applied in order to detect and remove the particles. However, they suffer from the limited generalization ability which has been dealt with using the same-resolution CNNs based on the synthetic datasets.

Fu et al. [1] utilized a combination of CNNs and handcrafted priors for removing rain particles from a single image. A large synthetic snowy image dataset was published in [15] by Liu et al. which was called Snow100K. They presented a multistage network architecture as DesnowNet and evaluated it qualitatively and quantitavely on the Snow100K dataset. However, this model is time-consuming with bad generalization ability and a very large size which made it inapplicable to the light-weight applications.

A two-stage network was proposed by Li et al. [13]. In this method, the first step was a physics-based backbone and the second step was a depth-guided generative adversarial network (GAN) refinement. Recently, Jaw et al. [5] proposed a simple, efficient single-image desnowing model based on a pyramidal hierarchical design and cross-resolution lateral connections.

2.2 Video-Based Snow/Rain Removal

Prior to the success of the deep learning-based methods, conventional computer vision and image processing technique-based approaches have been widely adopted for video- and image-based rain/snow removal.

Most of the video deraining approaches are based on the high correlation between the corresponding pixels in consecutive frames [2]. One of the earliest works in this field was proposed by Garg and Nayar [2] by capturing the dynamics of rain based on a correlation model and a physics-based motion blur model. Later, they proposed a method [4] to further reduce the impacts of rain before taking images/videos by adapting the parameters of the camera, e.g. exposure time. In another work, the sparsity of rain streaks along with the rain-perpendicular direction were considered by Jiang et al. [7] to propose a video rain streak removal approach based on tensor. Low-rank hypothesis of the background was employed by Ren et al. [18] to separate sparse and dense rain and deal with heavy rain/snow in dynamic scenes. In addition to deraining based on monocular videos, some studies have been carried out for deraining based on stereo videos [9] which can be applied widely in outdoor vision applications such as autonomous driving systems. These approaches include more information and details than the monocular videos thanks to the information provided from two cameras. However, the necessity of using two cameras results in additional cost.

Due to extremely fast improvements in deep learning models, e.g. CNNs and RCNNs, and their ability in investigating complex patterns, they have been extensively applied in variety of applications [6,17] as well as rain/snow removal systems. Liu et al. [14] proposed a deep RCNN for rain removal based on spatial texture appearances. In this method, the background detail was reconstructed by considering temporal coherence. A two-stage recurrent network was presented by Yang et al. [20] through which the inverse recovery process of the main synthesis model was performed for deraining. Additionally, they provided a new rain synthesis model in order to create more videos for training and evaluation.

In some recent studies [10–12], multi-scale convolutional sparse coding has been applied for rain/snow removal from both dynamic and static background scenes. Li et al. [11] proposed a method for dynamic background, in which the rain/snow was encoded based on an online multi-scale convolutional sparse coding (OMS-CSC) model. However, it still suffers from some limitations on handling the videos from non-surveillance cameras and videos with extensive moving objects, fast illumination changes, and fast moving cameras.

3 Dataset Development

Recently, a video dataset including synthetic snow and rain has been proposed in [11] which mainly focused on rain rather than snow. Additionally, the variations on the camera and background settings were not considered in this dataset. An image-based snow removal dataset, namely Snow100K [15] is available. Recently, the Canadian Adverse Driving Conditions (CADC) video dataset has been proposed in [16] which was collected during winter within the Region of Waterloo. It was specifically designed for autonomous driving in a variety of winter weather conditions. However, as it is the same as real snowy videos, it suffers from the lack of ground truth information. To the authors' best knowledge, there is no complete unique dataset for rain/snow removal from videos, especially for snow. We build a complete snow and rain dataset with distinguishable characteristics, called **Variants in Snow&Rain Videos**[1]. This dataset comprises three main sections: 1) videos with synthetic snow and rain, 2) videos with quasi-snow, and 3) videos with real snow and rain.

3.1 Videos with Synthetic Snow and Synthetic Rain

Ground-Truth Videos. Only two scenarios are considered for videos with synthetic snow/rain in the available datasets, i.e., static background and dynamic background. In our dataset, different background and camera settings and variations are considered in 46 recorded videos. We use a 25MP camera to record these videos with a frame rate of 30. These frames are saved in "JPEG" format as images with a size of 1080×1920 pixels. For the dynamic background, different scenarios are considered, such as slow movements (i.e., the tree leaves are swinging), fast movements (i.e., cars on the street or the movements of a swing in the park). The camera is also either dynamic or static. The dynamic camera refers to the scenarios as slow and fast translation, slow and fast rotation, slow and fast zooming, small and large shaking, slow and fast illumination changes, and simultaneous zooming and rotation. Different possible combinations of background and camera variations are also utilized, and the videos are recorded as ground truth. Additionally, some more videos are recorded from other locations such as the sea, roads, and parks to make the dataset rich in various locations

---

[1] The dataset is available at https://bit.ly/3BHKeRo. For any issues regarding downloading the dataset, please contact `arezoo.sadeghzadeh@bahcesehir.edu.tr` or `bislam.eng@gmail.com`.

Table 1. Total characteristics of the videos and the considered scenarios in the developed dataset.

Ground-truth videos for synthetic snow and rain				
Camera resolution	Camera variations	Background	Number of videos	Video length
25MP 1080 × 1920 pixels fps = 30	Static	Dynamic (slow)	3	35 s, 14 s, 13 s
		Dynamic (fast)	4	8 s, 8 s, 10 s, 8 s
	Dynamic (shaking and translation)	Dynamic (slow)	1	14 s
	Static and Dynamic (slow and fast translation, zooming, rotation, illumination changes, small and large shaking, both rotation and zooming)	Dynamic (fast)	13	11 s, 11 s, 14 s, 18 s, 11 s, 10 s, 13 s, 29 s, 9 s, 12 s, 11 s, 13 s, 11s
		Dynamic (slow)	13	14 s, 21 s, 14 s, 13 s, 18 s, 10 s, 10 s, 20 s, 10 s, 34 s, 11 s, 9 s, 13 s
		Static	12	22 s, 11 s, 18 s, 11 s, 25 s, 12 s, 37 s, 11 s, 10 s, 14 s, 18 s, 11 s
Videos based on quasi-snow				
8Mp 480 × 460 fps = 30	Static	Static	2	59 s, 23 s
	Dynamic (translation)		1	74 s
25MP 1080 × 1920 fps = 30	Static and Dynamic (slow and fast translation, zooming, rotation, illumination changes, small and large shaking, both rotation and zooming)		13	25 s, 19 s, 12 s, 10 s, 26 s, 16 s, 16 s, 10 s, 19 s, 28 s, 11 s, 26 s, 13 s
Videos with real snow and rain				
13MP 1080 × 1920 fps = 30	Static	Static	1 (snow)	8 s
25MP 1080 × 1920 fps = 30	Static	Static and Dynamic	8 (light and heavy rain)	21 s, 7 s, 21 s, 11 s, 12 s, 42 s, 11 s, 18 s

with a quiet or crowded background in nature and daily life. These scenarios and characteristics of the ground-truth videos are summarized in Table 1.

Augmentation for Synthetic Rain and Snow. Once the ground-truth videos have been recorded, the synthetic snow and synthetic rain are added to those videos using an augmentation library in Python as "image" [8], i.e.

"iaa.Snowflakes" for synthetic snow and "iaa.Rain" for synthetic rain. Ten different scenarios for snowflakes form the synthetic snow dataset: 9 combinations of snowflake sizes from small to big (i.e., 0.7, 0.85, and 0.95) and speed from slow to fast (i.e., 0.001, 0.01, and 0.03), and a scenario with randomly chosen snowflake size and speed in the range of [0.7, 0.95] and [0.001, 0.03], respectively. As in reality, rain has very random scattering. The synthetic-rain dataset is formed by one scenario of raindrops, randomly choosing raindrop size and speed in the range of [0.1, 0.2] and [0.1, 0.3], respectively. Consequently, in this section, in addition to 46 ground-truth videos, $46 \times 10 = 460$, and $46 \times 1 = 46$ videos have been created for synthetic-snow and synthetic-rain, respectively. Some samples of the synthetic-snow dataset are illustrated in Fig. 2(a).

Fig. 2. The sample videos of the developed dataset with a) synthetic-snow, b) quasi-snow, and c) real snow and rain for different scenarios.

3.2   Videos with Quasi-snow

Although the videos with synthetic snow are really rich in the possible variations for background and camera status, the shape and scattering pattern of the snowflakes cannot be as similar as those of the natural snowflakes. Therefore, in this part of the dataset, we simulate the real snowflakes by using the snow spray, which produces snowflakes with the most similar shape and scattering pattern and velocity to those of real snowflakes. A total of 16 videos was created with a static background and dynamic camera. All available scenarios are summerized in Table 1 and some sample videos are illustrated in Fig. 2(b). For the static background and camera, the first frames can be considered as ground truth.

3.3 Videos with Real Snow and Rain

There are many available videos for real rain and snow, only 9 videos are included in our dataset, 8 for real rain, and 1 for real snow. Different scenarios of real videos are listed in Table 1 with some sample videos illustrated in Fig. 2(c).

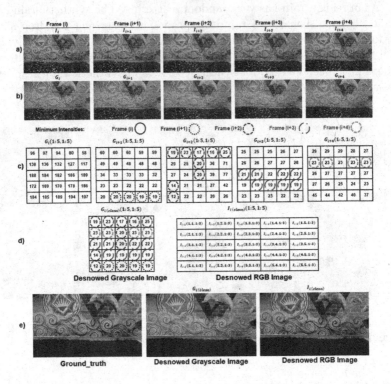

Fig. 3. The overall flowchart of the proposed desnowing/deraining method.

4 Proposed Method

Based on the studies, the rain streaks and snowflakes have sparse scattering, randomly distributed in the atmosphere. It is observed that rain streaks and snowflakes appear at different locations in temporally adjacent frames. Hence, it is unlikely for a single pixel to contain rain/snow in several consecutive video frames. Based on this fact, a simple but efficient method is proposed for snow removal using the temporal information of the adjacent frames and the color of the snowflakes. Generally, rainfall and snowfall on a digital image or a video frame have very similar characteristics, which causes desnowing techniques to be applied for deraining scenarios simultaneously and vice versa. The overall flowchart of the proposed method is illustrated in Fig. 3. In this method, after dividing the input video into frames, for ith frame of the video (Ii), a few consecutive frames (e.g. four frames in Fig. 3(a)) after that frame are selected and converted to grayscale images (Fig. 3(b)). In this step, the grayscale intensities of every single pixel in consecutive frames are compared. As the color of snowflakes and rain streaks are almost white, their intensity value is 255 or near 255. Therefore, for a single pixel in consecutive frames, the background pixel has an intensity less than the pixel's intensity including snowflakes, or at most near to the intensity of that pixel if the background is white.

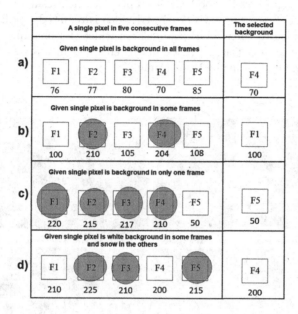

Fig. 4. The possible conditions for a single pixel in five consecutive frames.

On the other hand, based on the temporal information of the snowy videos, it is considered that for a given single pixel, it is clean of snow at least in one frame among a few consecutive frames. Accordingly, the pixel with the minimum intensity is selected as the background. This idea is investigated for different scenarios for a single pixel in five consecutive frames of a video in Fig. 4. In Fig. 4(a), the same pixel in all five consecutive frames is assumed to be without any snowflakes. So, all can be considered as the background pixel, and selecting the minimum intensity is also a background pixel. Another scenario is illustrated in Fig. 4(b), in which the same pixel in some frames contains snowflakes, and in some others, it does not. As illustrated, the snowy pixels have grayscale intensities near 255, and the clean pixels have intensities less than 200. Hence, selecting the pixel with minimum intensity results in choosing the background pixel.

In one of the most challenging scenarios, in which only one pixel is not snowy, the background can be easily detected based on the proposed method and selecting the pixel with the least intensity (Fig. 4(c)). Another essential scenario occurs when the background is white, as illustrated in Fig. 4(d). It is the most straightforward scenario because the snowy pixel is almost white. In this case, the background can be detected by selecting the pixel with minimum intensity because the intensities of all pixels are nearly 255, representing the white color. This pixel-wise selection is illustrated in Fig. 3(c) for the first 5 × 5 pixels of the input images (left top part of the images) in five consecutive frames of a video. As it is presented, for example, for the pixel of (1,2), the minimum value belongs to the third frame. So, the grayscale intensity value of that pixel in the final image equals the grayscale intensity of that pixel in the third frame. As shown in Fig. 3(d), this process is repeated for all pixels, which results in the desnowed grayscale image. Since the RGB desnowed video is required, the final desnowed image is extended to three RGB channels, in which, for example, for the given pixel of (1,2), the intensities of R, G, and B channels in desnowed image equal to those the same pixel in the third frame.

Fig. 5. Qualitative performance of the proposed method for static background and camera on quasi-snow videos, real-snow and rain videos, and synthetic-snow and rain videos.

5   Experimental Results and Comparison

5.1   Performance Evaluation

In this section, all the experiments have been implemented on a PC with 32G RAM and i7 CPU. As was mentioned above, one of the critical parameters is the number of consecutive frames considered in the analysis. This factor is essential because it defines the least number of consecutive frames among which all pixels appear at least once as background. Implementing different values for this parameter, we observe that 3, 7, and 10 frames are sufficient for light, heavy, and weighty snow/rain. In the following experiments, seven consecutive frames are considered for completely removing the snow/rain. The proposed

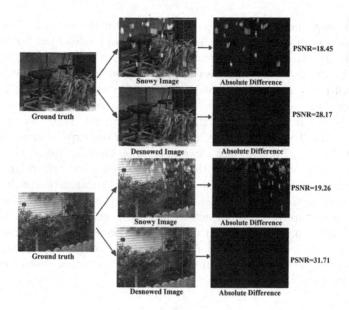

Fig. 6. Quantitive performance of the proposed method for static background and camera on quasi-snow videos.

method is tested and evaluated qualitatively for different scenarios in Fig. 5. It can efficiently remove the snow/rain for static background and camera. It can also remove the snow/rain when there is slight camera shaking while recording videos and is robust to illumination changes.

The quantitative evaluation of the proposed method is carried out on two different quasi snow frame sequences considering an image quality assessment metric called peak signal-to-noise ratio (PSNR) and the absolute difference between the desnowed frame and the ground truth frame. PSNR (in dB) is defined as $PSNR(x, y) = 10 \log_{10} \frac{max(x)}{\sqrt{MSE}}$ in which MSE is as $MSE = \frac{1}{mn} \sum_{i=1}^{m} \sum_{j=1}^{n} (x_{ij} - y_{ij})^2$, where x and y are the $m \times n$ ground truth image and its corresponding desnowed image, respectively. In Fig. 6, the PSNR is significantly improved after removing the snow (from 18.45 to 28.17 and from 19.26 to 31.71). Additionally, the visual results of the absolute difference between the desnowed image and the ground truth image, which is almost zero represented with black color, prove the effective performance of the proposed method in removing snow.

The average running times of the proposed method for removing the snow from a single frame with quasi-snow are presented in Table 2 for two different sizes of the image and three different numbers of the consecutive frames. From this table, the speed advantage of the proposed method is evident especially for the small size of the images. As the process is pixel-wise, increasing the size of the image can increase the computational time. However, even for the very big size of the image as 1080×1920 it takes at most 4.40 s to remove snow. Although increasing the number of the frames can slightly increase the running time, it significantly increases the accuracy of the final result.

The performance of the proposed method is further evaluated on two real snowy videos with dark and light backgrounds downloaded from YouTube[2] and compared with the other methods in the literature in Figs. 7 and 8, respectively. As the video in Fig. 7 contains heavy rain, its implementation is carried out using ten consecutive frames while the video in Fig. 8 is desnowed only with 7 frames. It is worth mentioning that the video of Fig. 8 composed of scenarios with both stable and dynamic cameras, though only the frames with static background and camera (i.e., $1480 - 1486^{th}$ frames) are selected for our experiments. Comparing the results in Figs. 7 and 8, it is clear to see that most of the other competing techniques cannot entirely remove the snowflakes and recover the original texture information with details, and some others cause blurring artifacts. In contrast, our proposed method can successfully remove the snowflakes and recover the background texture (even small details in Fig. 8) while the image's contrast is still kept high. No blurriness occurred in the desnowed image, no matter if the background is dark or light. Additionally, it is worth mentioning that this efficient performance is achieved by our method while its computational complexity is significantly less than that of other methods.

Table 2. Average running time of the proposed method for desnowing a single frame with two different sizes of images for 3 different numbers of consecutive frames.

Image size	3 consecutive frames	7 consecutive frames	10 consecutive frames
480 × 640	0.61 s	0.65 s	0.75 s
1080 × 1920	3.82 s	4.10 s	4.40 s

Fig. 7. Qualitative comparison with the methods in the literature on a video with dark background, (a) input, (b) Garg et al. [4], (c) Jiang et al. [7], (d) Ren et al. [18], (e) Wei et al. [19], (f) Liu et al. [14], (g) Li et al. [12], (h) the proposed method.

5.2   Failure Cases

As it was presented, the proposed method can successfully deal with the snowy video sequences with static background and camera containing light and heavy

---

[2] https://www.youtube.com/watch?{v=kNTYEKjXqzs,v=HbgoKKj7TNA}.

Fig. 8. Qualitative comparison between the proposed method and the methods in the literature on a video with light background, (a) input, (b) Garg et al. [4], (c) Jiang et al. [7], (d) Ren et al. [18], (e) Liu et al. [14], (f and g) Li et al. [12], (h) the proposed method.

snow/rain. However, it still suffers from limitations when there are extensive movements in the background and camera. As our method is a pixel-wise method based on the temporal information of the frame sequences, variations in spatial information can lead to slight blurriness, especially for heavy rain/snow when more frames are required for completely removing the snow. In our future work, we will attempt to improve the method by adding spatial information to make it more robust to background movements and camera translation, rotation, and zooming in the presence of heavy snow/rain.

6 Conclusion

This paper first built a snow and rain dataset by considering all possible background and camera scenarios. In this dataset, three kinds of particles were used, i.e., synthetic snow and rain with different sizes and speeds, quasi-snow, and real snow and rain. Additionally, a simple but very efficient desnowing/deraining method was proposed based on the temporal information of consecutive frames and the color of pixels for static background and camera. Experimental results and comparisons with the related works proved that our method could efficiently remove the snow/rain without causing any blurriness. It performed faithfully even for heavy snow scenarios and illumination changes and could recover the original background information. We will improve the method to deal with the dynamic background and moving cameras in our future research work.

References

1. Fu, X., Huang, J., Ding, X., Liao, Y., Paisley, J.: Clearing the skies: a deep network architecture for single-image rain removal. IEEE Trans. Image Process. **26**(6), 2944–2956 (2017)
2. Garg, K., Nayar, S.K.: Detection and removal of rain from videos. In: Proceedings of the 2004 IEEE Computer Society Conference on Computer Vision and Pattern Recognition, 2004. CVPR 2004, vol. 1, pp. I–I. IEEE (2004)

3. Garg, K., Nayar, S.K.: When does a camera see rain? In: Tenth IEEE International Conference on Computer Vision (ICCV 2005) Volume 1, vol. 2, pp. 1067–1074. IEEE (2005)
4. Garg, K., Nayar, S.K.: Vision and rain. Int. J. Comput. Vis. **75**(1), 3–27 (2007)
5. Jaw, D.W., Huang, S.C., Kuo, S.Y.: DesnowGAN: an efficient single image snow removal framework using cross-resolution lateral connection and GANs. IEEE Trans. Circuits Syst. Video Technol. **31**(4), 1342–1350 (2020)
6. Jeny, A.A., Sakib, A.N.M., Junayed, M.S., Lima, K.A., Ahmed, I., Islam, M.B.: SkNet: a convolutional neural networks based classification approach for skin cancer classes. In: 2020 23rd International Conference on Computer and Information Technology (ICCIT), pp. 1–6. IEEE (2020)
7. Jiang, T.X., Huang, T.Z., Zhao, X.L., Deng, L.J., Wang, Y.: A novel tensor-based video rain streaks removal approach via utilizing discriminatively intrinsic priors. In: Proceedings of the IEEE Conference on Computer Vision and Pattern Recognition, pp. 4057–4066 (2017)
8. Jung, A.B., et al.: imgaug (2020). https://github.com/aleju/imgaug. Accessed 01 Feb 2020
9. Kim, J.H., Sim, J.Y., Kim, C.S.: Stereo video deraining and desnowing based on spatiotemporal frame warping. In: 2014 IEEE International Conference on Image Processing (ICIP), pp. 5432–5436. IEEE (2014)
10. Li, M., Cao, X., Zhao, Q., Zhang, L., Gao, C., Meng, D.: Video rain/snow removal by transformed online multiscale convolutional sparse coding. arXiv preprint arXiv:1909.06148 (2019)
11. Li, M., Cao, X., Zhao, Q., Zhang, L., Meng, D.: Online rain/snow removal from surveillance videos. IEEE Trans. Image Process. **30**, 2029–2044 (2021)
12. Li, M., et al.: Video rain streak removal by multiscale convolutional sparse coding. In: Proceedings of the IEEE Conference on Computer Vision and Pattern Recognition, pp. 6644–6653 (2018)
13. Li, R., Cheong, L.F., Tan, R.T.: Heavy rain image restoration: Integrating physics model and conditional adversarial learning. In: Proceedings of the IEEE/CVF Conference on Computer Vision and Pattern Recognition, pp. 1633–1642 (2019)
14. Liu, J., Yang, W., Yang, S., Guo, Z.: Erase or fill? Deep joint recurrent rain removal and reconstruction in videos. In: Proceedings of the IEEE Conference on Computer Vision and Pattern Recognition, pp. 3233–3242 (2018)
15. Liu, Y.F., Jaw, D.W., Huang, S.C., Hwang, J.N.: DesnowNet: context-aware deep network for snow removal. IEEE Trans. Image Process. **27**(6), 3064–3073 (2018)
16. Pitropov, M., et al.: Canadian adverse driving conditions dataset. Int. J. Robot. Res. **40**(4–5), 681–690 (2021)
17. Redmon, J., Farhadi, A.: YOLOv3: an incremental improvement. arXiv preprint arXiv:1804.02767 (2018)
18. Ren, W., Tian, J., Han, Z., Chan, A., Tang, Y.: Video desnowing and deraining based on matrix decomposition. In: Proceedings of the IEEE Conference on Computer Vision and Pattern Recognition, pp. 4210–4219 (2017)
19. Wei, W., Yi, L., Xie, Q., Zhao, Q., Meng, D., Xu, Z.: Should we encode rain streaks in video as deterministic or stochastic? In: Proceedings of the IEEE International Conference on Computer Vision, pp. 2516–2525 (2017)
20. Yang, W., Liu, J., Feng, J.: Frame-consistent recurrent video deraining with dual-level flow. In: Proceedings of the IEEE/CVF Conference on Computer Vision and Pattern Recognition, pp. 1661–1670 (2019)

Computer Vision Systems in Agriculture

Robust Counting of Soft Fruit Through Occlusions with Re-identification

Raymond Kirk[1]([✉]) [iD], Michael Mangan[2] [iD], and Grzegorz Cielniak[1] [iD]

[1] Lincoln Centre for Autonomous Systems, University of Lincoln, Lincoln, UK
{rkirk,gcielniak}@lincoln.ac.uk
[2] Department of Computer Science, University of Sheffield, Sheffield, UK
m.mangan@sheffield.ac.uk

Abstract. Fruit counting and tracking is a crucial component of fruit harvesting and yield forecasting applications within horticulture. We present a novel multi-object, multi-class fruit tracking system to count fruit from image sequences. We first train a recurrent neural network (RNN) comprised of a feature extractor stem and two heads for re-identification and maturity classification. We apply the network to detected fruits in image sequences and utilise the output of both network heads to maintain track consistency and reduce intra-class false positives between maturity stages. The counting-by-tracking system is evaluated by comparing with a popular detect-to-track architecture and against manually labelled tracks (counts). Our proposed system achieves a mean average percentage error (MAPE) of 3% ($L1$ loss = 7) improving on the baseline multi-object tracking approach which obtained an MAPE of 21% ($L1$ loss = 41). Validating this approach for use in horticulture.

Keywords: Computer vision · Multi-object tracking · Mobile robotics

1 Introduction

Fruit counting is a critical process in effective management of a fruit crop. It informs decisions on harvesting, labour management and yield estimates. Labour constitutes for 65% of the total fruit harvesting cost and yield estimates typically have high uncertainty, motivating the need for accurate counting systems. With the advent of mobile agricultural robots and the success of convolutional neural network (CNN) based detectors, traditionally laborious tasks such as flower counting (a strong indicator of future yield) can now be automated.

Insight into the capabilities of a vision-based tracking system on a mobile robot is yet to be evaluated for fruit counting. Multi-object trackers in the detect-to-track paradigm have shown promise applied to people tracking, and some of these approaches have been successfully applied to fruit counting [1,13,18].

Tracking fruit, for the purpose of counting, faces many challenges due to the nature and complexity of farm environments. A tracking algorithm must be able to disambiguate near identical instances of fruit, handle changing appearances, manage varying factors such as illumination or altering-viewpoint, and

© Springer Nature Switzerland AG 2021
M. Vincze et al. (Eds.): ICVS 2021, LNCS 12899, pp. 211–222, 2021.
https://doi.org/10.1007/978-3-030-87156-7_17

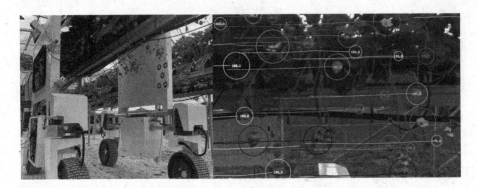

Fig. 1. Mobile robot tracking platform in the *Katrina-1* Strawberry row (left). Fruit counting-by-tracking (Ripe, Unripe and Flower) visualisation (right). The circles show the tracked fruit identities over time and tracks generated from our proposed method. Strawberry maturity classes are omitted for visualisation purposes, individual instances are in the format *TrackID_ClassID* where 1, 2, 3 are ripe, flower and unripe respectively.

re-identify after disappearances due to other issues such as occlusion. Examples are depicted in Fig. 1. Recently proposed solutions [4,8] leverage deep learning to accurately detect fruit in varying conditions, with newer models subsequently adding detect-to-track based approaches as the counting method [11,12]. These approaches generally deal with a single class for each fruit: we investigate the utilisation of fruit maturity stage and a mobile robot to enable more effective tracking.

A comparison of SOTA trackers [9] in the MOT challenge attribute the recent rise in tracker performance to the inclusion of stronger affinity and appearance models in tracking architectures. Enabling tracks to be maintained over more complex sequences. We explore this insight in this paper extending an appearance model-based tracking framework for improved counting of objects in horticultural environments.

The main contributions of our paper are: (1) a novel first re-identification and label probability based tracking framework applied on mobile robots for the purpose of counting fruits (2) extension of a popular re-identification tracking framework to embed contextual, shape and class information into association cost (3) four sequences of hand labelled Strawberry data for tracking in complex environments shared for bench-marking with the community and (4) validation of the counting accuracy for the purpose of yield estimation. A video of the tracking system and the code to run, train and reproduce the experiments can be found at the fruit_tracking repository.

2   Related Work

Recent object tracking frameworks follow the detect-to-track paradigm [2,3,15, 19] following the success of deep object detectors. Regional-based convolutional

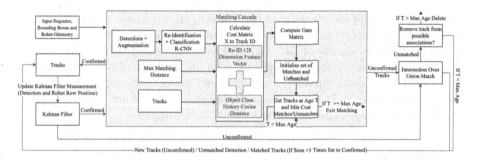

Fig. 2. The proposed fruit counting pipeline. The pipeline consists of three main stages, starting with the input of detections in the format of bounding boxes and the corresponding images, generation of re-identification feature vectors and class descriptors and then finally a matching cascade prioritising newer tracks with IoU matching.

neural networks (R-CNN) were introduced in 2013 [5] which used convolutional networks to extract features from region proposals instead of relying on hand-crafted low-level features such as edges, gradients and corners to detect objects. Several improvements were made over the next two years with the introduction of Faster R-CNN [17] which focused on improving the accuracy and speed of R-CNN.

More recently, approaches have moved from two-stage architectures (CNN + RPN) to single-stage architectures (CNN) such as RetinaNet [10] and YOLOv3 [16] to improve the speed of the network while maintaining similar architectures. Due to the advent of these accurate and fast object detectors, tracking objects through detection has become a well instated method for tracking and counting fruit. Most approaches are generally formulated by combining object detectors, motion models, appearance models and data association algorithms.

Separation of target objects from distractors such as false positives is a challenging part of the association problem in the detect-to-track paradigm. At the time of publication, previous work focusing on simple tracking architectures have achieved state-of-the-art results. IoU Tracker [3] uses simple intersection over union matching as the cost for matching objects across frames, however it requires an extremely high frame rate detector. SORT [2] used the Hungarian data association algorithm with a Kalman filter cost to model the motion of defections and was at the time the best in class online tracking method.

DeepSORT [19] improved on SORT by adding a cosine similarity cost between appearance vectors from a re-identification deep network used in the data association metric, while still running in real time.

This paradigm is applied to Mangos in [11] where a Faster R-CNN model detects regions of interest and a combination of Kanade-Lucas-Tomasi (KLT) optical flow estimator, Kalman Filters, and the Hungarian Assignment algorithm are used to associate detections to tracks, finally a structure from motion (SfM) algorithm is applied to reduce the effect of double-counting achieving an overall mean error of 27.8.

Oranges and apples are counted per frame in [4] utilising a neural network to produce detections and to regress the final image count, resulting in an overall $L2$ error (least square errors) of 13.7 and 10.5 for oranges and apples. The authors in [12] extend this work from counting fruit in single images to sequences of images. The proposed pipeline integrates deep neural network detections with SfM algorithms to count fruit from a single camera, achieving a $L1$ error (least absolute deviations) of 203 for oranges and 322 for apples.

3   Methods

This section describes our solution to counting rows of fruit in table-top farm environments autonomously from a mobile robotic platform with a mounted colour camera. We're interested in obtaining the total fruit count (flower, unripe, ripe) per row for the purpose of informing farmers decisions on yield and labour. To count fruit, our solution aims to associate bounding boxes between cameras frames where the total number of unique associated detection IDs provides the total count. The basis of our approach is inspired by DeepSort [19] a tracking framework from the Multi-Object Tracking (MOT) challenge [14], that has outperformed much more complex architectures on the MOT benchmark. We introduce a set of novel components to bolster the tracking accuracy, (1) we update the CNN architecture (2) we add a novel classification branch to deal with multi-class data and force more distinct embeddings in the appearance feature space (3) we integrate robot odometry data (position along row) into the Kalman filter state space and (4) we augment the input data with contextual and aspect preserving qualities. The proposed pipeline is shown in Fig. 2. We detail the various changes in the following section, at its core the problem formulation as in [12] is for a set of images $\mathbf{I} = (I_k)_{k=1}^{n}$ containing n consecutive frames collected from a moving robotic platform and $c \in N$ fruit we are looking to find the mapping between the true fruit count c and estimated count $\hat{c}$.

3.1   Tracking

Our formulation for track handling and Kalman filtering is similar to SORT [2] and other MOT benchmarks. We assume no ego-motion information is available, but odometry information relating to robot position along a fruit row is provided. Note that the camera is not calibrated. We only utilise standard Kalman filters with a constant velocity motion model. The Kalman filter state space is defined as the 10 dimensional vector $(u, v, \gamma, h, r, \dot{u}, \dot{v}, \dot{\gamma}, \dot{h}, \dot{r})$ where (u, v) are the bounding box co-ordinates, (γ, h) are the aspect ratio and height and finally (r) is the row position of the robot. Row position r is a unit length from the start of robot operation at the start of the row.

Co-ordinates (u, v, γ, h, r) are the respective object state and the following are respective velocities in image coordinates.

To accurately solve assignment between newly arrived detections and existing tracks, we formulate our approach into an assignment problem solvable by the

Hungarian algorithm. We use multiple models to represent motion, appearance and class description. Motion is incorporated in the model as squared Mahalanobis distance between predicted Kalman states dictated by $d^{(1)}$ in Eq. 1, where the i-th track distribution projection is denoted in measurement space as $(\mathbf{y}_i, \mathbf{S}_i)$ and the j-th new observation $\mathbf{d}_j$. Using this metric with a 10-dimensional measurement state space allows us to easily filter highly improbably associations with the 95% quartile of the Chi-square distribution $t^{(1)} = 11.07$ with 10 degrees of freedom, metrics are admissible if they are within this threshold by the indicator from Eq. 2 where $x = 1$.

$$d^{(1)}(i,j) = (\mathbf{d}_j - \mathbf{y}_i)^T \mathbf{S}_i^{-1}(\mathbf{d}_j - \mathbf{y}_i) \tag{1}$$

$$z_{i,j}^{(x)} = 1[d^{(x)}(i,j) \leq t^{(x)}] \tag{2}$$

Mahalanobis distance for multi-object data association might fail in situations while tracking on a mobile robot, such as when small angular/Cartesian movements of the camera are introduced. This can result in large shift in position in image space. Due to this, we incorporate two more models for improving the assignment problem. From the baseline implementation in [19] we keep the appearance descriptor shown in Eq. 3 and extended in Eq. 4 where the smallest cosine distance between i-th tracks and j-th bounding boxes is measured. For the appearance descriptor, r_j we keep a gallery $\mathbf{R}_k = \{\mathbf{r}_k^{(i)}\}_k^{O_k}$ of the last $O_k = 100$ observations for each track k. We extend the model by adding a new class description metric that considers the probability of different maturity stages. For a given observation with constant motion, occlusion can alter the intra-class appearance (i.e. covering the red part of a Strawberry may make it appear as unripe instead of ripe), to ensure consistent re-identification we compute a class description of all previous class observations.

$$d^{(2)}(i,j) = min\{1 - \mathbf{r}_j^T \mathbf{r}_k^i \mid \mathbf{r}_k^i \in \mathbf{R}_i\} \tag{3}$$

We compute the class description metric w_j from the map of label probabilities of the classification head projected onto the unit hyper-sphere of previous class observations where $||\mathbf{w}_j|| = 1$, similarly to computing the appearance metric, we utilise a gallery $\mathbf{W}_k = \{\mathbf{w}_k^{(i)}\}_k^{O_k}$ of previous observations of each track k, trivially inconsistent tracks before weighting with similar appearance but differing classes the total metric will be $\mathbf{w}_j + \mathbf{r}_j \leq \mathbf{r}_j + 1$. Equation 4 denotes the cosine distance between label probabilities and previous label probability observations.

$$d^{(3)}(i,j) = min\{1 - \mathbf{w}_j^T \mathbf{w}_k^i \mid \mathbf{w}_k^i \in \mathbf{W}_i\} \tag{4}$$

Combining the metrics ensures the association is more robust, taking into account motion, appearance and class description. As with squared Mahalanobis distance a binary variable is introduced to discount improbable associations for both appearance $t^{(2)}$ and class description $t^{(3)}$ in Eq. 2. The association problem cost matrix m is the combination of all the metrics with a weight parameter λ

where $x = 3$ and the association is admissible if it is within the gating region in Eq. 6.

$$m_{i,j} = \lambda d^{(1)}(x - 1) + \sum_{p=2}^{x}(1 - \lambda)d^{(p)}(i, j) \tag{5}$$

$$z_{i,j} = \prod_{p=1}^{3} b^{(p)} \tag{6}$$

Suitable thresholds $t^{(x)}$ for each gating function $z_{i,j}^{(x)}$ can be found. For the motion metric chi-square distribution threshold will remove unlikely associations, for the appearance metric values of cosine similarity of similar bounding boxes from training data can be computed to find a suitable threshold and finally for the class description metric values $t^{(3)} \leq 1$ is a suitable value where closer to zero forces more consistent label probability history. The weight variable λ can be optimised depending on the domain, small values will prioritise appearance and class description over motion and higher values close to 1 will use mostly motion information to calculate the association and gating cost. We use the same matching cascade as in [19] extended with the new cost matrix m defined in Eq. 5.

3.2   Re-identification and Class Description Network

To discriminate between different identities, we train a recurrent neural network to generate feature vectors r_j and w_j that minimise the cosine similarity between j-th bounding boxes of the same instance. The feature extraction stem architecture is described in Fig. 3. To train the network, we add two classification heads. The re-identification classification head attempts to map the identities vector r_j to the ground truth instance ID. The objective loss is Cosine Soft Max (Cross Entropy Loss). The label classification head maps r_j to label probabilities w_j, Cross Entropy Loss is used to minimise the most probable class to the ground truth maturity stage (flower, unripe, ripe). The training procedure attempts to minimise both losses. For a batch size of 128 one forward pass of the network takes $412\,\mu s$ per bounding box on a modern GPU (Nvidia GeForce GTX 3090) making the method suitable for online tracking, with a max capability of >2400 bounding boxes per second.

To deal with multi-class tracking as well as multi-object, we added the label classification head in order to coerce more separable features depending on fruit maturity stage. Figure 4 visualises the Principal Component Analysis of learned feature vectors from a trained network with (bottom) and with (top) this extra label classification step. We visualise 128 dimension feature vectors as two principal components and colour the x, y components with the label class. It can be seen adding the extra network head creates much more separable features. To visualise the component space we plot a grid of 100 points around the extrema regions of principal components then take the PCA inverse transform of u, v

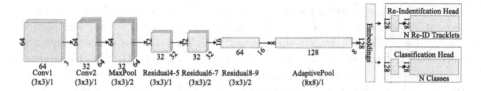

Fig. 3. Recurrent Neural Network Re-ID feature extractor. Input is a 64×64 patch of a bounding box detection and output is a 128 length feature vector projected onto the unit hyper sphere (for use with cosine similarity metric $d^{(2)}$). Each convolutional block (1, 2) is a 2D convolution followed by 2D batch normalisation and ReLU activation function. Each residual block (4, 5, 6, 7, 8, 9) is a basic ResNet block [7]. There are two heads to coerce more separable feature embeddings while training, a re-identification head and maturity classifier head. Total trainable parameters are 825,152.

components to get a representative feature vector. Once we have the representative features, we build a k-d tree of the original feature vectors and take the smallest cosine distance to the representative feature vectors to visualise an example bounding box (shown on the right) from the low dimensional u, v components. Much tighter and logical groupings are observed and the weight of different labels is more uniform, creating a more stable cosine distance between classes.

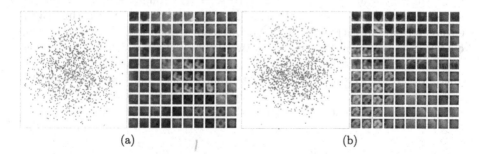

(a)   (b)

Fig. 4. Principal Component Analysis (left) and inverse mapping of 10 by 10 grid points (right, denoted by black crosses). Best viewed online. Analysis performed on the re-identification network feature vector of (a) baseline network and (b) improved network with classification head. The PCA (left) shows us the classification network (b) has better separation between classes (green = flower, blue = unripe, red = ripe) when the inverse of the PCA function is applied to the X and Y positions of each grid point. (Color figure online)

3.3   Tracking Sequences

Image sequences of commercial strawberry plants were collected at the University of Lincoln's research farm at Riseholme, UK from a RGBD camera (Intel RealSense D435i) mounted on the agricultural robot Thorvald [6] (see Fig. 1).

The robot was deployed in two 8×24 m poly-tunnels containing 5 table-top rows separated by a distance of 1.5 m. The central row of each tunnel was used to capture the *Driscoll's Amesti* and *Driscoll's Katrina* data sequences. Sequences were collected one day apart late in the season (September) with the camera's height aligned to the strawberry soil bags. The data was acquired at 7 Hz with the robot traversing the rows at 0.1 ms (*Amesti-1, Katrina-1, Katrina-2*) and 0.2 ms (*Amesti-2*) at a resolution of 1920×1080. Data was annotated manually with expert knowledge into 3 distinct classes: Ripe (>85% red coverage), Flower (white petals with no calyx shown) and Unripe (small to large immature green calyx visible). Each of the sequences capture was stopped at 500 frames. These images were captured and aligned using the RaymondKirk/topic_store and IntelRealSense/realsense-ros packages hosted on GitHub.

Four sequences were collected to validate our approach, containing two sides of table-top poly tunnel grown Strawberries of Amesti and Katrina variety. We will refer to the sequences in the format of *Variety-Side* where 1 and 2 are left and right sides of each row respectively. Amesti1-2 and Katrina 1-2 contain 12219, 4895, 15850 and 14507 bounding box annotations with 233, 172, 299 and 326 tracklets (count) respectively. To evaluate our proposed method, we define a *training* and *testing* split of a 75% to 25% ratio, to ensure no bias in evaluation of the system and promote generalisation when tracking. The training split consists of the images from *Katerina-1, Katerina-2* and *Amesti-2* sequences, whereas the testing split consists of *Amesti-1* image sequences. The training set was then split again by 75% and 25% to serve as training and validation data for optimising the re-identification model. The splits were chosen this way to ensure no bias in the final testing set used for evaluation. Some experiments contain data augmentation, we apply two different types which we deem square and padding, these transformations given in Eq. 7 and 8 of the raw bounding boxes are to preserve aspect ratio of textual features and embed surrounding environment context respectively. We share the data to support bench-marking in the community, since we found no other sequences openly available.

$$s(x, y, w, h) = \{(x, (y + \frac{h}{2}) - \frac{w}{2}, w, w)w > h((x + \frac{w}{2}) - \frac{h}{2}, y, h, h)w \leq h\} \quad (7)$$

$$pad(x, y, w, h, p) = (x - p, y - p, w + 2p, h + 2p) \quad (8)$$

3.4 Evaluation Metrics

Let $f : \mathbf{I}^{(j)} \rightarrow c \in N$ for a sequence $\{\mathbf{I}^{(j)}\}_{j=1}^{500}$ we evaluate our proposed methods as the Least Absolute Deviation ($L1$ loss) of $c^{(j)}$ and $\hat{c}^{(j)}$.

$$\sum_{j=1}^{500} |f(\mathbf{I}^{(j)}) - \hat{c}^{(j)}| \quad (9)$$

For specific classes, we consider only c, $\hat{c}$ fruit belonging to the specific class and ignore others. We use this loss in model selection and to validate the proposed system. Specifically Eq. 9 concerns the testing set *Amesti-1* for evaluation.

4   Results

In this section, we now evaluate our counting-by-tracking pipeline. We first detail the training regime for each experiment. We then compare the baseline system to seven other experiments with the following modifications: (1) addition of a label probability cosine cost $d^{(3)}$ and label classification head to the re-identification network (2) detection augmentations *square* in Eq. 7 and *pad* in Eq. 8 and (3) a combined improvements network consisting of the all modifications that resulted in an improved score shown in Fig. 5. We apply all evaluations in this section to the hand labelled *Amesti-1* data sequence which was hidden during network training against the predicted count data per-frame and total per-sequence.

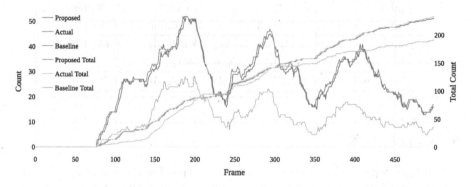

Fig. 5. Counting-by-tracking performance of the baseline approach and our proposed combined method, detailed in Table 1. Total counts over time are given, and also frame by frame counting results for all classes combined (class agnostic tracking). It can be seen our proposed system (dark blue, purple) performs much better and achieves almost perfect frame-by-frame counting. Whereas the baseline system (light blue, green) has a much lower overall count accuracy. (Color figure online)

To train the models we input a batch of 128 bounding boxes per iteration and train for a total of 6400 iterations, reducing the base LR of 0.1 by a factor of 10 at 80% and 90% of total iterations. To ensure consistent results, we apply the data augmentation to the data directly before training and output the re-identification accuracy and label classification accuracy (relevant only for the Sub-Net experiment) every 400 iterations. The re-identification accuracy during training for the baseline model and Sub-Net model were 97% and for all other experiments the accuracy was >99% when rounded to two significant figures.

Table 1 describes the results of the experiments, we present the results per-class and class agnostic since intrinsically the baseline tracking system is class agnostic. The results show a strong improvement over the baseline experiment across all experiments. Bold values of $L1$ loss indicate the best experiment for each evaluation metric.

Table 1. $L1$ loss of berry count on Amesti-1

Experiment	Class			
	Agnostic	Flower	Ripe	Unripe
Baseline	41 (192/233)	**1 (23/24)**	19 (69/50)	59 (100/159)
Maintaining aspect ratio				
Square	57 (176/233)	2 (26/24)	3 (53/50)	62 (97/159)
Classification network cost matrix				
Sub-Net	31 (202/233)	**1 (25/24)**	3 (53/50)	35 (124/159)
Embedding context in detection				
Pad-8	33 (266/233)	14 (38/24)	29 (79/50)	10 (149/159)
Pad-16	86 (319/233)	13 (37/24)	36 (86/50)	37 (196/159)
Pad-32	25 (258/233)	3 (27/24)	12 (62/50)	10 (169/159)
Pad-64	8 (241/233)	3 (27/24)	4 (54/50)	**1 (160/159)**
Combined improvements				
Combined	**7 (240/233)**	2 (26/24)	**2 (52/50)**	3 (162/159)

5   Conclusion

We have presented a framework for accurately tracking and counting fruit in a complex scene from bounding boxes, extending on current tracking architecture. Our system utilises re-identification features and label probability vectors with cosine similarity as well as robot odometry formatted as row position and data augmentation methods to maintain track consistency through occlusions and to maintain tracks in densely clustered detection regions.

The results demonstrate that our system is capable of reliably tracking and counting multiple classes in clusters from multiple view points. We use an off the shelf cheap computer vision camera and modern GPUs so that our system can be applied easily. Our results indicate an improvement of $L1$ loss from 41, 1, 19 and 59 (all classes, flower, ripe, unripe) to 7, 2, 2, 3 error in counting 500 frames of the *Amesti-1* sequence not used in training. On a modern GPU we are able to process >2400 bounding box detections per-second in a single forward pass of the network, enabling online tracking applications.

Future work will include further evaluation of the proposed system and further ablation studies into tracking by using additional cues, utilising different feature extraction networks, class embeddings and extending to full 3D space with approaches such as depth data integration or recent structure from motion approaches. We applied our counting system to soft-fruit, however the generic nature of the proposed solution makes it applicable to a wide range of object counting applications beyond the soft-fruit scenario where a mobile robot can operate.

Acknowledgement. This work was partially funded by the RASberry project at the University of Lincoln in affiliation with the Collaborative Training Partnership for Fruit Crop Research.

References

1. Bellocchio, E., Ciarfuglia, T.A., Costante, G., Valigi, P.: Weakly supervised fruit counting for yield estimation using spatial consistency. IEEE Robot. Autom. Lett. **4**(3), 2348–2355 (2019). https://doi.org/10.1109/LRA.2019.2903260
2. Bewley, A., Ge, Z., Ott, L., Ramos, F., Upcroft, B.: Simple online and realtime tracking. CoRR abs/1602.00763 (2016). http://arxiv.org/abs/1602.00763
3. Bochinski, E., Eiselein, V., Sikora, T.: High-speed tracking-by-detection without using image information. In: International Workshop on Traffic and Street Surveillance for Safety and Security at IEEE AVSS 2017, Lecce, Italy, August 2017. http://elvera.nue.tu-berlin.de/files/1517Bochinski2017.pdf
4. Chen, S.W., et al.: Counting apples and oranges with deep learning: a data-driven approach. IEEE Robot. Autom. Lett. **2**(2), 781–788 (2017). https://doi.org/10.1109/LRA.2017.2651944
5. Girshick, R.B., Donahue, J., Darrell, T., Malik, J.: Rich feature hierarchies for accurate object detection and semantic segmentation. CoRR abs/1311.2524 (2013). http://arxiv.org/abs/1311.2524
6. Grimstad, L., From, P.J.: The Thorvald II agricultural robotic system. Robotics **6**(4) (2017). https://doi.org/10.3390/robotics6040024. https://www.mdpi.com/2218-6581/6/4/24
7. He, K., Zhang, X., Ren, S., Sun, J.: Deep residual learning for image recognition. CoRR abs/1512.03385 (2015). http://arxiv.org/abs/1512.03385
8. Kirk, R., Cielniak, G., Mangan, M.: L*a*b*fruits: a rapid and robust outdoor fruit detection system combining bio-inspired features with one-stage deep learning networks. Sensors **20**(1) (2020). https://doi.org/10.3390/s20010275. https://www.mdpi.com/1424-8220/20/1/275
9. Leal-Taixé, L., Milan, A., Schindler, K., Cremers, D., Reid, I.D., Roth, S.: Tracking the trackers: an analysis of the state of the art in multiple object tracking. CoRR abs/1704.02781 (2017). http://arxiv.org/abs/1704.02781
10. Lin, T., Goyal, P., Girshick, R.B., He, K., Dollár, P.: Focal loss for dense object detection. CoRR abs/1708.02002 (2017). http://arxiv.org/abs/1708.02002
11. Liu, X., et al.: Monocular camera based fruit counting and mapping with semantic data association. IEEE Robot. Autom. Lett. **4**(3), 2296–2303 (2019). https://doi.org/10.1109/LRA.2019.2901987
12. Liu, X., et al.: Robust fruit counting: combining deep learning, tracking, and structure from motion. CoRR abs/1804.00307 (2018). http://arxiv.org/abs/1804.00307
13. Mekhalfi, M.L., et al.: Vision system for automatic on-tree kiwifruit counting and yield estimation. Sensors **20**(15) (2020). https://doi.org/10.3390/s20154214. https://www.mdpi.com/1424-8220/20/15/4214
14. Milan, A., Leal-Taixé, L., Reid, I., Roth, S., Schindler, K.: MOT16: a benchmark for multi-object tracking. arXiv:1603.00831 [cs], March 2016

15. Ning, G., Zhang, Z., Huang, C., He, Z., Ren, X., Wang, H.: Spatially supervised recurrent convolutional neural networks for visual object tracking. CoRR abs/1607.05781 (2016). http://arxiv.org/abs/1607.05781
16. Redmon, J., Farhadi, A.: YOLOv3: an incremental improvement. CoRR abs/1804.02767 (2018). http://arxiv.org/abs/1804.02767
17. Ren, S., He, K., Girshick, R.B., Sun, J.: Faster R-CNN: towards real-time object detection with region proposal networks. CoRR abs/1506.01497 (2015). http://arxiv.org/abs/1506.01497
18. Santos, T.T., de Souza, L.L., dos Santos, A.A., Avila, S.: Grape detection, segmentation, and tracking using deep neural networks and three-dimensional association. Comput. Electron. Agric. **170**, 105247 (2020). https://doi.org/10.1016/j.compag.2020.105247. https://www.sciencedirect.com/science/article/pii/S0168169919315765
19. Wojke, N., Bewley, A., Paulus, D.: Simple online and realtime tracking with a deep association metric. CoRR abs/1703.07402 (2017). http://arxiv.org/abs/1703.07402

Non-destructive Soft Fruit Mass
and Volume Estimation for Phenotyping
in Horticulture

Raymond Kirk[1]([⊠])(iD), Michael Mangan[2](iD), and Grzegorz Cielniak[1](iD)

[1] Lincoln Centre for Autonomous Systems, University of Lincoln, Lincoln, UK
{rkirk,gcielniak}@lincoln.ac.uk
[2] Department of Computer Science, University of Sheffield, Sheffield, UK
m.mangan@sheffield.ac.uk

Abstract. Manual assessment of soft-fruits is both laborious and prone to human error. We present methods to compute width, height, cross-section length, volume and mass using computer vision cameras from a robotic platform. Estimation of phenotypic traits from a camera system on a mobile robot is a non-destructive/invasive approach to gathering quantitative fruit data which is critical for breeding programmes, in-field quality assessment, maturity estimation and yield forecasting. Our presented methods can process 324–1770 berries per second on consumer grade hardware and achieve low error rates of $3.00\,\text{cm}^3$ and $2.34\,\text{g}$ for volume and mass estimates. Our methods require object masks from 2D images, a typical output of segmentation architectures such as Mask R-CNN, and depth data for computing scale.

Keywords: Computer vision · Phenotyping · Reconstruction

1 Introduction

  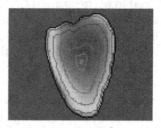

(a) Actual = 35.00 cm³   (b) 34.11 cm³   (c) 34.53 cm³

Fig. 1. Volume predictions of the Strawberry in image (1a) via methods deemed disc summation (1b) and surface area integration (1c) described in Sect. 3

Image-based fruit recognition is an area fast gaining interest in the horticultural industry. The environmental challenges posed by the fast growing population

M. Vincze et al. (Eds.): ICVS 2021, LNCS 12899, pp. 223–233, 2021.
https://doi.org/10.1007/978-3-030-87156-7_18

and climate concerns are spurring new innovative approaches to fruit detection, harvesting and yield estimation using computer vision, e.g. [2,11,16]. Phenotypic information about the fruit is important for all of these approaches and is crucial for effective breeding programmes. For harvesting, it allows to automatically grade and harvest specific type of berries, for yield more specific estimates such as detection of waste strawberries or estimating a total yield volume can be computed and for quality more accurate assessments can be made.

We present methods for estimating phenotypic traits using models derived in laboratory conditions and validate them in the in-field conditions. We estimate these traits from images based on the intuition that most fruits and berries such as kiwi, strawberries and grapes are ellipsoidal in nature and symmetrical around their major-axis, meaning the methods presented are applicable to most of the soft-fruit family. Geometrically, the major axis is the longer axis of an ellipse passing through its foci or centre of gravity in the case of our planar segment; the minor axis is the shorter axis directly perpendicular to the major. We restrict our methodologies and findings in this paper to strawberries as they are one of the more difficult crops in the soft-fruit family to phenotype due to high variation in shape, irregular protrusions and size due to maturity.

Traditionally, fruit phenotyping requires a human agent to manually derive fruit quality attributes, which commercially is not viable due to an already increasing labour demand and the subjectivity between agents in different lighting and environmental conditions. Robotic monitoring platforms are a promising solution to automating these processes and removing human error. We apply our methods to data captured in-field from a mobile robotic platform, and analyse the suitability for use as an online phenotyping tool over multiple maturity stages. Current phenotyping techniques are generally restricted to in-lab conditions [6,14], restricting the collection of large quantities of statistical data necessary for commercial application and in-field use where the relationship between plants and fruit is more accurately modelled.

Recent data driven approaches have shown automation of the phenotyping process using computer vision to be a powerful tool for many of the challenges faced in horticulture [14]. Automation of this process will allow high-bandwidth and high-fidelity phenotyping in real agri-food environments. Robotic monitoring platforms allow us to do apply these processes over large areas in a shorter amount of time, concurrently to other tasks such as harvesting and fruit counting. Our methods can be applied using cheap off the shelf components that are widely available, since the minimum requirements are only colour imagery obtained from consumer cameras. With further investigation, these methods can be used as a cost-effective phenotyping technique for use at commercial scale. The contributions of our research are detailed below:

1. We present three novel approaches to estimate phenotypic traits width, height, cross-section length, volume and mass from only image segments and depth information of strawberries.
2. A thorough evaluation of the proposed methods in lab conditions against ground truth data.

3. Application and validation of the proposed methods in-field from a robotic platform.

This paper is organised as follows: a discussion of the related work in automated phenotyping and related methods is presented in Sect. 2, the proposed methodologies for quality trait estimation are then introduced in Sect. 3. Section 4 then follows, detailing the experiments performed for validation and prediction of the phenotypic traits. A suitability study is presented in this section in the form of an analysis of in-field application, which is used to determine the applicability of our methods from mobile robotic platforms. Section 5 and 6 then summarises the work and discusses future improvements.

2 Related Work

Estimation of fruit quality information and phenotypic traits is a crucial component in translating genomic knowledge into useful information for an efficient strawberry breeding programme [13] and moreover successful robotic fruit harvesters [16] and yield estimators. The estimated traits are grouped by region in terms of suitability for the respective industry and are currently reliant on the human eye to make assessments [13]. Recent work has expressed the importance of automating these processes for enhanced breeding efficiency, using information only computer vision sensors can provide [15]. As stated in [4] this technique to phenotypic trait estimation is more likely influenced by human bias and is not suitable for generation of commercial scale quantitative prediction models.

Vision systems aim to segment, classify and localise fruit instances in the environment and provide meaningful semantic information such as area, position, size and maturity [11]. The proposed methods depend on detected strawberry regions, and previous work indicates good detection accuracy using a variety of techniques. The authors in [3] use the HSI colour space to segment and calculate maturity of strawberries. Maturity is calculated based on the ratio of red pixels (ripe) to green in laboratory conditions. The principle axis of moment of inertia is then used for pose estimation and stem segmentation. In [1] the normalised green-red difference index [8] is used to distinguish the background and vegetation. Both texture and colour features can be integrated to increase segmentation and classification accuracy [12]. Smoothness and colour features are used to find fruit pixels, these sets of pixels are then expanded using k-d-trees for efficiency and contour arcs in close proximity are merged and compared against an ideal apple contour model. This was an effective way of segmenting the apples, an 85% and a 95% accuracy was obtained when capturing the images in natural lighting with some pre-processing to underexpose the images. More recently, in our previous work, deep networks have also been used as a method to detect the initial strawberry regions [11] with good accuracy.

Approaches to compute industrial quality metrics describing strawberries have also been previously proposed. One such approach [9] classifies the shape of strawberries into nine different groups using machine learning, and the results show that eight of the shape classifications can successfully be determined from image features. Strawberry orientation, major axis length and minor axis length computation methods based on image level features for picking point (stem) detection have also been proposed [7]. The best performing method in their approach simply intersects the lowest detected point with the centroid of the berry to determine the search region for the picking point detection method.

Previous work has used 3D information to estimated phenotypic traits of strawberries in laboratory conditions using point clouds [6]. The strawberry point clouds are constructed from a stereo imaging platform. The platform consists of a 360° revolving object and a high resolution RGB camera to match features between many RGB camera frames and calculate the 3D point information. Using this point information they calculate a mesh of the strawberry calyx (leaf) and exocarp (skin including achene regions) through Poisson Surface Reconstruction [10] to estimate berry height, width, length, volume, calyx size and achene number. They show good agreement between ground truth data and predicted values, showing great promise for our proposed methods extending from 2D to the same height, width, length and volume measurements. It is noted a further feasibility study is required to optimise this approach for application in current strawberry breeding programmes, however they state an average processing time of ten seconds per berry, outperforming the same manual assessment by three times.

3   Methods

In the following section, we introduce the methods used to extract phenotypic information from 2D binary segments. A segment (planar RGB slice) is a binary mask detailing all of the pixels that belong to an object in an image. We obtain these segments from ground truth data, where each strawberry pixel was labelled. From these segments we trivially compute the width, height and cross-section length of strawberries by computing the minor and major axis of each segment. The cross-section length is equivalent to the minor axis length for most soft-fruits, so we use this value as standard, when depth information is available we compute the cross-section length as two times the difference in min and max of the depth values contained in each segment instead.

The motivation of calculating phenotypic traits this way is that the computational resources required to process these segments are very low and are a typical output of modern object detectors in this field, meaning this approach is easily integrated with existing work with negligible overhead. The computation statistics are later presented in Table 2. Each of the volumetric estimator methods will use the minor, major and cross length estimates of the segment, so the assumption is made that for most soft-fruits the surface bounded by each segment is symmetric, as the hidden surface is estimated to be the same volume as the visible surface.

3.1   Volume Estimation

In this section we present three methods to extract the volume of a segment, the three evaluated methods are ellipsoidal, surface area integration and disc summation. The ellipsoidal method for brevity, trivially computes the volume as $\frac{4}{3}\pi m_i m_a d$ where m_i is the minor axis, m_a is the major and d is the cross-section lengths. These measurements are computed from both the segment data and optionally measurements extracted from the depth map.

When depth information is available, we can also compute the scale of the estimates. The presented methods approximate the volume in pixels (px^3), to calculate the volume in centimetres (cm^3) we can simply deproject the segment contour c by the camera intrinsic parameters focal length f_x, f_y, principal point p_x, p_y and an estimated distance z_{max} from the camera obtained from the max value bounded by the segment. For the disc method, the z_{max} value is equal to the local max at each row rather than the entire segment. The deprojection step is shown in Eq. (1) and is applied prior to volume estimation.

$$c'_x = \frac{z_{max}}{f_x}(c_x - p_x) \qquad\qquad c'_y = \frac{z_{max}}{f_y}(c_y - p_y) \qquad (1)$$

Surface Area Integration. The method we deem surface area integration uses the relationship between surface area and volume. For an ellipsoid, the volume is the integral of the surface area with respect to the radius. In our case we know the radius to be the cross-section length, however soft-fruits are not perfectly spherical or ellipsoidal and have deformities around the contour, strawberries in particular have a more teardrop profile. To account for this, we need to instead calculate the surface area of the actual contour of each segment rather than the bounding ellipse to compute a more accurate volume estimate. The centre of mass is also not guaranteed to be half of the dimensions of each segment either, as with a perfect ellipse, so we also need to consider the scaled contour around our segment centre of mass when scaling the contour with respect to the cross-section length. For a contour, c we can scale it around it is centre of mass with respect to the cross-section length r by applying the function $f(c,r)$ as shown in Eq. 2.

$$f(c,r) = \frac{r}{m_i}\left(\frac{\sum_{k=1}^{n}(c_{xk}, c_{yk})}{n} - c\right) + c \qquad (2)$$

To calculate the surface area of each scaled contour, s we can use the shoelace algorithm $a(s)$ for finding the area of a simple polygon (no intersection or holes) expressed as Cartesian coordinates of a segment, as shown in Eq. 3. To use this method, we first have to order the points in the scaled contour counter-clock wise. The surface area of the segment could also be expressed as the sum of all the binary pixels, however the shoelace method is more generalisable when also computing scaled volumetric estimates using depth information.

$$a(s) = \frac{1}{2} \left| \sum_{i=1}^{n-1} s_{xi}s_{yi+1} + s_{xn}s_{y1} - \sum_{i=1}^{n-1} s_{xi+1}s_{yi} - s_{x1}s_{yn} \right| \tag{3}$$

To compute the volume estimate V of the segment, we can compute the integral of the scaled contours surface areas with respect to the estimated cross-section length. We show the integral for computing the volume V of an irregular segment in Eq. 4 by taking the product of dx, the height of each slice and the contour c, which is scaled by each slice radius r in function $f(c, r)$ (2) and calculating its surface area $a(f(c, r))$. We use the integral range $[0, r]$ and multiply the result by 2 to only consider positive scaling of the initial contour values.

$$V = 2 \int_0^r 2a(f(c, r)) dx \tag{4}$$

Disc Summation. The disc summation method estimates the volume of the segment by treating each row of the contour c of size d_y as a cylinder. Where each cylinder height is d_y, the unit distance between each row, and radius is half the row width. When depth information is available, the row can also be treated as a cylinder with an elliptical cross-section, since the cross-section length can be different to the minor axis length for each row. The volume of each cylindrical row can now be computed as $\pi r^2 d_y$. This method should be more robust than the integration step in cases when the orientation estimate error is large or when the volume of the object's hidden surface is very different to the volume of the visible surface. Since each row is treated independently, a more complete surface not dependent on axial symmetry can be reconstructed, whereas with integration the entire contour is used with a singular estimate of the cross length. We show the method for computing the volume V from a contour c in Eq. 5.

$$v_i = \sum_{j=1}^{n} c_{ij} \qquad v = \left(\pi \frac{v_i^2}{4} d_y \right)_{i=1}^{n} \qquad V = \sum_{k=1}^{n} v_k \tag{5}$$

3.2   Mass Estimation

To calculate the mass of an object m from a volume estimate, V one can take the product of volume and density. The average density p_{avg} of the all ground truth samples we collected was $0.858\,\mathrm{g/cm^3}$, therefore the estimated mass is $m = p_{avg}V$. Our density measure only considers mature Beltran berries, however in-field this measurement is dependent on many varying factors such as water content, environmental conditions, growth stage and variety.

4   Experiments and Results

In the following section we introduce the dataset we collected, an evaluation of the methodologies presented above, the phenotyping metrics, and validation of our methods applied to real in-field data.

4.1   Data Collection

In order to evaluate our methods, we required mass and volumetric data of soft fruit. We chose to evaluate strawberries as they are readily available and have one of the most challenging shapes in the soft fruit family compared to blackberries, blueberries etc. their surface is not as ellipsoidal and has a more teardrop profile. We collected 20 samples of class 1 ripe strawberries, shown in Fig. 2b. The strawberries we collected were of the Beltran (Fragaria Hybrid) variety purchased from local supermarkets a couple of hours before the data collection. Each berry was stored in 3 °C until measurements were taken to ensure the best quality and to minimise potential deformations.

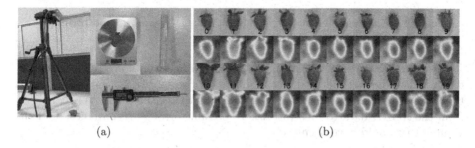

(a)   (b)

Fig. 2. Data collection equipment 2a and colour/depth Strawberry images 2b

To capture the data necessary we used a $2\,cm^3$ precision volumetric beaker, a 5 g confidence scale accurate to 1 g, a 0.01 mm accurate digital caliper and an Intel Realsense D415 computer vision camera to capture RGB images and depth information, pictured in Fig. 2a. Each strawberry was measured in three dimensions manually through its minor, major and cross-sections which are the widest, tallest and deepest lengths of the berry respectively. Then it was weighed and placed in the volumetric beaker containing 20 °C water and a control rod of a known volume was used to fully submerge the berry to get more accurate readings. Finally, the berry was placed at a set distance away from the downwards facing camera, flat on a table to simulate the conditions met in-field (hanging from the stem) and the colour and depth information was captured and logged.

4.2   Phenotypic Trait Predictions

To evaluate our methods, we compare our predicted volume and mass estimates against our ground truth data and take the median absolute error $V_{err} = median(|\hat{V}_1 - V_1|, ..., |\hat{V}_n - V_n|)$ and $m_{err} = median(|\hat{m}_1 - m_1|, ..., |\hat{m}_n - m_n|)$, where a value of 0 would indicate a perfect estimate. Additionally, to measure agreement and correlation between the values, we used the coefficient of determination (R^2). Figures 3a and 3b show the estimated values against the actual ground truth.

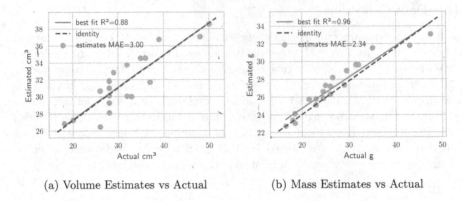

(a) Volume Estimates vs Actual   (b) Mass Estimates vs Actual

Fig. 3. Surface area integration estimates agreement against ground truth data

In Table 1 we present the statistical analysis of the methods. In this case *GT* denotes that the method used measurements for minor, major and cross lengths that are from ground truth data and *Depth* denotes measurements were extracted from the RGBD data to illustrate where possible error in reconstruction of the volume that could have occurred.

Table 1. Median Absolute Error of volume and mass estimation methods, bold indicates the best method

Trait	Ellipsoid		Integration		Disc summation	
	GT	*Depth*	*GT*	*Depth*	*GT*	*Depth*
Volume	$3.28\,cm^3$	$3.94\,cm^3$	$3.11\,cm^3$	$\mathbf{3.00\,cm^3}$	$3.75\,cm^3$	$3.20\,cm^3$
Mass	2.62 g	4.34 g	2.46 g	**2.34 g**	2.99 g	2.39 g

4.3   In-Field Experiments

The application of these phenotyping methods will be best used on a robotic platform for online trait estimation while performing tasks such as: harvesting, yield estimation, quality assessment, automated weighing and disease detection. To illustrate the effectiveness of the approach, we collected image data at a local strawberry farm from a mobile agricultural robot Thorvald [5], pictured in Fig. 4a. The RGBD camera was placed 30–50 cm from the Strawberry row and 80 images were captured containing 1250 examples ripe and unripe berries of varying sizes and shapes. The strawberry varieties captured was Amesti.

Figure 5 shows volume and mass predictions made on the data collected in-field. It is evident from this initial tests that this method can be used successfully in-field to estimate these attributes online. Table 2 shows the performance speed of each of our proposed methods, any value greater than 30 estimates per second

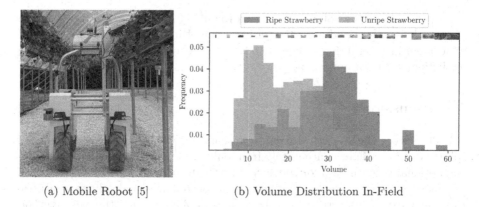

(a) Mobile Robot [5]   (b) Volume Distribution In-Field

Fig. 4. In-field volume distribution 4b over 2 classes and 1250 samples ran from a mobile robotic platform 4a in strawberry polytunnels.

is appropriate for online application. The camera used is an off the shelf sensor that can be easily added to already existing platforms. The average strawberry size in the 1250 in-field data samples was 50.21 px^2. The ellipsoid, disc summation and integration methods could respectively process 1770, 1623 and 324 strawberries per second at this scale.

Table 2. Performance of phenotyping methods in calculations per second on an Intel Core i7-8700 CPU. 50.21 px^2 was the average in-field berry size.

Method	Object sizes							
	$16\ px^2$	$32\ px^2$	$50\ px^2$	$64\ px^2$	$128\ px^2$	$256\ px^2$	$512\ px^2$	$1024\ px^2$
Ellipsoid	3341	2407	1770	1601	682	232	62	13
Disc summation	2862	2278	1623	1427	675	231	64	13
Integration	424	362	324	269	172	90	36	11

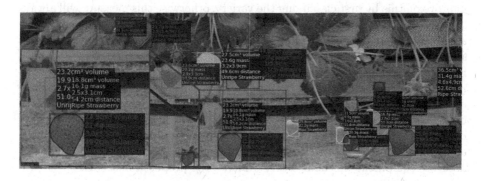

Fig. 5. In-field volume estimation results

Figure 4 shows the volume estimation frequency distribution for both unripe and ripe berries grouped into 20 inter-class bins. Ripe strawberries are expected to be larger in general than unripe, and this separation is confirmed in the volume predictions for both berry types.

5   Discussion

It is clear from the statistical results presented in Table 1 that both mass and volume can be estimated accurately from only two-dimensional data (segments) and optionally depth data for converting pixels to cm^3 and mass measures. Both methods have very low errors relative to the expected mass and volume measures. The median absolute error for volume is only $3.00\,cm^3$ for the best method surface area integration, which is only $1.00\,cm^3$ above the maximum precision of the volumetric measurements. The results for mass estimation are also very similar having only $2.34\,g$ of error for the same method, which is well below the $5\,g$ confidence interval of the $1\,g$ accurate scales we used. Our results show a compelling case for integration of RGB data when depth data is too noisy to reconstruct a surface in outdoor environments.

6   Conclusions and Future Work

We have presented a non-invasive/destructive, inexpensive method for volume and mass estimation in-field designed for use on a robotic platform. The evaluation of the methods have shown they are accurate in lab conditions and also work successfully in outdoor scenarios mounted on a Thorvald robot. We have shown that the in-field estimates are in the range of expected values and that the methods can process between 324–1770 strawberries per second on consumer hardware. Future work will include gathering images and ground truth data in-field, so we can fully evaluate the overall accuracy of the methods. The density value used in the mass calculation is also specific to only one variety of strawberry and may not generalise well to other varieties. Further work could improve on this by first classifying the variety, otherwise this measure will always need changing on a per-application basis. The current approach works under the assumption that the surface that is hidden is symmetric to the surface that is seen, future work would try to reconstruct the berry from partial view to get a more complete accuracy measurement from different orientations or to first correctly orient the berry segment to correct for the viewpoint. In situations where depth data is noisy this method is best applied as it's only dependent on depth data for the extraction of berry measurements, future work could include validation of other sensors to estimate these parameters. Finally, our data collection equipment was characterised by low precision, with sub-gram/sub-millimeter accurate equipment we could better evaluate the proposed methods.

References

1. An, N., et al.: Plant high-throughput phenotyping using photogrammetry and imaging techniques to measure leaf length and rosette area. Comput. Electron. Agric. **127**, 376–394 (2016). https://doi.org/10.1016/j.compag.2016.04.002
2. Chen, Y., et al.: Strawberry yield prediction based on a deep neural network using high-resolution aerial orthoimages. Remote Sens. **11** (2019). https://doi.org/10.3390/rs11131584
3. Feng, G., Qixin, C., Masateru, N.: Fruit detachment and classification method for strawberry harvesting robot. Int. J. Adv. Robot. Syst. **5**(1), 41–48 (2008). https://doi.org/10.5772/5662
4. Goddard, M., Hayes, B.: Genomic selection. J. Anim. Breed. Genet. **124**(6), 323–330 (2007). https://doi.org/10.1111/j.1439-0388.2007.00702.x
5. Grimstad, L., From, P.: The Thorvald II agricultural robotic system. Robotics **6**(4), 24 (2017)
6. He, J., Harrison, R., Li, B.: A novel 3D imaging system for strawberry phenotyping. Plant Methods **13** (2017). https://doi.org/10.1186/s13007-017-0243-x
7. Huang, Z., Wane, S., Parsons, S.: Towards automated strawberry harvesting: identifying the picking point. In: Gao, Y., Fallah, S., Jin, Y., Lekakou, C. (eds.) TAROS 2017. LNCS (LNAI), vol. 10454, pp. 222–236. Springer, Cham (2017). https://doi.org/10.1007/978-3-319-64107-2_18
8. Hunt, E.R., Cavigelli, M., Daughtry, C.S.T., McMurtrey, J.E., Walthall, C.L.: Evaluation of digital photography from model aircraft for remote sensing of crop biomass and nitrogen status. Precis. Agric. **6**(4), 359–378 (2005). https://doi.org/10.1007/s11119-005-2324-5
9. Ishikawa, T., et al.: Classification of strawberry fruit shape by machine learning. In: ISPRS - International Archives of the Photogrammetry, Remote Sensing and Spatial Information Sciences, vol. XLII-2, pp. 463–470, May 2018. https://doi.org/10.5194/isprs-archives-XLII-2-463-2018
10. Kazhdan, M., Bolitho, M., Hoppe, H.: Poisson surface reconstruction. In: Proceedings of the Fourth Eurographics Symposium on Geometry Processing, SGP 2006, pp. 61–70. Eurographics Association, Goslar (2006)
11. Kirk, R., Cielniak, G., Mangan, M.: L*a*b*fruits: a rapid and robust outdoor fruit detection system combining bio-inspired features with one-stage deep learning networks. Sensors **20**(1) (2020). https://doi.org/10.3390/s20010275. https://www.mdpi.com/1424-8220/20/1/275
12. Linker, R., Cohen, O., Naor, A.: Determination of the number of green apples in RGB images recorded in orchards. Comput. Electron. Agric. **81**, 45–57 (2012)
13. Mathey, M., et al.: Large-scale standardized phenotyping of strawberry in Ros-BREED. J. Am. Pomol. Soc. **67**, 205–216 (2013)
14. Pound, M., et al.: Deep machine learning provides state-of-the-art performance in image-based plant phenotyping. GigaScience **6** (2016). https://doi.org/10.1101/053033
15. Vázquez-Arellano, M., Griepentrog, H.W., Reiser, D., Paraforos, D.S.: 3-D imaging systems for agricultural applications-a review. Sensors **16**(5), 618 (2016)
16. Xiong, Y., Peng, C., Grimstad, L., From, P.J., Isler, V.: Development and field evaluation of a strawberry harvesting robot with a cable-driven gripper. Comput. Electron. Agric. **157**, 392–402 (2019). https://doi.org/10.1016/j.compag.2019.01.009

Learning Image-Based Contaminant Detection in Wool Fleece from Noisy Annotations

Timothy Patten[1,2](✉) [ID], Alen Alempijevic[1] [ID], and Robert Fitch[1] [ID]

[1] Robotics Institute, Faculty of Engineering and Information Technology,
University of Technology Sydney, Ultimo, NSW 2007, Australia
{timothy.patten,alen.alempijevic,robert.fitch}@uts.edu.au
[2] Automation and Control Institute, Faculty of Electrical Engineering
and Information Technology, TU Wien, 1040 Vienna, Austria

Abstract. This paper addresses the problem of detecting natural contaminants in freshly shorn wool fleece in RGB images using deep learning-based semantic segmentation. The challenge of inconsistent annotation is overcome by learning the probability of contamination as opposed to a discrete class. From the continuous value predictions, contaminated regions can be extracted by selectively thresholding on the probability of contamination. Furthermore, the imbalance of the class distributions is accounted for by adaptively weighting each pixel's contribution to the loss function. Results show that the adaptive weight improves the prediction accuracy and overall outperforms learning an approximated representation by quantising the distributions.

Keywords: Wool · Contaminant detection · Semantic segmentation · Deep learning · Annotation noise

1 Introduction

Wool handling is a highly manual and repetitive task. A major bottleneck in this activity is the identification of contaminants [6] that must be removed by hand, known as *skirting* (Fig. 1). Automation of this process can improve both efficiency and accuracy, which is anticipated to increase productivity and thus translate to significant savings in cost for wool growers.

A vision system that identifies contaminants in wool is a crucial aspect of the automation process. The system should capture images and specify the regions that contain contaminants and those that have clean wool. Previous studies on contaminant detection in wool from monocular cameras [18,25] consider non-organic substances such as fibres from packing material, fertiliser bags or hay bale twine. These methods use thresholding to identify image pixels with colour properties different to the background wool. The *natural* contaminants that are removed from fresh wool during skirting, such as urine-stain, dung, pigmentation/medullation and vegetable matter, are less distinguishable by their colour and, therefore, prior work is unsuitable for the task.

© Springer Nature Switzerland AG 2021
M. Vincze et al. (Eds.): ICVS 2021, LNCS 12899, pp. 234–244, 2021.
https://doi.org/10.1007/978-3-030-87156-7_19

Fig. 1. The manual skirting process of contaminated wool fleece [1]. Left: Two wool handlers move along the edge of the fleece. Right: Close up of the hand position and gripping.

Machine learning, in particular deep learning, has profoundly improved the performance of visual perception [8] for a broad range of applications such as recognition, classification and segmentation [20]. Recently, deep learning has been applied in the related task of foreign fibre detection in cotton [21,22]. We conjecture that the application of deep learning to contaminant detection in wool fleece will not only deliver highly accurate results but also generalise to more difficult scenarios, where colour differentiation, as in [18,25], is unsuited.

This work addresses the challenge of learning to identify natural contaminants in wool fleeces from RGB images. A strong prerequisite for this task is access to a large, annotated dataset, which constitutes pixel-level annotation of the contaminated wool. Unfortunately, annotation may be inconsistent due to the difficulty of identifying contamination in images. Furthermore, some contaminants are continuous in nature – contamination is in the spectrum from "light" to "heavy". As such, annotators may disagree on what parts of the fleece should be removed. The end result is that multiple annotations are presented to the learning algorithm from which a meaningful output should be derived; see Fig. 2. Consequently, our system learns to predict the continuous blending between the classes based on noisy pixel labels. More specifically, a deep learning architecture for pixel-wise classification is employed to predict the probabilities of each class. We propose to weight the influence of each pixel in the loss function according to the frequency of the distribution in the dataset by extending the formulation in [13].

We report the performance of deep learning-based semantic segmentation on newly collected and annotated datasets that represent two scenarios: (1) Delineation around the edge of wool fleeces that separates the portion that is skirted and (2) Bathurst burr (a species of weed) contamination on fleece off-cuts. In comparison to predicting a quantised set of classes, the probabilistic output is more general. We show how adjusting the contaminant threshold can promote more aggressive or conservative contaminant removal. This is highly useful in industry as external factors, such as the daily market value or lot size, contribute to the degree at which wool handlers remove contaminants.

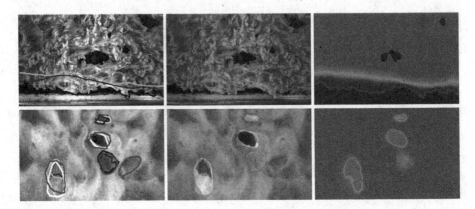

Fig. 2. Examples of wool contamination and annotation. *Dubbo* dataset on top row and *Bathurst burr* dataset on bottom row. Left: Inconsistent annotations of contaminated wool, background and vegetable matter. Middle: Discrete class representation from the combinations of the annotations. Right: Probabilistic prediction of each class encoded to RGB.

The remainder of this paper is organised as follows. Section 2 discusses related work. In Sect. 3, we present our approach for predicting class probabilities from noisy labels. Section 4 introduces the new datasets of wool contamination. Section 5 presents the experiments and finally in Sect. 6 we conclude the paper.

2   Related Work

2.1   Contaminant Detection in Wool

Detection of contaminants in wool from vision sensors has been a topic of research in wool technology for decades [4]. In this early work, an NIR camera observes the wool and then PCA with soft independent modelling of class analogies is applied to discriminate between polymeric material (polyethylene and polypropylene) and uncontaminated wool. More recently, Zhang et al. [25] present a system that uses RGB cameras, in which the polypropylene contaminants are identified through global and local adaptive thresholding in the RGB and HSV colour spaces. This vision system is integrated with a mechanical system in [24] to remove and sort the contaminants in real time. Similarly, Su et al. [18] develop an online system to detect and remove contaminants in wool. As in [24,25], thresholding on the RGB values identifies the contaminants.

While these systems show strong results, they focus on detecting contaminants that are vastly different to the wool. The approaches do not detect natural contaminants, which appear as stains or more subtle colour/textural changes compared to plastic material. A more promising direction is the use of modern deep learning techniques, which has been applied to the related task of detecting foreign fibres in cotton [16,21,22]. Indeed, this task has attracted significant attention that dedicated datasets have been compiled for developing and training learning algorithms [12].

2.2   Semantic Segmentation

Within the computer vision community, the task of assigning a class label to every pixel in an image is known as *semantic segmentation*. This differs from classification for which an entire image is assigned a single class label. In the context of deep learning, seminal work by Long et al. [10] adapted existing convolutional neural networks (CNNs) for classification to the task of semantic segmentation by converting them to fully convolutional architectures through the replacement of the classification layer(s) with an upsampling convolutional layer. Exploiting CNNs means that spatial information is incorporated. Ronnenberg et al. [13] introduce U-Net, which extends [10] by mirroring the convolution structure in the upsampling stage with consecutive convolutional layers. The larger number of feature channels in the decoder, as compared to [10], propagates contextual information to higher resolution layers, yielding more precise segmentation with fewer training images. A plethora of adaptations and modifications now exist, which is motivated by the broad range of applications that this technique can be applied, for example, autonomous driving [7,15].

Supervised learning from noisy pixel-wise labels is a growing trend because it is often difficult to avoid annotation error in complex, real-world data [5,17]. Zheng and Yang [26] show that incorporating predicted uncertainty in the optimisation procedure leads to better domain adaptation when learning from pseudo labels. In similar work, noisy pre-segmentation masks in the target domain are refined by a label cleaning network that is trained jointly with the segmentation network using the same feature encodings [9]. Similar to our work, the problem of noise at boundaries (i.e., label transition) due to poor image resolution or mistakes made by an annotator is addressed in [2]. By introducing a pixel-weight that is determined by the pixel's distance to its nearest pixel of another class, the loss function is less affected by potential incorrectly labelled pixels. Cheng et al. [3] train a GAN to both revise spatially noisy labelling and output a label weight that, similar to [2], reduces the influence of untrustworthy samples. This method, however, requires access to the underlying ground truth during training in order to learn the mapping between clean and noisy samples.

3   Semantic Segmentation from Noisy Annotations

3.1   Problem Definition

Classical semantic segmentation assumes a dataset $\mathcal{D} = \{\mathcal{X}, \mathcal{Y}\}$ that consists of images $\mathcal{X}$ with corresponding labels $\mathcal{Y}$. Each pixel $\mathbf{x} \in \Omega \in \mathcal{X}$ has a corresponding unique label $y_\mathbf{x}$ belonging to one of the known set of classes $\mathcal{C} = \{1, \ldots, C\}$. The task during inference is to predict the label $y_\mathbf{x}$ for each $\mathbf{x}$ for any test image.

In this work, labelled images are provided by N annotators, in other words, $\tilde{\mathcal{D}} = \{\mathcal{X}, \mathcal{Y}^1, \ldots, \mathcal{Y}^N\}$. Each $\mathbf{x}$ is assigned a set of potentially different labels, thus no single class can be assumed. Instead, each pixel has a corresponding probability distribution over the classes $\mathcal{C}$. Formally, the dataset consists of images where each $\mathbf{x} \in \Omega \in \mathcal{X}$ has an associated probability distribution $p(\mathbf{x}) = F(y_\mathbf{x}^1, \ldots, y_\mathbf{x}^N)$

where $F : \mathbb{Z}^{C \times C} \to \mathbb{R}^C$ maps the set of annotated labels to a probability distribution over $\mathcal{C}$ such that

$$\sum_{c \in \mathcal{C}} p(x_c) = 1, \tag{1}$$

is satisfied where $x_c \in \mathbf{x}$ are the individual class probability values. The task during inference is to predict the probability $p(\mathbf{x})$ for each $\mathbf{x}$ for any test image.

3.2 Learning Probabilistic Output

Pixel-wise prediction using deep convolutional networks was first introduced by Long et al. [10]. The fully convolutional network learns a pixel-to-pixel mapping through an encoder (the feature extraction layers of a classification CNN) and a decoder to upsample the feature map to the original input resolution. The output is a class prediction for each pixel and the parameters are optimised according to a classification loss applied over every pixel in the input image. Numerous modifications and enhancements have been applied to extend this basic principle. A good discussion is given in [11].

Our work learns to predict a distribution instead of a discrete class, which is trivially achieved by using the *softmax* activation as final layer. The activation function outputs the value of each class $z_c \in \mathbf{z}$ in the range $[0, 1]$. Equation (1) is satisfied due to the normalisation in the denominator

$$\sigma(\mathbf{z})_c = \frac{e^{z_c}}{\sum_{c \in \mathcal{C}} e^{z_c}}. \tag{2}$$

A variety of loss functions can be applied to minimise the difference between the input probability distributions and the corresponding predictions. Prior work for classical semantic segmentation show that the issue of class imbalance should be addressed by assigning a weight to each class [13, 19] so that classes represented by very few samples have more contribution during learning. As such, the more common classes do not dominate the optimisation, enabling less common classes to also be precisely learned. For the discrete class scenario, the inverse of the volume of each class is used as the weight. For the probabilistic scenario, computing the weight is less straight forward because it is uncountable.

We propose a weighting scheme based on the frequency of the probability distribution for each pixel in the ground truth images. For each pixel $\mathbf{x}$, the weight is computed by

$$w(\mathbf{x}) = \prod_{c \in \mathcal{C}} G_c \left(p(x_c) \right)^{-\gamma}, \tag{3}$$

where $G_c : \mathbb{R} \to \mathbb{R}$ maps a pixel's ground truth probability of class c to a frequency value and $\gamma \geq 0$ is a constant. The functions G_c are approximated by fitting Gaussian processes (GPs) to the histograms of the counts per probability value. We use 10 bins and GPs with the Matérn kernel with length scale 1.0 and smoothing factor 1.5. Although we use GPs, other approximators could be used so long as they output a smooth function.

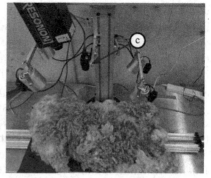

Fig. 3. Acquisition of wool datasets (camera indicated by **c**). Left: Camera mounted on trolley that is pushed parallel to freshly shorn wool fleeces. Right: Plate mounted on linear actuator that moves wool samples below static camera.

The weights are applied to each pixel when computing the loss during training. The pixel-wise loss for image Ω

$$L\left(\Omega\right) = \sum_{\mathbf{x}\in\Omega} \ell\left(p(\mathbf{x}), f(\mathbf{x})\right), \tag{4}$$

becomes

$$L_w\left(\Omega\right) = \sum_{\mathbf{x}\in\Omega} w(\mathbf{w})\ell\left(p(\mathbf{x}), f(\mathbf{x})\right), \tag{5}$$

where ℓ is a loss value computed for pixel $\mathbf{x}$ and $f(\mathbf{x})$ is the model output.

4   Wool Datasets

Datasets of RGB images of wool fleece were collected to evaluate our proposed work. A Flir Blackfly S USB3 RGB camera[1] was used with a resolution of 1440×1080 pixels. Example images with annotation are provided in Fig. 2.

The *Dubbo* dataset consists of images of freshly shorn Merino fleece collected on site in Dubbo, NSW, Australia. The camera was mounted on a trolley that was pushed by a human operator along the edge of the skirting table; see Fig. 3 (left). Scanning was conducted at a slow pace to minimise motion blur. In total, five fleeces were scanned four times, i.e., once per edge. For each scan, images were hand selected such that visual overlap was minimised, resulting in a dataset consisting of 126 images. The skirting lines were annotated by two expert wool handlers. As discussed, the annotations do not necessarily agree due to differing opinions and the difficulty to identify the boundary between the "good" and contaminated wool in the images. In addition, the background was also annotated. This was performed by non-wool handlers as domain experience

---

[1] https://www.flir.com.au/products/blackfly-s-usb3/.

was not required. However, disagreement also exists in this annotation due to human error or ambiguity, e.g., thin wool that appears translucent over the background. The final result was a set of masks, from each annotator, that depicts the regions of the images that are either good wool (above the skirting line) or background (below the background line). The remaining class of contaminated wool is derived from the unlabelled pixels of the merged masks.

The *Bathurst burr* dataset consists of images of Merino fleece off-cuts. Each off-cut was placed on the rig in Fig. 3 (right), which moves the wool underneath the downward-facing statically mounted camera. Ten pieces of wool were scanned and for each scan, three images were hand selected to minimise image overlap. Due to the small number of images, 320×320 crops were extracted from the full images to yield a total of 380 images. In this dataset, the wool pieces were taken from different parts of the fleece and contain heavy Bathurst burr contamination. Each annotator was requested to label the instances of burr that they were confident about as well as those that they were uncertain about, by assigning a different label. A total of five people performed the annotation.

The probabilistic annotation was obtained by merging the masks of each image. Then, for each pixel, the number of class votes were counted and normalised to obtain the probability distribution. For the *Bathurst burr* annotation, each pixel assigned the uncertain label contributed a vote of 0.5.

Due to the small size of the datasets and to avoid samples from the same fleece or piece of wool appearing in both the training and test sets, we provide multiple splits for k-fold cross-validation. For the *Dubbo* dataset, for each fold, one fleece is held out for testing while the remaining four fleeces are used for training. For the *Bathurst burr* dataset, pairs of scans, i.e., 1–2, 3–4, ..., 9–10, are held out for testing and all remaining scans are used for training.

5   Experiments

5.1   Implementation Details

This work is implemented in PyTorch using the segmentation models library [23]. We use a lean network composed of the U-Net architecture [13] with MobileNetV2 encoder [14]. Using a lean network with fewer parameters than alternative architectures is both suitable for training on our datasets that have few training images as well as for time-constrained real-world applications. Models are pre-trained on ImageNet then trained on the wool datasets with a batch size of 4 for 30 epochs with an initial learning rate of 10^{-3} that is divided by 10 at epoch 15 and 25. All layers use *ReLu* activation except the last layer that uses *softmax* activation. Batch normalisation is applied between the convolutional and activation layers in the decoder. The L_2 loss is applied to regress the probability values, which showed best performance even compared to more intuitive distribution-based losses such as cross entropy. Images in the *Dubbo* dataset are input to the network with the dimension 640×640 by padding the shorter dimension and resizing. Images in the *Bathurst burr* dataset are input at the patch resolution of 320×320. All training and testing is performed on an NVIDIA RTX 2080 Ti.

Table 1. Mean KL divergence for subsets of pixels for varying values of γ in Eq. (3) applied to the L_2 loss. $\gamma = 0.0$ is equivalent to the unweighted loss.

Dataset	Dubbo				Bathurst burr			
γ	0.0	0.1	0.5	1.0	0.0	0.1	0.5	1.0
good	**0.007**	**0.007**	0.012	0.020	**0.001**	**0.001**	0.002	0.004
cont.	0.044	**0.039**	0.072	0.148	0.196	0.093	0.086	**0.075**
mix	0.072	0.057	0.028	**0.014**	0.045	0.043	0.034	**0.025**
all	0.015	**0.013**	0.020	0.045	0.004	**0.003**	**0.003**	0.005

5.2 Results and Discussion

Weighted Loss Function. The performance of the proposed weighting scheme for various values of γ in Eq. (3) applied to the L_2 loss in Eq. (5) is provided in Table 1. We report the mean Kullback–Leibler (KL) divergence as measured using the predicted and ground truth probability distributions for each pixel[2]. The results in Table 1 are shown for fully-uncontaminated (*good*), fully-contaminated (*cont.*) and partially-contaminated (*mix*) pixels. The bottom row shows overall performance (*all*). Note that fully-uncontaminated pixels are significantly more common than fully- or partially-contaminated pixels. For both datasets, increasing γ improves the predictions of the contaminated and mixed pixels at a sacrifice in performance on the good pixels. This is expected because larger γ means a more extreme difference in the weights between the dominant and less common distributions. With $\gamma = 1.0$, although the gains on the contaminated and mixed pixels are significant, the reduction of the more present good pixels results in worse overall performance compared to no weighting scheme (i.e., $\gamma = 0.0$). A smaller value of γ is less aggressive and strikes a balance, which achieves best performance for *all* pixels.

Comparison to Classification: We compare the performance of learning continuous probabilities as opposed to learning a discrete set of quantised classes on the *Bathurst burr* dataset. For discrete learning, we create sets of classes that quantise the probabilities to different resolutions. The dice loss is employed for learning classification. As shown in Fig. 4, when considering all pixels (in grey), the performance between continuous and discrete learning is highly similar. However, for the pixels that have a mixed class probability distribution (in yellow), there is a notable difference. Discrete learning has worst performance when the number of classes is small. This is because the resolution is insufficient to predict the continuous values. As the number of classes increases, the performance improves. However, with even more classes, the performance begins to decrease because the classification task is more difficult. Overall, directly learning the probabilities performs better than learning any discrete representation.

---

[2] Common metrics for evaluating pixel-wise class prediction, such as intersection-over-union or accuracy, do not apply since our model predicts a probability distribution instead of a single class.

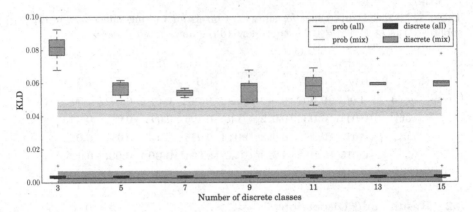

Fig. 4. Performance of learning continuous probabilities in comparison to discretising and learning to classify on the *Bathurst burr* dataset. KL divergence computed on *all* pixels in grey and partially-contaminated (*mix*) in yellow. Shaded regions around the lines is the standard deviation from results on different splits. For each level of discretisation, box plots are shown (as derived from results on different splits) with the median in red. (Color figure online)

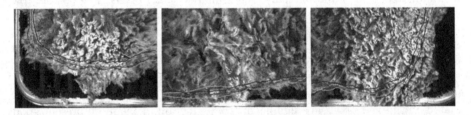

Fig. 5. Examples of predicted skirting lines for contamination probability of 25, 50 and 75% in increasing shade of green (light, mid and dark). Annotated skirting lines shown in red and magenta for reference. (Color figure online)

Flexible Contaminant Detection: An advantage of learning a probabilistic representation is that the contamination boundary can be flexibly extracted from a single trained model. An adjustable threshold can be applied such that a different skirting line is generated based on the contour in the predicted probability map as shown in Fig. 5. This allows more conservative or aggressive contaminant removal. With a low probability of contamination, e.g., 25%, the predicted skirting line (in light green) follows the region where all annotators agree on contamination. On the other hand, for a higher contamination probability, e.g., 75%, the predicted skirting line (in dark green) follows the boundary where at least one annotator indicates contamination. In between the extremes, e.g. 50%, the predicted skirting line (in mid green) is approximately between the annotated lines.

6   Conclusion

This paper analysed the capability of deep learning-based semantic segmentation for detecting natural contaminants in wool fleece from RGB images. To account for the ambiguous annotation, we learned probabilistic outputs rather than discrete class labels. The imbalance of the probability distributions was addressed by a weighting scheme to bolster the loss function to the less occurring probabilities. Our experiments on two new wool datasets showed that the weighting scheme improves accuracy and that learning probabilities is more accurate than learning discrete representations.

In future work we will expand the datasets to thoroughly analyse the model's generalisation. Furthermore, we will incorporate more contaminants such as dermatitis, wool rot and other varieties of vegetable matter. We also plan to investigate the capability of detecting contaminants in hyperspectral images. Finally, the vision system will be integrated with a mechanical system to physically remove contaminants in the automated skirting process.

Acknowledgement. This work is supported by funding from Australian Wool Innovation Limited, grant number ON-00713. The authors thank Craig French and Penny Clout for their expert annotation.

References

1. Australian Wool Innovation Limited (2015). https://www.wool.com/people/ shearing-and-woolhandling/training-resources/
2. Bressan, P.O., et al.: Semantic segmentation with labeling uncertainty and class imbalance. arXiv arXiv:2102.04566 (2021)
3. Cheng, G., Ji, H., Tian, Y.: Walking on two legs: learning image segmentation with noisy labels. In: Proceedings of UAI, pp. 330–339 (2020)
4. Church, J., O'Neill, J.: The detection of polymeric contaminants in loose scoured wool. Vib. Spectrosc. **19**(2), 285–293 (1999)
5. Han, B., et al.: A survey of label-noise representation learning: past, present and future. arXiv arXiv:2011.04406 (2020)
6. Hansford, K.: Contamination. University of New England, WOOL472: Wool biology and metrology (coursenotes) (2012). https://www.woolwise.com/wp-content/ uploads/2017/07/WOOL-472-572-12-T-12.pdf
7. Kaymak, Ç., Uçar, A.: A brief survey and an application of semantic image segmentation for autonomous driving. In: Balas, V.E., Roy, S.S., Sharma, D., Samui, P. (eds.) Handbook of Deep Learning Applications. SIST, vol. 136, pp. 161–200. Springer, Cham (2019). https://doi.org/10.1007/978-3-030-11479-4_9
8. Krizhevsky, A., Sutskever, I., Hinton, G.E.: ImageNet classification with deep convolutional neural networks. In: Proceedings of NeurIPS, pp. 1097–1105 (2012)
9. Li, Y., Jia, L., Wang, Z., Qian, Y., Qiao, H.: Un-supervised and semi-supervised hand segmentation in egocentric images with noisy label learning. Neurocomputing **334**, 11–24 (2019)
10. Long, J., Shelhamer, E., Darrell, T.: Fully convolutional networks for semantic segmentation. In: Proceedings of IEEE CVPR, pp. 3431–3440 (2015)

11. Minaee, S., Boykov, Y.Y., Porikli, F., Plaza, A.J., Kehtarnavaz, N., Terzopoulos, D.: Image segmentation using deep learning: a survey. IEEE Trans. Pattern Anal. Mach. Intell. (2021). [early access]
12. Pelletier, M.G., Holt, G.A., Wanjura, J.D.: A plastic contamination image dataset for deep learning model development and training. AgriEngineering **2**(2), 317–321 (2020)
13. Ronneberger, O., Fischer, P., Brox, T.: U-Net: convolutional networks for biomedical image segmentation. In: Navab, N., Hornegger, J., Wells, W.M., Frangi, A.F. (eds.) MICCAI 2015. LNCS, vol. 9351, pp. 234–241. Springer, Cham (2015). https://doi.org/10.1007/978-3-319-24574-4_28
14. Sandler, M., Howard, A., Zhu, M., Zhmoginov, A., Chen, L.C.: MobileNetV2: inverted residuals and linear bottlenecks. In: Proceedings of IEEE CVPR, pp. 4510–4520 (2018)
15. Siam, M., Elkerdawy, S., Jagersand, M., Yogamani, S.: Deep semantic segmentation for automated driving: taxonomy, roadmap and challenges. In: Proceedings of IEEE ITSC, pp. 1–8 (2017)
16. Siddaiah, M., Prasad, N.R., Lieberman, M.A., Hughs, S.E.: Identification of trash types and computation of trash content in ginned cotton using soft computing techniques. In: Proceedings of MWSCAS, pp. 547–550 (1999)
17. Song, H., Kim, M., Park, D., Shin, Y., Lee, J.G.: Learning from noisy labels with deep neural networks: a survey. arXiv arXiv:2007.08199 (2021)
18. Su, Z., Tian, G.Y., Gao, C.: A machine vision system for on-line removal of contaminants in wool. Mechatronics **16**(5), 243–247 (2006)
19. Sudre, C.H., Li, W., Vercauteren, T., Ourselin, S., Jorge Cardoso, M.: Generalised dice overlap as a deep learning loss function for highly unbalanced segmentations. In: Cardoso, M.J., et al. (eds.) DLMIA/ML-CDS -2017. LNCS, vol. 10553, pp. 240–248. Springer, Cham (2017). https://doi.org/10.1007/978-3-319-67558-9_28
20. Voulodimos, A., Doulamis, N., Doulamis, A., Protopapadakis, E., Andina, D.: Deep learning for computer vision: a brief review. Comput. Intell. Neurosci. **2018**, 7068349 (2018)
21. Wei, W., Deng, D., Zeng, L., Zhang, C., Shi, W.: Classification of foreign fibers using deep learning and its implementation on embedded system. Int. J. Adv. Robot. Syst. **16**(4), 1–20 (2019)
22. Wei, W., Zhang, C., Deng, D.: Content estimation of foreign fibers in cotton based on deep learning. Electronics **9**(11), 1795 (2020)
23. Yakubovskiy, P.: Segmentation models Pytorch (2020). https://github.com/qubvel/segmentation_models.pytorch
24. Zhang, L., Dehghani, A., Su, Z., King, T., Greenwood, B., Levesley, M.: Development of a mechatronic sorting system for removing contaminants from wool. IEEE/ASME Trans. Mechatron. **10**(3), 297–304 (2005)
25. Zhang, L., Dehghani, A., Su, Z., King, T., Greenwood, B., Levesley, M.: Real-time automated visual inspection system for contaminant removal from wool. Real-Time Imaging **11**(4), 257–269 (2005)
26. Zheng, Z., Yang, Y.: Rectifying pseudo label learning via uncertainty estimation for domain adaptive semantic segmentation. Int. J. Comput. Vis. **129**(4), 1106–1120 (2021). https://doi.org/10.1007/s11263-020-01395-y

Active Learning for Crop-Weed Discrimination by Image Classification from Convolutional Neural Network's Feature Pyramid Levels

Usman A. Zahidi$^{(\boxtimes)}$ and Grzegorz Cielniak

Lincoln Agri-Robotics, University of Lincoln, Lincoln, UK
{uzahidi,gcielniak}@lincoln.ac.uk

Abstract. The amount of effort required for high-quality data acquisition and labelling for adequate supervised learning drives the need for building an efficient and effective image sampling strategy. We propose a novel Batch Mode Active Learning that blends Region Convolutional Neural Network's (RCNN) Feature Pyramid Network (FPN) levels together and employs t-distributed Stochastic Neighbour Embedding (t-SNE) classification for selecting incremental batch based on feature similarity. Later, K-means clustering is performed on t-SNE instances for the selected sample size of images. Results show that t-SNE classification on merged FPN feature maps outperforms the approach based on RGB images directly, random sampling and maximum entropy-based image sampling schemes. For comparison, we employ a publicly available data set of images of Sugar beet for a crop-weed discrimination task together with our newly acquired annotated images of Romaine and Apollo lettuce crops at different growth stages. Batch sampling on all datasets by the proposed method shows that only 60% of images are required to produce precision/recall statistics similar to the complete dataset. Two lettuce datasets used in our experiments are publicly available (Lettuce datasets: https://bit.ly/3g7Owc5) to facilitate further research opportunities.

Keywords: Image sampling · Robotic weeding · Deep learning · Convolutional Neural Network

1 Introduction

Accurate and reliable weeding is crucial for crop care in modern precision farming. Robotic weeding is an enabling technology and emerging alternative to herbicides. It is reported that herbicides may potentially have carcinogenic ingredients and are also susceptible to resistance and mutations [1]. Precise robot platforms, weed destruction mechanism and Computer Vision (CV) systems are the core components of integrated robotic weeding platforms. CV, in particular, is vital for intelligent control required for such weed scouting and removal (see

© Springer Nature Switzerland AG 2021
M. Vincze et al. (Eds.): ICVS 2021, LNCS 12899, pp. 245–257, 2021.
https://doi.org/10.1007/978-3-030-87156-7_20

for example Fig. 1). A high-performance semantic segmentation for classifying any weed type from an early-stage crop is an essential success criterion. Data-driven supervised Deep Learning (DL) approaches such as CNN are known to outperform other learning alternatives, particularly in CV [2]. Supervised learning in essence comes with the need of a distinctive minimal data source and its annotation for success, which is both time and human resource intensive.

Active Learning (AL) is an approach to overcome these issues, it aims to explore effective alternatives for selecting distinctive data points for labelling from a pool of unlabelled data. A universally good AL strategy is not possible to achieve [20] but many heuristic-based approaches are known to perform well in CNN model predictions. We propose an AL algorithm that suits CNN based learning, particularly CNN-based semantic segmentation and Mask-RCNN.

Region CNN (RCNN) is a successful architecture of DL which applies region proposal algorithms to CNN feature maps. It has several Residual Networks (Resnet) that construct a Feature Pyramid Network (FPN) of various scaled feature maps as its levels. We incorporate a combination of variable receptive fields of feature maps for selecting exemplar images from the unlabelled pool. The state-of-the-art RCNN with Feature Pyramid Networks are used as these receptive fields. A high-resolution pyramid layer is used for detecting smaller sized features. Therefore we employ only P2 and P3 layers as shown in Fig. 2, as we seek detection of early-stage (smaller) crop and small to medium weed sizes. These feature maps are then further input to Resnet101 [22] to output a 2048 dimensional feature vector for one FPN layer. Two such layers are merged and their corresponding Resnet101 feature vector is 4096 dimensional which is projected to 2D by t-SNE [4] embedding. The two-dimensional points are then classified by K-means to extract the most salient images with a batch.

We articulate yet another heuristic strategy for AL on CNN architecture. Our main contributions are as follows: 1) We propose a heuristic-based AL algorithm and show that a blend of feature maps provide more refined information content and leads to better similarity ranking, which is employed for superior classification and sample selection when compared to baselines. 2) We perform the experimental evaluation of the proposed method on the real data for a crop-weed discrimination task including different crops and weeds at different growth stages and illumination conditions. 3) Eventually, we release Romaine and Apollo lettuce image datasets together with their annotations to facilitate further research opportunities in weeding applications.

In Sect. 2 we provide relevant literature review whilst the core of the proposed method is presented in Sect. 3. Sect. 4 contains details about the experimental setup followed by results and experimental evaluation presented in Sect. 5. The paper is concluded in Sect. 6 providing some discussion on future work.

2 Literature Review

2.1 Robotic Weeding

Automated robotic weeding is a vital component in modern precision farming, enabling farmers to remove weeds in a time-efficient manner. It is a

Fig. 1. Robot used for data collection (top left), an example input ·image of Apollo lettuce (top right), its ground truth annotation (bottom left) and the prediction output of a model trained by FPN-tSNE selected samples (bottom right).

multi-disciplinary domain including autonomous robots, weed removal mechanics and CV. CV systems are employed for optimal localising, mapping, traversing decisions [6,7]. Some weed scouting applications seek classification to ascertain the type of weeds while others treat any weed type as a single class [8]. Figure 1 shows robotic weeding field test and predictions from the CV system.

2.2 Active Learning

Classical active learning algorithms retrieve each training sample from unlabelled images pool incrementally, this is not feasible when training CNNs since a single point instance are not statistically significant on the model parameters due to potential local minima trapping of optimization algorithms, moreover it is infeasible to train models incrementally for every instance hence making it impractical in larger datasets [9]. Therefore, recently substantial research interest is observed in Batch Mode Active Learning (BMAL) which select a batch from unlabeled instances based on heuristics. A popular approach to active learning relies on the uncertainty and diversity of the model [18,19]. The overall performance of the AL is dependent on minimal generalisation and training error, which is studied in literature [3,10]. [9,10] transformed these metric to formulate AL as an optimization problem and established mathematical bounds on the quality of AL. [3] concluded that uncertainty based approaches are ineffective in coverage of complete image features space. [11] applied bayesian inference in active learning for CNN, however it is reported to be ineffective when sample size gets larger [3]. There are several weakly-supervised learning-based approaches to AL [12,13] that require tentative labelling by oracle before sample rankings may be suggested. [12] for example used labelling of vegetation from the background by K-means clustering, they employed this approach for computing norm of gradients and gradient projections on the weight space of the CNN model. Moreover, they formulated AL for robotic weeding applications. They propose weakly supervised learning as part of their active learning pipeline. First unsupervised learning based pseudo ground truth is created, then AL is performed and evaluated against it.

2.3   Convolutional Neural Networks and Features Pyramid Network

Instance segmentation in images encounter three major challenges, firstly, localising the objects, secondly finding the periphery of these objects and eventually applying labels to them. Region proposal algorithms [24] and [23] define a set of candidate detection regions in an image. Region CNN (RCNN) applies these region proposals to CNN feature maps for object detection i.e. without periphery [14,15]. RCNN is a deep convolutional layer network, when the deeper network starts to converge, a degradation problem occurs i.e. with the increase in network depth, accuracy gets saturated and then degrades rapidly. To overcome these issues, Resnet [22] adds shortcut connections that skip one or more layers. They perform identity mapping, and their outputs are added to the outputs of the stacked layers. Resnets make it easier to optimize and gain accuracy from the greatly increased depth of CNN. Therefore RCNN employs many Resnets as shown in Fig. 2. A variant of RCNN called Mask-RCNN [16] was designed to overcome this issue and enables instance segmentation through RCNN. There are several popular architectures of Resnet that are employed in CNNs, they typically vary due to the number of layers such as Resnet 18,34,50,101 and 152 layers. Resnet 101 is used in our experiments which has $(1 \times 1 \times 2048)$ conv5 output layer, more details can be found at [22]. Feature pyramids are a basic component in recognition systems for detecting objects at different scales. A top-down architecture with lateral connections developed by [17] for building high-level semantic feature maps at all scales. Resnet outputs in RCNN construct a Feature Pyramid Network (FPN), it has significant improvement as a generic feature extractor in several applications. An overview of FPN is shown in Fig. 2, showing pyramids and their lateral connections. Through scaling FPN

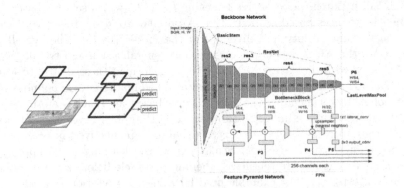

Fig. 2. An overview of FPN with lateral connection (left) and the Generalized RCNN architecture illustrating layers of pyramids from P2 to P6 (right).

captures different perceptions, one pixel of 'P6' feature corresponds to broader area of input image than 'P2', that is 'P6' has a larger receptive field than 'P2'. FPN can extract multi-scale feature maps with different receptive fields [17].

AL strategies based on uncertainty and diversity of the model network are not effective with CNN due to the lack of uncertainty based approaches to cover the space of the image. On the other hand, AL based on weakly supervised learning and gradient-based metrics elongate the AL pipeline by appending additional oracle effort for pseudo-labelling. Some aforementioned approaches [3,11,25] are not suitable for pixel-wise semantic segmentation of images with CNNs or they are time and memory intensive. Our proposed strategy is well-suited for CNN architectures and does not require any weak supervision. The RCNN feature extraction and FPN construction are not computationally expensive. However, the dimensionality reduction by t-SNE is a computational bottleneck that is overcome by employing CUDA-based t-SNE library [26]. We compared our result with a) random sampling, b) uncertainty based sampling, c) Our approach applied directly on RGB images (called RGB-tSNE) and eventually d) our FPN based approach. We present that both our approaches overperform random and entropy-based approaches, our FPN based approach has a steep performance improvement compared to the counterpart RGB base method.

3   Proposed Method

The lack of image feature space coverage by uncertainty methods in CNN is the prime motivating factor for this work. We explore the feature space in state-of-the-art Generalised Region-based Convolutional Neural Networks (RCNN) instead of the raw image. The block diagram of Generalised RCNN is given in Fig. 2, which shows multiple Resnets and construction of a Feature Pyramid Network (FPN). FPN levels represent several scales of feature maps that perceive different receptive fields. The FPN feature maps are passed to the Region Proposal Network where objectness maps are constructed together with the bounding boxes. The Low-resolution FPN layer captures larger objects in the image while the higher resolution level captures small objects and features. We are particularly interested in early-stage crops, therefore we propose a two-layer pyramid i.e. the output from res2 and res3 is computed for all unlabelled images. These images are loaded as a test dataset and predicted by a standard COCO pre-trained model. So, the FPN is constructed during prediction through the pre-trained model which is merely employed as a feature extractor. These two feature maps are further processed by another feature extractor called Resnet101, which outputs a 2048 dimensional feature vector for each input image. Each feature extracted from Resnet101 is denoted as f_i^l, where i represent the number of images and l denotes the number of layers. The proposed n dimensional feature space $\mathcal{F}^n$ is given in Eq. (1).

$$\mathcal{F}^n = \{f_b^1 f_b^2 : f_b^1 \in L_1, f_b^2 \in L_2\} \tag{1}$$

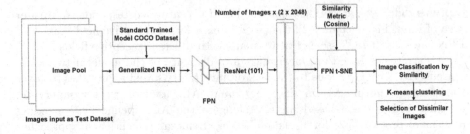

Fig. 3. The Proposed Active Learning algorithm flow with unlabelled image pools as input which is passed to Generalized RCNN to create the Feature Pyramid Network and Resnet 101 model before classification and selection.

where, f_b^l denotes features of images belonging to batch b. f_b^1 and f_b^2 are the first (P2) and second (P3) FPN layer feature maps belonging to the universal set of feature map pools L_1 and L_1, respectively. $\mathcal{F}^n$ is mapped to a two dimensional embedding by t-SNE, denoted in Eq. (2). K-means clustering is finally run

$$T : \mathcal{F}^n \longrightarrow \mathcal{F}^2 \tag{2}$$

on $\mathcal{F}^2$ for selected number of samples. A flow diagram is shown in Fig. 3.

3.1 Workflow Description

The input to the sample selection method is images from the unlabelled pool, in batches. These batches are constructed as a test dataset for feature extraction by Generalized RCNN. The model on which GRCNN is trained is from the standard model zoo of the COCO dataset. Particularly the model was obtained from reference [27]. We employed Detectron2 Mask-RCNN FPN-101 as a feature extractor that outputs five-level feature pyramids. One input image generates five pyramid levels, if a batch has n images then the total number of levels is $n \times 5$. As mentioned earlier, our method utilises only two levels of the pyramid as shown in Fig. 3. Each individual level is reduced to a feature vector of 2048 dimensions by employing Resnet101 as shown in Fig. 3. Two feature vectors are merged together by Eq. 1, hence the output feature vector for one image is 4096 dimensional. Therefore, for n images there are n vectors that are further reduced in dimension by t-SNE 2D embedding. Although initially, we chose Feature Similarity Index (FSIM) as the similarity metric for tSNE, however, it was substantially slower than cosine with a minor gain in classification performance. Therefore, we eventually settled to cosine metric for t-SNE with the perplexity of 30, in our experiments. T-SNE outputs a 2D point for each image and places it according to feature similarity, an example is Romaine lettuce images that are shown in Fig. 5, where images with two different growth stages are segregated. The oracle defines the number of images that are selected by K-means clustering such that the images are diverse within the image set.

3.2 Model Training Setup

Once the images are selected, they are forwarded to the oracle for annotation. The annotated images are then used in supervised learning. In our training setup, we use Mask-RCNN for instance segmentation. The Mask-RCNN is based on Faster-RCNN which is built upon the Generalised RCNN backbone network. therefore, the constructed feature map FPNs are the same which input into the Region Proposal Network (RPN), hence the proposed method is a suitable active learning approach for this setup. In our experiments, we employed Facebook's Detectron2 Mask-RCNN implementations [27].

4   Experimental Setup

Data Sets: Several field tests were rendered for data acquisition. During this process, images of two different crop categories such as Romaine and Apollo Lettuces were collected at the Riseholme facility of the University of Lincoln. These images are taken from an industrial-grade Intel$^{\circledR}$ RealSense^{TM} camera having RGB, infrared and depth channels. The camera was mounted on a mobile robot traversing the rows of the crop with a downward-facing orientation. Characteristic features of the collected datasets include different growth stages, hard shadows with crisp boundaries and intense, blocking direct light, different times of the day and outdoor illumination conditions.

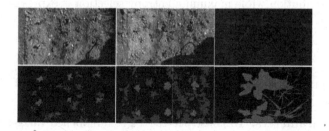

Fig. 4. Examples from the three considered datasets: images of Romaine lettuce, Apollo lettuce and Sugar beet (top row), and corresponding ground truth annotations (bottom row).

Table 1. Summary of the datasets used for experimental comparisons.

Dataset	Image #		Instances		Ratio (weed/crop)	Growth stages	Resolution
	Train	Test	Crop	Weed			
Sugar beet	500	400	2191	19462	8.88	1	1296 × 966
Romaine lettuce	500	150	4578	29007	6.34	2	848 × 480
Apollo lettuce	200	100	2040	13057	6.40	1	848 × 480

For our experiments, we selected 950 images for annotation by professional annotators to create the ground truth as shown in Fig. 1. The annotations include crop and weed classes with the outline of individual plants indicated. In our experiments, we also include the University of Bonn's Sugar beet 2016 dataset which is publicly available at [5]. The summary of annotated datasets is included in Table 1 and selected examples are shown in Fig. 4.

The Sugar beet dataset has medium to large crop sizes frequently but weeds typically have smaller sizes, however, some large size weeds are also found. Contrarily, both Romaine and Apollo lettuce have smaller crop sizes and the weeds are also following a trend similar to the Sugar beet dataset. Table 1 also lists the instance count of crop and weed in all crops. All datasets exhibit distribution imbalance with crops having a share between 11%–15% while weed is between 85%-89%. The ratio of weed and crop is also listed in Table 1 to show the degree of instance imbalance in each dataset.

Evaluation Metrics: We employ the standard evaluation metrics for the experimental comparisons. A pixel-wise True Positives (T_P) and False Negatives F_N are computed for all images, this allows to define the measures of precision $= \frac{T_P}{T_P+F_P}$ and recall $= \frac{T_P}{T_P+F_N}$ which were calculated for each class (i.e. crop/weed) separately. Results covered in Sect. 5 are computed pixel wise for all datasets.

Baseline Methods for Comparison: We compared the proposed method with baseline random sampling, maximum entropy [3] method and our own algorithm with RGB image as an input to tSNE classification instead of feature maps, this method is termed as RGB-tSNE in Sect. 5. Random sampling is based on Gaussian distribution while maximum entropy selection is expressed as:

$$H(\mathbf{x}) = -\frac{1}{N} \sum_{i=1}^{N} \sum_{c} p\left(c \mid x_i\right) \log p\left(c \mid x_i\right), \tag{3}$$

where x_i is pixel i in image x, c is the class and N is the number of pixels in the image. Image samples that have the highest entropy are selected.

Training Parameters: To construct the FPN, unlabelled images are loaded as test datasets where the base trained model is Mask RCNN R101 FPN 3x, which is used as the feature extractor. The final training of Mask-RCNN is performed with the learning rate of 0.0025, the number of iteration is 90000, the test threshold is set to 0.5 and the model optimizer is Stochastic Gradient Descent.

5   Experimental Evaluation

In this section, we demonstrate the effectiveness of the proposed approach and compare it with baseline methods such as random and maximum-entropy-based batch sampling. We empirically assert that applying t-SNE on feature maps FPN improves sampling quality rather than directly on RGB images. A set of example results illustrating t-SNE mapping to 2D for three different crops is shown in Fig. 5 depicting samples selected and excluded after K-means clustering.

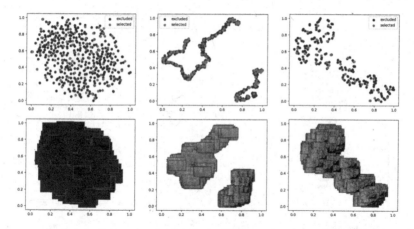

Fig. 5. The t-SNE mapping to 2D for three different crops depicting 20% of samples selected by K-means clustering (red) including Sugar beet (left column), Romaine lettuce (middle column), and Apollo lettuce (right column). (Color figure online)

The average size of the crop is larger than weeds which are smaller and more varied in size but larger in numbers, as mentioned in Sect. 4. Figure 6(a) shows the result for Sugar beet dataset. Here both precision and recall in the crop are above 0.90 for all methods. The precision of weed detection for all methods except FPN-tSNE is lower than 0.75. Latter is the top performer with precision above 0.8 in all sample sizes. A similar performance of FPN-tSNE is observed in recall compared to other methods. Figure 6 also shows that the proposed method performance with a complete dataset approaches all images when the sample size is close to 60% of that size.

Similarly, in the case of Romaine lettuce, it is observed that both precision and recall in the crop is above 0.85 in all methods. In weeds, however, precision is above 0.75 and recall is above 0.70 for all methods, as shown in Fig. 6(b). Table 1 shows the imbalance in class instances of the Romaine dataset, moreover, its number of instances is also significantly larger than other datasets instance distributions. Furthermore, the crop bed in Romaine is an uneven terrain causing the presence of self and external shadows cast from robot inclusively. Our Lettuce datasets have a large number of small weeds therefore they are more likely to come under these shadows, hence increasing the diversity in pixels intensity and colour of weed instances, which may cause lower recall statistics due to increasing False Negative possibility. In the case of FPN-tSNE, it is observed that FPN-tSNE has a monotonic decrease in weed precision but a similar increase in weed recall. Although in precision it is performing better than other methods in the first two sample instances, however, it gets worse at the sample size of 300. A monotonic contrast of trends in weeds for FPN-tSNE shows that the model is sensitive in detection gaining higher False Positives and lower False Negatives. The Apollo lettuce dataset has fewer images for training and testing than the aforementioned experiments. A similar trend of precision and recall above 0.9 for

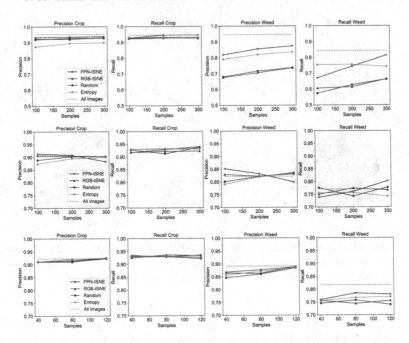

Fig. 6. Precision/recall of crops and weeds: (a) Row 1: Sugar beet; (b) Row 2: Romain lettuce; (c) Row 3: Apollo lettuce

the crop is observed in the results of this dataset, which is shown in Fig. 6(c). In weeds precision and recall of all methods are above 0.85 and 0.7, respectively. A reciprocal trend in precision and recall of weed is observed through the number of samples. However, in both cases, the proposed method performs better results than other methods. In FPN-tSNE classification is performed on refined feature maps having enhanced features in multiple levels, contrarily RGB-tSNE, process t-SNE based classification directly on RGB images therefore it is vulnerable to shadows more than FPN feature maps. As RGBs are full-resolution, therefore they have a higher potential of redundant pixels. Due to their higher resolution detection on batches are less sensitive than for the FPN counterpart, therefore showing better overall statistics in precision but values are lower in recalls.

6   Conclusions and Future Work

In this paper, we proposed an active learning method that employs multiple levels of the feature map pyramid of CNNs to select the most distinctive images which are then used for training. Three different datasets for a crop/weed discrimination task were used for evaluation of the proposed method which was compared to a set of standard baseline methods. Our results show that the proposed t-SNE classification on merged FPN feature maps outperforms corresponding RGB images, and random sampling and maximum entropy-based image sampling schemes.

The proposed method is heuristic-based therefore there is no guarantee of the optimal sample selection. Moreover, our experimental results show that the method is more sensitive to shadows and variable illumination. The input RGB image pool may be altered to other colour-space such as HSL to filter out illumination effects in future to overcome this issue. We also observe that the weed to crop ratio does not seem to influence the performance of our algorithm but the total number of weeds does affect the detection capacity as it becomes highly probable to have weeds under shadow region. It is noticed that our method is lagging behind in weed precision of the Romaine lettuce dataset only, therefore it should be investigated whether having multiple growth stages of the crop in the training dataset has any effect on these statistics. We have tested a combination of two pyramid layers, however, more layers could be tested in future. The intuition of having two layers is to keep the vector dimension lower so that 2D mapping perform better, secondly, it is also computationally efficient to have fewer layers. Performing a comparative analysis with only one level of the pyramid would also be interesting future work.

References

1. Gilbert, N.: A hard look at GM crops. Nature **497**(7447), 24–26 (2013)
2. Cooper, G.: New vision technologies for real-world applications. Semiconductor Engineering website, October 2019. https://semiengineering.com/new-vision-technologies-for-real-world-applications/
3. Sener, O., Savarese, S.: Active learning for convolutional neural networks: a core-set approach. arXiv preprint arXiv:1708.00489 (2017)
4. Van der Maaten, L., Hinton, G.: Visualizing data using t-SNE. J. Mach. Learn. Res. (2008)
5. Chebrolu, N., Lottes, P., Schaefer, A., Winterhalter, W., Burgard, W., Stachniss, C.: Agricultural robot dataset for plant classification, localization and mapping on sugar beet fields. Int. J. Robot. Res. **36**, 1045–1052 (2017)
6. Lottes, P., Behley, J., Chebrolu, N., Milioto, A., Stachniss, C.: Robust joint stem detection and crop-weed classification using image sequences for plant-specific treatment in precision farming. J. Field Robot. **37**, 20–34 (2020). https://doi.org/10.1002/rob.21901
7. Lottes, P., Höferlin, M., Sander, S., Stachniss, C.: Effective vision-based classification for separating sugar beets and weeds for precision farming. J. Field Robot. **34**, 1160–1178 (2017). https://doi.org/10.1002/rob.21675
8. Bosilj, P., Aptoula, E., Duckett, T., Cielniak, G.: Transfer learning between crop types for semantic segmentation of crops versus weeds in precision agriculture. J Field Robot. **37**, 7–19 (2020). https://doi.org/10.1002/rob.21869
9. Guo, Y., Schuurmans, D.: Discriminative batch mode active learning. In: Proceedings of the 20th International Conference on Neural Information Processing Systems (NIPS 2007). Curran Associates Inc., Red Hook, NY, USA, pp. 593–600 (2007)

10. Chakraborty, S., Balasubramanian, V., Sun, Q., Panchanathan, S., Ye, J.: Active batch selection via convex relaxations with guaranteed solution bounds. IEEE Trans. Pattern Anal. Mach. Intell. **37**(10), 1945–1958 (2015). https://doi.org/10. 1109/TPAMI.2015.2389848

11. Gal, Y., Ghahramani, Z.: Dropout as a Bayesian approximation: representing model uncertainty in deep learning. In: International Conference on Machine Learning (2016)

12. Sheikh, R., Milioto, A., Lottes, P., Stachniss, C., Bennewitz, M., Schultz, T.: Gradient and log-based active learning for semantic segmentation of crop and weed for agricultural robots. In: IEEE International Conference on Robotics and Automation (ICRA) 2020, pp. 1350–1356 (2020). https://doi.org/10.1109/ICRA40945. 2020.9196722

13. Kwak, S., Hong, S., Han, B.: Weakly supervised semantic segmentation using superpixel pooling network. In: Thirty- First AAAI Conference on Artificial Intelligence (2017)

14. Girshick, R., Donahue, J., Darrell, T., Malik, J.: Rich feature hierarchies for accurate object detection and semantic segmentation. In: IEEE Conference on Computer Vision and Pattern Recognition (CVPR) (2014)

15. Girshick, R.: Fast R-CNN. In: IEEE International Conference on Computer Vision (ICCV) (2015)

16. He, K., Gkioxari, G., Dollár, P., Girshick, R.: Mask R-CNN. In: IEEE International Conference on Computer Vision (ICCV) 2017, pp. 2980–2988 (2017). https://doi. org/10.1109/ICCV.2017.322

17. Lin, T., Dollár, P., Girshick, R., He, K., Hariharan, B., Belongie, S.: Feature pyramid networks for object detection. In: IEEE Conference on Computer Vision and Pattern Recognition (CVPR) 2017, pp. 936–944 (2017). https://doi.org/10.1109/ CVPR.2017.106

18. Zhou, Z., Shin, J., Zhang, L., Gurudu, S., Gotway, M., Liang, J.: Fine-tuning convolutional neural networks for biomedical image analysis: actively and incrementally. In: Proceedings of the IEEE Conference on Computer Vision and Pattern Recognition (CVPR), pp. 7340–7351 (2017)

19. Yang, L., Zhang, Y., Chen, J., Zhang, S., Chen, D.Z.: Suggestive annotation: a deep active learning framework for biomedical image segmentation. In: Proceedings of the International Conference on Medical Image Computing and Computer-Assisted Intervention, pp. 399–407 (2017)

20. Dasgupta, S.: Analysis of a greedy active learning strategy. In: Conference on Neural Information Processing Systems (2004)

21. Chakraborty, S., Balasubramanian, V., Sun, Q., Panchanathan, S., Ye, J.: Active batch selection via convex relaxations with guaranteed solution bounds. IEEE Trans. Pattern Anal. Mach. Intell. **37**, 1945–1958 (2015)

22. He, K., Zhang, X., Ren, S., Sun, J.: Deep residual learning for image recognition. In: IEEE Conference on Computer Vision and Pattern Recognition (CVPR) 2016, pp. 770–778 (2016). https://doi.org/10.1109/CVPR.2016.90

23. Alexe, B., Deselaers, T., Ferrari, V.: Measuring the objectness of image windows. IEEE Trans. Pattern Anal. Mach. Intell. **34**(11), 2189–2202 (2012). https://doi. org/10.1109/TPAMI.2012.28

24. Uijlings, J.R.R., van de Sande, K.E.A., Gevers, T., et al.: Selective search for object recognition. Int. J. Comput. Vis. **104**, 154–171 (2013). https://doi.org/10. 1007/s11263-013-0620-5

25. Yoo, D., Kweon, I.S.: Learning loss for active learning. In: Proceedings of the IEEE Conference on Computer Vision and Pattern Recognition (CVPR), pp. 93–102 (2019)
26. Chan, D.M., Rao, R., Huang, F., Canny, J.F.: GPU accelerated t-distributed stochastic neighbor embedding. J. Parallel Distrib. Comput. **131**, 1–13 (2019)
27. Wu, Y., Kirillov, A., Massa, F., Lo, W.-Y., Girshick, R.: Detectron2. Facebook Research (2019)

Author Index

Printed in the United States
by Baker & Taylor Publisher Services